YORKSHIRE FOOTBALL A HISTORY

Cameron Fleming

Scratching Shed Publishing Ltd

First published by Scratching Shed Publishing Ltd in 2010
Registered in England & Wales No. 6588772.
Registered office:
47 Street Lane, Leeds, West Yorkshire. LS8 1AP

www.scratchingshedpublishing.co.uk

ISBN 978-0956252654

A catalogue record for this book is available from the British Library.

Typeset in Warnock Pro Semi Bold and Palatino

Printed and bound in the United Kingdom by
L.P.P.S.Ltd, Wellingborough, Northants, NN8 3PJ

YORKSHIRE FOOTBALL
A HISTORY

For my wife Linda and young son Jack,
the twin loves of my life.

Contents

1

In The Beginning

YORKSHIRE, as every right-minded soul knows, is God's Own Country. So to describe Sheffield as a Yorkshire Bethlehem does not stretch the imagination unduly, not when the Steel City can claim to be the birthplace of the global religion that is club football.

Here, in the industrialised footholds of the Peak District, Sheffield FC, the world's first official football club, sprung into life on 24th October, 1857. Its conception was forged not in the blasting furnaces of working class toil - the days when players would emerge from coal mines, steelworks and factories lay very much in the future - but in the more genteel fires of the prosperous mercantile and skilled professional classes.

The club's founding fathers were two young gentlemen whose enthusiasm, drive and leadership skills would soon be put to good use as army officers in the newly formed Hallamshire Volunteer Rifles[1]. William Prest, a man born in York, was a thriving wine merchant while his friend Nathaniel Creswick was a Sheffield solicitor and member of a distinguished family firm of silver plate craftsmen dating back to the Middle Ages. Both men loved to play sport, turning their hands and feet to fencing, athletics and, above all, cricket. Their summers were devoted to Sheffield Cricket Club, the ancestor of Yorkshire CCC. Indeed Prest, a contemporary of a youthful WG Grace, was so adept with bat and ball that he played first-class cricket for Yorkshire Gentlemen and the North of England, no mean feat in the years before Test matches.

In May 1857, reputedly during a walk in the countryside, the friends discussed forming a football club as a way of keeping fit during the cold winter months as they awaited the return of their beloved leather on willow. Sheffield FC thus became the first but by no means last Yorkshire football club to owe a debt of gratitude to followers of the summer game.

'The Club', as Sheffield FC quickly became known, was established at a meeting held in Parkfield House, the suburban home of Harry Waters Chambers, a fellow solicitor. Prest was happy to remain in the administrative background but Creswick eagerly took on the dual posts of Honorary Secretary and Treasurer. Meanwhile, Fred Ward, a wealthy young man who ran Eyre, Ward & Co. in the town, was installed as club president. His first act was to present the committee with a permanent headquarters - a large greenhouse at the bottom of his garden.

Let us not be carried away by the notion that Messrs Creswick and Prest *invented* what they knew as 'Foot-Ball'. A violent street form had, for centuries, been played on festival days between rowdy mobs of brawling youths and, in recent years, become all the rage with young toffs attending public schools and the universities. The first known recorded match locally was a six-a-side affair between Sheffield and Norton in 1793. Creswick himself practised the game when a student at Sheffield Collegiate

School and he and Prest had both competed in off-the-cuff matches with their cricketing colleagues at Sheffield CC.

The duo's landmark achievement was rather to *formalise* the rough and ready pastime into a structured system of regular matches. For an annual subscription of 2s 6d (12½p), they and their friends could play football every Saturday afternoon (no Sunday sport in these God-fearing times) from foggy November right through to Easter. In the absence of any other clubs to compete against, the members split into teams along the lines of Married versus Singles, Professional Occupations against the Rest and Smokers v. Non-smokers. Matches were played on several local fields and parks. One butted up to Ward's house on East Bank Road, another was on Strawberry Hall Lane, around the corner from Bramall Lane; all were situated away from the thick smoke and grime belched out by Sheffield's industrial East End.

Entry into The Club was strictly by invitation. Support came from 'most of the leading men in the neighbourhood' - manufacturers, lawyers, surgeons, brewers - a number of whom were, like Creswick, Collegiate old boys. Ten years later the *Sheffield Daily Telegraph* described Sheffield FC as 'almost exclusively of the middle class', a sure sign that the rigid class system and social bars that pervaded Victorian life were firmly in place. No room at The Club for poorly paid labourers.

Grainy black and white photographs of early football teams are about as rare as finding a Yorkshireman with a good word to say about Mancunians, but they do exist. Looking suspiciously like escaped convicts, players are clothed in ill-fitting shirts and baggy knickerbockers held up by fabric belts tied about their waists. Many of them sport twirled moustaches and mutton chop whiskers as were the fashions of the day while others have upon their heads a bizarre assortment of spotty caps and striped fezzes. And to a man they stare intently, menacingly even, into the camera lens, as if challenging the viewer to come and have a go if they think they're hard enough.

Having posed for stilted photos, members of The Club would have gone off to play a game of football governed by Sheffield Rules. Drawn up by committee on 21st October, 1858 and based upon a variety of codes already in place at Cambridge University and some of the leading fee-paying schools, Sheffield Rules were as follows:

1. Kick off from the middle must be a place kick.
2. Kick out must not be from more than 25 yards out of goal.
3. Fair catch is a catch direct from any player, provided the ball has not touched the ground and has not been thrown from touch which is entitled to a free-kick.
4. Charging is fair in case of a place kick but he may always draw back unless he has actually touched the ball with his foot.
5. Pushing with the hands is allowed but no hacking or tripping up is fair under any circumstances whatsoever.
6. No player may be held or pulled over.
7. It is not lawful to take the ball off the ground (except in touch) for any purpose whatever.
8. The ball may be pushed on or hit with the hand but holding the ball, except in the case of a fair catch, is altogether disallowed. [This rule was amended in 1860 to disallow all handling of the ball].
9. A goal must be kicked but not from touch nor by a free-kick from a catch.
10. A ball in touch is dead, consequently the side that touches it down must bring it to the edge of the touch and throw it straight out from touch.

11. Each player must provide himself with a red and dark blue flannel cap, one colour to be worn by each side.

These eleven simple rules offer a tantalising glimpse into their bygone age. Some aspects are familiar. The pitch is delineated by touch lines. Kick offs, goal kicks, free kicks and throw-ins are all in place. Teams are colour coded, albeit by caps rather than full strips, and the overriding aim of the game is to score goals by dribbling the ball in between two posts. We can imagine players barging one another to the ground (a rude characteristic inherited from mob football) but, already, holding the ball and running with it, as practised by those young scamps at Rugby School, was outlawed. So too was hacking, the deliberate walloping of an opponent's shins, which in the autumn of 1863 became such a highly contentious issue that it cleaved Foot-Ball, the common ancestor, once and for all into ball-handling Rugby football and its ball-dribbling cousin, the Association variety.

The Club's version of the game has a certain familiarity but it differed substantially too in many important respects to its modern equivalent. Thirteen to twenty-a-side matches were commonplace and often lasted for three hours on a pitch twice as long as its modern counterpart. There was no dedicated goalkeeper nor any defined outfield positions for that matter. The goal was just two wooden sticks hammered into the ground without a crossbar, the ball resembled a medicine ball, there were no penalties and the thorny issue of the offside rule had yet to rear its ugly head. As for on-field disputes, they were settled not by a referee but by the random judgment of any committee member who happened to be playing that day.

Then there were tactics, which were primitive to say the

least. Wearing their long, fleecy knickerbockers, coloured caps and sturdy hobnailed boots, neither Prest nor Creswick or any of their chums would have thought much about passing the ball to one another. The odd kick through to a goal-hanging forward, maybe, but by and large individualism was the thing, not expansive team play. Players put faith in their own bravery, skill and sheer brute strength to transport the ball through a scrum of opponents, manfully dodging body charges and bone-crunching tackles in the hope of winning a punt at goal at the end of it all. Team-mates acted as a hustling posse of minders, protecting the man with the ball while also being poised to take up the attack should he lose possession. Little wonder there was often no end product; goalless draws were exceedingly frequent.

Yet, in the age of steam when Britannia ruled the waves and private enterprise gained her an Empire, it was such dashing displays of personal courage that won roars of approval. Sheffield FC's middle-class members were products of their time, self-made men who relied upon their own wits and resourcefulness to carve out profitable careers. A naturally gung-ho and individualistic attitude towards football merely reflected their everyday business lives.

In 1860, the inevitable happened; a rival football club, Hallam FC, appeared on the scene. What is more, that club was formed at the instigation of two former Sheffield members, Thomas Vickers, a steel magnate and one of The Club's original committee, and John Charles Shaw, an attorney's clerk who, in 1862, launched the daunting Hallam Chase fell-run - winning it himself, by some margin, the next year. 'The Countrymen', as Hallam became known, were an adjunct to the long-established Hallam Cricket Club. They even shared the latter's ground on Sandygate Road, close to where Sheffield Hallam University stands today, a ground which, remarkably, remains their home 150 years on.

The first inter-club clash - and thus the first official county derby - was not long in coming. Shortly after Christmas 1860 a few hundred curious, frost-bitten spectators gathered at a snowbound Sandygate to watch the 'old boys' of Sheffield, clad in scarlet caps, defeat the young whippersnappers of Hallam, wearing blue, 2-0. The match was noted for being 'conducted with good temper and in a friendly spirit', but the gritty, niggling, competitive spirit of the true Yorkshire derby arrived soon enough. Two years later, a second reporter described the pugnacious match he had just witnessed - a thirteen-a-side yuletide encounter so disorderly that it has gone down in the annals as the 'Battle of Bramall Lane'[2] - as 'the day the waistcoats came off and the fighting began'.

Hostilities commenced on the afternoon of 29th December, 1862 - Boxing Day might have been a more appropriate date - at the Duke of Norfolk's swanky new cricket ground on Bramall Lane. Since its grand unveiling in April 1855, William Prest participating in the first cricket match, dirty football boots had not once soiled the square. Permission was grudgingly granted now only because the proceeds would benefit thousands of cotton weavers in Lancashire, impoverished by a collapse in the cross-Atlantic cotton trade following the outbreak of the American Civil War.

Sadly the match itself, which lasted fully three hours and ended without a goal being scored, proved far less charitable. Sheffield-Hallam games gained repute as tough, 'bull-strength' affairs with no quarter given and none asked for, as Sheffield secretary William Chesterman described: 'I have often seen the ball lying on the pitch totally ignored while half a dozen players have been preoccupied with butting each other.' But no other match plunged to such riotous depths as this one did midway through the second half. At the heart of the tumult was Creswick, the Sheffield captain and by now a major in the Hallamshire Volunteers. In response to the dastardly crime of being deliberately held back he thumped the miscreant, William Waterfall, full in the face. Unintentionally, according to the *Sheffield Independent* whose former editor just so happened to be Fred Ward's father. 'Deliberately!' retorted the livid Countrymen.

Whatever the rights and wrongs of the situation, something snapped inside Waterfall's head. Enraged, he 'threw off his waistcoat', raised his fists and 'began to show fight', returning several punches of his own. Any festive spirit on offer at the start of play must have distilled by half-time because the bust-up escalated into a free-for-all with players from both sides joining in the fray. The *Sheffield Independent* noted, however, that Major Creswick 'preserved his temper admirably and did not return a single blow.'

Excited by the wild fisticuffs, spectators invaded the pitch and waded into the brawl, a very early example of football hooliganism. Further play was impossible until 'older and cooler heads prevailed'. Once the chaos had given way to order an aggrieved Waterfall, who continued to blame the major for starting the fracas, was put in goal for the remainder of the game as punishment. Since the keeper was normally whoever happened to be nearest to his goalposts that was chastisement indeed. That Creswick, who escaped reprimand, was now an army officer and able to pull rank did not help his cause.

Whoever was to blame, and there was plenty of mudslinging in the local papers afterwards, the fallout was dismal. Shaw, the Hallam captain, resigned his position on the club board, temporarily as it happened, until harmonious relations were re-established between the two clubs which, unhappily, took a number of years. The unsavoury incident thrust football onto Sheffield's back pages. Readers would have been dismayed but also fascinated by how such a simple game could arouse passions so feverishly, both on and off the pitch. Rather than dampening enthusiasm for the sport, the 'Battle of Bramall Lane' helped to stimulate its growth. Football fever gripped the town and almost overnight another dozen clubs popped up out of nowhere. Against the backdrop of Charles Darwin's recently published and groundbreaking theory of evolution, football in Yorkshire could be said to be winning its fight for sporting life.

FOOTNOTES

[1] The Hallamshire Volunteer Rifles was one of numerous territorial units raised nationwide in 1859, three years after the end of the Crimean War, to combat an imminent invasion by Napoleon III of France, the grandson of the emperor Napoleon Bonaparte, which in the event never came.

[2] Not to be confused with a second 'Battle of Bramall Lane' fought between Sheffield United and West Bromwich Albion on 16th March, 2002. With West Brom leading 3-0 this bruising encounter was abandoned ten minutes from time when the Blades ended up with just six players on the pitch. The farcical situation arose from United having three sent off and then two more taken injured from the fray after they had used all their substitutes. West Brom boss Gary Megson was far from happy. 'There will be no replay,' he fumed. 'If we are called back to Bramall Lane we shall kick-off and then walk off the pitch.' Following an investigation, the Football League declared that the result should stand and punished United with a £10,000 fine for indiscipline.

2

Football's A Stage

THE explosion of interest in football in Sheffield ignited a keen sense of rivalry between the new clubs. No longer was a game merely a fun knockabout between friends during the cricket close season. Local bragging rights were now at stake, glory ready to be won. But where were the cups, the trophies, the silver pots to prove who was the best?

By the time the Christmas feasts were consumed in 1866, there was still no tangible reward for one club beating any other. What Sheffield football needed was someone with the vision and the flair to take it onto the next level. Step forward Irishman Tommy Youdan, the flamboyant owner of the Alexandra Music Hall and popular town councillor. In March 1864 he had lost a good deal of chattels in the Great Sheffield Flood when the newly-built Dale Dyke Dam failed and sent 700 million gallons of water coursing down the Loxley valley and into the centre of Sheffield. Some 270 people were killed and 800 properties destroyed. But the resilient Youdan bounced back and, in the New Year of 1867, the gregarious showman was in such a position again to be able to sponsor a knockout tournament for the vogue sport of the moment. Paying for everything out of his own pocket, including a sparkling silver trophy, the Youdan Cup was a clever marketing exercise, designed to advertise its patron and his theatre. But it also marked a milestone for organised football because here was its first silverware, predating the FA Cup by five years.

A dozen clubs were lured by the prospect of winning local fame: Broomhall, Fir Vale, Garrick, Hallam, Heeley, Mackenzie, Mechanics, Milton, Sheffield Norfolk, Norton, Pitsmoor and Wellington. One side conspicuous by its absence was Sheffield FC which had taken the extraordinary decision to withdraw from all local matches in favour of challenging teams from across the county border, Nottingham being favourite opponents.

Kicking off in early February, the Youdan Cup was played for under Sheffield Rules. Within a month the sides whittled themselves down, round by round, to two finalists, Hallam, captained by JC Shaw, and Norfolk. On 6th March, 1867 around 3,000 paying spectators watched The Countrymen draw 0-0 with Norfolk on goals scored but emerged victorious and inaugural Cup winners by virtue of slamming in two late rouges.

Borrowed from Eton school rules, rouges were a short-lived feature of the Sheffield game which were scored by kicking the ball through large outer posts and used as a back-up system in the event of a draw on goals. Unfortunately, the silversmiths failed to craft the Youdan Cup in time for the presentation and so Shaw was frustratingly left without a trophy to lift. When he did finally get his hands on the claret jug it soon went walkabouts, mysteriously resurfacing more than a century later in a

Scottish antiques shop and obliging Hallam to fork out £2,000 to be reacquainted with their lost heirloom.

Almost immediately after the one-off tournament ran its triumphal course, the dozen cup chasers joined with The Club in forming a permanent alliance, the Sheffield Football Association. The Sheffield FA, which from 1869 was led by Shaw, was an instant threat to another federation of football clubs based in London and known as *The* Football Association. Co-founded in 1863 by a London-based solicitor from Hull called Ebenezer Cobb Morley and dominated by Oxbridge graduates, the FA had one aim, to unite under one umbrella the dribbling code that was beginning to flourish also in the Home Counties. Morley, as FA secretary, drafted the first laws which, as with Sheffield Rules, banned the disagreeable activities of hacking and running with the ball held in the hand. These restrictions on 'manliness', in particular hacking, angered a good number of the FA's own member clubs who resigned in protest and went off to develop the game of 'rugger'. In a parting salvo, Mr FW Campbell of the Blackheath club warned those they left behind: 'You will do away with all the courage and pluck of the game, and I will be bound to bring over a lot of Frenchmen who would beat you with a week's practice.' A damning verdict if ever there was one.

Morley and his cohorts at the FA suddenly found themselves fighting for survival. Membership dwindled to ten clubs (interestingly, Sheffield FC was one of them) of which only three bothered to abide by the FA's own regulations. This was not wholly surprising considering the rules included a stifling three-man offside, a constraint on attacking play that was anathema to Sheffield Rules. In the industrialised towns and cities of the North and Midlands many new clubs, such as Stoke City (formed 1863), Nottingham Forest (1867) and Rotherham FC (1870), rejected

FA rules in favour of those operating in Sheffield. It seemed only a matter of time before the teetering London faction toppled into the abyss.

Then, out of the wings, strode Charles Alcock, a young and dynamic successor to Morley as FA secretary. This 'colossus of Victorian sport', as he was described by his biographer Keith Booth, focused his initial efforts on saving the London association from extinction. That goal was soundly achieved by the introduction of a knockout competition that was modelled on the Cock House Cup at Harrow, his old public school, and which in due course became the most prestigious trophy in English football - the FA Challenge Cup. The first Final was held at The Oval cricket ground on 16th March, 1872 and featured the officers of the Royal Engineers and Wanderers, an aristocratic team packed with ex-university chaps and captained by none other than Alcock. In the Golden Age of the gentleman amateur, Wanderers were the Chelsea of their day, winning the 'Little Tin Idol', as the FA Cup was popularly known, five times in the 1870s, starting with a 1-0 victory in the first Final. In these early years the decider was often played on the morning of the Varsity boat race, thereby giving spectators the opportunity to attend both spectacles. Such scheduling speaks volumes for the elite class of player and spectator the game of football attracted in the capital.

North and South became entangled in a mellow power struggle. An *entente cordiale* clearly existed though, for in spite of a divergence in their respective rules, mainly over offside and throw-ins, an annual Sheffield-London fixture was established in December 1871 to showcase Association football, or soccer as it was shortened to. When it came to the important matter of cup competition, however, the friendship garnered by these annual encounters was suspended. The Sheffield FA discouraged its affiliated clubs from entering the FA Cup, fearing they could become infatuated with the London code. So instead an alternative and very local tournament was inaugurated, unimaginatively called the Sheffield Challenge Cup.

The committee grandees, headed up by Shaw, must have raised their glasses in celebration and slapped each other heartily on the back when a considerable crowd of 8,000 - almost treble the size of that attending the FA Cup Final - descended on Bramall Lane for the first Sheffield Challenge Cup Final in spring 1877. The fans were treated to a sumptuous seven goal feast, Wednesday FC, another club with a fine cricketing heritage and the forebears of Sheffield Wednesday, mounting a dramatic fight back from three goals down to beat Heeley 4-3 in extra-time. 'We firmly believe there is a much greater vitality in the cutlery town's society than there is in the so-called national one of the London Association,' boasted a cocksure Sheffield committee member at their end-of-season Annual Dinner. Clearly the Sheffield FA regarded itself as the leading man, but things were about to change radically.

Despite a comparative lack of support at its matches, the FA Cup was trumpeted as a big success by many influential personages within the game. The number of entrants for the competition had doubled since 1872 and Alcock had cast his net far and wide to land such prize catches as Queen's Park from Glasgow, Welsh side Druids, Shropshire Wanderers and, in a *coup de grâce*, Sheffield FC. The seeds of a truly nationwide competition had been sown.

A groundswell of public opinion welled up demanding, for the good of the game, that soccer everywhere adopt a once-and-for-all common set of rules. In reality, it was a thinly veiled call for the London code to be implemented across the country in order for the FA Cup to blossom unimpeded. The Sheffield FA, with an affiliation of some 40 clubs and 5,000 players, became a victim of its own insularity. As early as 1877 - just a few months after that triumphant first Sheffield Challenge Cup Final - they threw in the towel, exchanging their status as Northern moguls for that of FA provincial satellite. Sheffield Rules were abolished, the hated three-man offside rule was introduced to Yorkshire and the old boy network at the Football Association was left to assume the guardianship of a unified and national sport. Tommy Youdan might have brought knockout competition to the football stage, but Charles Alcock had shrewdly used it to steal all the limelight.

3

Napoleon Of Football

NOT content with winning fame for introducing the FA Cup, Charles Alcock took a second bite at football greatness when he launched an annual fixture which rapidly established itself as the pinnacle in any British soccer season; the England v Scotland international.

Liaising with bigwigs from Queen's Park, then the leading soccer club north of Hadrian's Wall, the Sunderland-born secretary of the FA advocated the tie, 'in order to further the interests of the Association in Scotland'. The momentous fixture took place on St. Andrew's Day, 30th November, 1872 at the West of Scotland cricket ground in Glasgow; even here, in a country not exactly renowned for it, the summer game intrudes.

Scotland, resplendent in dark blue shirts and scarlet pixie-like nightcaps, were merely the Queen's Park team in another guise. In contrast the England team, managed by Alcock and kitted out in navy blue caps and white shirts emblazoned with the three lions' badge, were a mixed bunch picked from nine different clubs. One was 22-year-old Sheffielder John Charles Clegg, a nippy, gaunt looking, long-striding forward for the Wednesday Football Club with a keen eye for goal. Born on 15th June, 1850, the eldest son of Alderman William Johnson Clegg, Charles, as he was always known, was the only player from a club based outside the FA's southern heartlands. His England colleagues included well-to-do types like Cuthbert Ottaway, an Old Etonian and the England captain; Arnold Kirke-Smith, a theologian student at Oxford University; Charles Morice, a team-mate of Ebenezer Morley's at the Barnes club, and Reginald de Courtenay Welch, from landed gentry stock and a star of the all-conquering Wanderers.

As the match progressed, Clegg became increasingly frustrated by some of his upper-class team-mates who refused to pass or even talk to him. They were, he later recalled, 'awful snobs and not much troubled about a man fra' Sheffield'. Such aloofness, it would seem, arose from Clegg being born on the wrong rung of the all-important social ladder. He was neither schooled at one of the leading public establishments, nor was he an Oxford or Cambridge man; little use him being the son of a future mayor of Sheffield. To his snooty team-mates he was just a trainee solicitor from somewhere 'oop north' who spoke with a funny accent.

On a cold, wet afternoon, 4,000 shivering spectators, unaware of the tension in the England camp, paid a shilling each to watch their nation go to war with the Auld Enemy. Except this was no battle. The match was, in fact, played in the Corinthian spirit as befitted gentlemanly amateurs. It illustrated too how football had progressed in the fifteen years since William Prest and Nathaniel Creswick had had their *tête-à-tête*. The game lasted ninety minutes rather than three hours. Both sides fielded eleven players, including a dedicated goalie, defenders (called cover-goals) and half-backs. A designated referee, ably assisted by two umpires acting suspiciously like linesmen, officiated. And the offside rule, controversial and unloved by many, particularly in Sheffield, was played.

The Scots were a revelation. Rejecting England's 1-1-8 line-up for a more balanced 2-2-6 formation, admiring reporters dubbed them 'Scotch Professors' for the way they practised the 'scientific art' of passing the ball. Football's first international match may have ended in yet another 0-0 draw but from that moment onwards mobile 'combination' play, as Alcock coined it, was roundly applauded by all. Scotland lost only three of the next 18 encounters between the two countries, proof, if it were needed, that their system worked. By the mid-1880s exhibitions of one-man dribbling had been marginalised to the wings and the slightly more defensive 2-3-5 pyramid formation had taken the tactical high ground, a position it would not relinquish for another forty years.

For JC Clegg, a non-smoking, teetotal Methodist - 'no one ever gets lost on a straight road' was his cautionary motto - his joyless experience with England was best forgotten. He was not awarded a second chance to make amends but his younger brother William Edwin, a fellow solicitor in the family law firm, did play in the next international in 1873. Considering the siblings' early exposure to 'combination' play it cannot be coincidental that the passing game caught on quicker in Sheffield than anywhere else in England.

Putting his international misery to one side, Charles proved himself as one of the very best footballers in his home town. A regular participant for Sheffield in fixtures against London and Glasgow, he was also a prominent member of the Wednesday side that won the Sheffield

he displayed a freedom of loyalties that is all but impossible to imagine in these hardened days of partisan support. Stranger still is how, after years of passionate campaigning against the payment of players, he remained involved with both clubs when they took to professionalism in the late 1880s. By that time he had succeeded Shaw as chairman of a reorganised and renamed Sheffield & Hallamshire FA. His unwavering and disciplined leadership alerted the mandarins at the Football Association and, in 1886, he was appointed to the FA Council. Four years later, aged forty and with his waxed hair and moustache now burnished like Sheffield steel, he was promoted to the post of FA Chairman. Those elitist snobs who had once snubbed him on the pitch certainly had use now for a lawyer from Sheffield.

Although he could be as strait-laced as a virgin's corset and possessed a rather dour outlook on life, as did many Victorians, Charles Clegg was not without humour. Taking charge of a disciplinary hearing, Clegg asked a young player who had been sent off for uttering un-gentlemanly remarks, what he had said to the match official. After a pause the nervous player rather tremulously replied, 'I've shit better referees'. Sitting back and musing for a moment, Clegg then pronounced: 'I see. All right, I'll tell you what I'll do. I'll give you a week to prove you can do just that. But if you can't, I'm afraid you'll have to pay a £1 fine.'

A great supporter of social causes, including the Temperance Society and the YMCA movement, Clegg was not one to rant and rave but he nevertheless had an iron will and the courage to pursue his convictions. Such was the powerbase he diligently built up in the inner sanctums of the Football Association that he earned the moniker, 'The Napoleon of Football'. During his long tenure, the FA became increasingly autocratic and inflexible. After entering FIFA in 1905 they withdrew their membership in 1928, not to return until after the Second World War. When the World Cup was introduced by Frenchman Jules Rimet in 1930 it was treated with such suspicion that the FA did not enter an England team for another 20 years. Footballers behind the formation of a Players Union in December 1907 were promptly banned from the game and, in 1921, women were barred from playing at Football League grounds, effectively strangling the life out of the ladies' game which had begun to flower during the Great War.

Clegg truly became emperor of all he surveyed in 1923 when he succeeded Lord Alfred Kinnaird, a grand old figure who played in an unsurpassed total of nine FA Cup Finals (1873-83), as President of the FA. A distinguished career was crowned in 1927 when King George V bestowed a knighthood upon him. By now an old man, Sir Charles Clegg soldiered on for another decade, dying, aged 87, at his Sheffield home on 26th June, 1937. His death was met with widespread sorrow. The commanding and hardworking Yorkshireman had shaped and influenced the game of Association football, for better or for worse and sometimes against his own better judgement, as few people have done before or since. At his funeral in Sheffield Cathedral the Rev H Tyler Lang paid tribute to his 'work to maintain the integrity of sport and to keep football clean of prostitution.'

Sir Charles Clegg was an outstanding if domineering administrator and a talented footballer, portrayed in Alcock's *Football Annual* as 'very fast with the ball, passing it with great judgment and, when within sight of the enemy's goal-posts, an unerring kick'. In his youth he was a champion sprinter, the finest amateur quarter-miler in the country. To such an impressive bow he added yet another string, that of top-class referee. He was in charge when Old Etonians became the last amateur side to win the FA Cup in 1882. A decade later he refereed the last Cup Final to be held at The Oval, watched by a 25,000 crowd, the largest yet for English football's blue ribbon event. More prestigious still, he officiated the England-Scotland international in 1893 in which Fred Spiksley, a slightly-built forward from Wednesday, scored twice in a 5-2 hammering of the Scots. Small recompense, perhaps, for the miserable time he had endured as a Wednesday player in an England shirt all those years before.

4

Pay To Play

BY THE late 1870s, Yorkshire football - indeed football in general - had successfully navigated the white rapids of invention, dispute and change, emerging in tact and fashioned to such a degree that it was readily identifiable from its fierce half-brother rugby, and more than recognisable as the sport adored by billions of fans around the world today.

Considering the huge development it had undergone over such a short space of time, club football must have felt in need of a breather, time to take stock. Yet the next test was not only imminent but the sternest it had faced so far, one which but for a great dollop of good luck and some old-fashioned commonsense would have fractured the game before it had hardly begun.

The story begins in the autumn of 1876 with James Lang, a one-eyed former shipbuilder from Scotland who earned his weekly wages in a Sheffield knife-making works. A riveter from the Clyde, Lang was on the books of a company owned by Walter Fearnehough, a board member of Wednesday FC, performing a job that entailed no formal duties. Lang had landed himself a cushy number, swapping back-breaking labours in the shipyards for apparently nothing much more strenuous than reading the papers with his right eye, as an industrial accident had cost him the sight in his left one.

So what prompted a Sheffield manufacturer to take on a half-blind Glaswegian when someone closer to home could surely have done the job? The answer is football. In spite of his disability, Lang was one of the finest players of his generation. He starred for Clydesdale against Queens Park in the first Scottish Cup Final in 1874, twice played for Scotland and appeared in numerous Glasgow representative teams. His employment in Sheffield was a smokescreen, a fudge to get round the knotty problem of soccer supposedly being, as James Catton, editor of *The Athletic News* wrote, 'the innocent diversion of the upper and middle classes who had no thought other than to pay for their own boots and clothes, take their own railway tickets, discharge their own hotel bills and entertain the teams which visited them.'

Lang was recruited not because he possessed an extraordinary talent as a cutler but for the dynamite he had in his boots. In return for an easy working life it was 'understood' that he would turn out each Saturday in the blue and white hoops of the Wednesday Football Club. Lang was a 'shamateur', football's first professional player in all but name. And he knew it, admitting later that he, 'hadn't crossed the border to play for nothing.'

He impressed his future employer while playing for Glasgow against Sheffield at Bramall Lane in February 1876. Contact was made, an offer proposed and 'Reddie', as Lang was nicknamed, presumably for a shock of red hair, immediately upped sticks and resettled in South Yorkshire.

Well versed in the combination play of his compatriots, he became a central figure alongside Charles and William Clegg in the Wednesday side that won the first Sheffield Challenge Cup. Interestingly, Heeley fielded their own Scottish international in that Final, Peter Andrews, who when not playing soccer, worked as an insurance agent in Leeds. Indeed many of football's early 'professionals' were Scotsmen, bribed by the prospect of better paid jobs in the North of England and by the covert stuffing of a silver half-crown or two in their boots after matches, so-called boot money.

Heeley and Wednesday secured the services of their big-name 'foreigners' to help them challenge for trophies, a move which paid handsome dividends: one or other, sometimes both, reached the Sheffield Challenge Cup Final in each of the tournament's first eight seasons. In addition to their Scottish imports both clubs could call upon England internationals such as Jack Hunter (seven caps), a rock-steady half-back for Heeley, and Billy Mosforth (nine caps, three goals), the 'Little Wonder', an inventive forward who played for Hallam as well as Wednesday, and whose quick feet, pinpoint crosses and corkscrew shots at goal were a real wow with the crowds.

Unsurprisingly, Sheffield's top two teams attracted the largest attendances as, all over town, football was being devoured by a new generation of fan. The Industrial Revolution transformed Sheffield into a northern boom town and the *nouveaux riches* it created became the first patrons of football. But by the 1870s a social revolution - one which would turn football from posh pastime into the epitome of working-class sport - was having a far more profound effect on the size of crowds.

Trade union agitation and a stack of factory laws effectively curtailed the working week, resulting in many common workers having Saturday afternoons off for the first time in living memory. The cooperative way in which they toiled was perfectly suited to the new 'combination' style of play and the game was eagerly taken up, as Catton said, 'by the mechanics, the artisans, the clerks, and thousands of others who depended upon weekly wages.' Albert Jenkins, an 18-year-old fitter for the Great Northern Railway, founded Doncaster Rovers in 1879. Lockwood Brothers, a team of file steel and cutlery workers from Sheffield, enjoyed bountiful success which culminated in a run to the last sixteen of the FA Cup in 1886/87. Works teams flourished in and around the county capital too with employees at York railway station, Joseph Rowntree's chocolate factory and John Smith's brewery all forming football clubs.

Thousands more men from this liberated industrial labour force spent the little spare brass they had in their pockets on going to watch a match, swapping the daily grind for ninety minutes of escapism. Boozed up and boisterous, they congregated on uncovered terraces and sang lewd songs and shouted at the referee and the opposition, and all the while roared on their own team to score. The raw passion at the heart of modern football crowds was already alive and kicking.

Football was changing fast but after many years of enlightenment those running the game in Sheffield now dug in their heels. Ignoring the cloak-and-daggers surrounding James Lang's recruitment and the situation then prevailing in Yorkshire cricket - the County XI was comprised almost entirely of paid professionals - the Sheffield FA committed itself to upholding the amateur game. In 1881 they suspended eleven leading players, including Hunter (Billy Mosforth escaped a ban by the skin of his teeth), for allegedly profiteering from exhibition matches organised to raise funds for the families of soldiers killed in the Zulu War of 1879. These charity games were bizarre black and white minstrel shows featuring 'The Zulus', a team of white men blackened up with burnt corks, decked out in African tribal costume and brandishing native shields. The players were even announced to the crowds with Zulu warrior names; Hunter, for example, was Dabulamanzi, the brother of King Cetewayo. For three years they toured the North of England and never lost a game.

Over the Pennines in Lancashire there were no such qualms about footballers lining their pockets. In 1883, after Preston North End were chucked out of the FA Cup for fielding two professionals, Major William Sudell, the Lilywhites' boss, stated quite frankly that the custom of paying players was rife, even in Sheffield. The brief era of the closeted shamateur was over. The game now faced a full-frontal assault by professionalism.

Tensions escalated in 1884 when Lancashire's leading clubs threatened to go it alone if the payment of players remained outlawed. Unwilling to see the game it had strived so hard to unite splinter in two, the FA offered a political compromise: 'It is now expedient in the interests of Association football to legalise the employment of professional football players, but only under certain restrictions'. Restrictions or no restrictions, the proposal outraged the Sheffield FA and a host of other traditionalists, including representatives of the Birmingham FA, who swiftly voted it down. Professionalism was, 'an evil which must be repressed,' huffed Charles Clegg's brother-in-law, the unfortunately named William Pierce-Dix. Clegg spoke for many when he argued that legalisation would, 'place greater power in the hands of the betting men and, if ever the gamblers got control of the game, I wouldn't give tuppence for it.'

Charles Alcock disagreed. Understanding that professionalism was a monster that needed to be tamed rather than exterminated, the FA secretary contended that professionals were not the, 'utter outcasts some people represent them to be' and neither was it immoral for working men to, 'labour at football as at cricket'. After much volatile debate, Alcock persuaded sufficient liberals to squeeze the legalisation of professionalism through in July 1885, albeit with stringent stipulations; wages, contracts, registration, working conditions and transfers would be strictly regulated. The labouring player had won the right to be paid a few shillings each week but in doing so he had shackled himself to the Football Association, an iron bond which took almost a century to break.

Alcock's judiciousness averted a damaging rift such as the one that befell rugby in 1895, when northern rugby clubs split from the amateur Rugby Football Union and formed their own self-regulated professional Northern Union, the forerunner to Rugby League. Yet Clegg and his colleagues in Sheffield remained bitter about the outcome. Honesty and fair play - the amateur ideals of sportsmanship - were, they thought, under threat. Their defiance, though, was as futile as King Canute's attempts at commanding the tides, for within a year open professionalism sprouted up like an ugly weed in their own back yard.

Hunter, angered by his treatment over Zulu-gate, had already left town to take over as player-manager of Blackburn Olympic, a team of tradesmen and weavers whom he lead to a historic victory over Old Etonians in the 1883 FA Cup Final. An ageing Lang followed, escaping the persecution when he joined Burnley in 1886. But Mosforth, the darling of the Sheffield crowds, chose to prospect for gold closer to home. Constantly scheming to make a few extra quid on the side, he was well known for placing wagers on himself to score and would swap sides if it was to his advantage, as in one match between Wednesday and Hallam when a supporter shouted out from the crowd, 'Ten bob and free drinks all week, Billy, if you'll change your shirt'. Mosforth was a non-conformist in the best Yorkshire tradition. He stood on ceremony for no one, not even the aristocratic Hon Alfred Lyttleton, a future Cabinet minister, who copped a voluble earful from him for hogging the ball in an England-Scotland international.

What Billy really desired was a slice of the Wednesday gate money. His demand was rebuffed by the board, but rather than meekly backing down, Sheffield's best footballer simply shrugged his shoulders and left, taking with him a crop of other players to form Sheffield Rovers, a short-lived professional team. Wednesday's form collapsed during the 1886/87 season, culminating in an embarrassing 16-0 drubbing by Halliwell. As the old saying goes, everyone has their price and ultimately Wednesday had theirs. If they kept on losing matches they would lose their hard won support and with that much of their revenue. Backed into a corner, the committee reluctantly voted to adopt professionalism in April 1887.

In light of the James Lang saga it is perhaps fitting that *Sheffield* Wednesday (as they were now known by the man on the street, even though an official name change did not come about until 1929) should become Yorkshire's first openly professional football club. A topsy-turvy season ended on a high when Mosforth, the prodigal son, returned - for a match fee, of course, amounting to the princely sum of five shillings - in time to inspire the team to another Sheffield Challenge Cup victory.

Charles Clegg must have been sorely disappointed by Wednesday's conversion. Yet two years later he gave his full backing to the founding of Sheffield United, a semi-professional outfit from the word go. Somewhere along the line Clegg reconciled his strong principles with the reality that professionalism was here to stay, a fact made more palatable by the knowledge that the game had not self-combusted in a fireball of greed and gamesmanship. And while the Golden Age of the gentleman amateur had come to an end, amateur players still peppered the England team for some years to come. One of them, GO Smith, a celebrated forward for the Corinthians, graciously conceded in 1899 that professionalism had, 'made it possible for thousands to enjoy a game which would otherwise have been altogether out of their reach.'

Lang, Hunter and Mosforth had all hung up their mercenary boots when, in September 1892, Wednesday and United entered a new all-professional tournament called the Football League. Instigated four years earlier by Aston Villa director William McGregor, the intention of the League was to exploit football's new wage-earning labour force for all it was worth. The home-and-away format was a big hit with the masses, not least in Sheffield where they clicked through the turnstiles in their thousands, rewarding Wednesday and United with bumper crowds and bulging bank balances. Sheffield FC, Hallam, Heeley, Lockwood Brothers and the rest were left behind, relics of a bygone amateur age. The big gamble on professionalism had paid off.

5

Olives To Owls

PROFESSIONALISM ushered in a turbulent period in which Sheffield Wednesday experienced more booms and busts than the UK economy. Like clambering aboard a white knuckle ride, thrilling highs of back-to-back Championships and a brace of FA Cup victories were checked by the stomach churning lows of relegation, eviction, and a ritual humiliation in another Cup Final. Throw in the beginnings of the Steel derby and the result was a bubbling cauldron of sweet success and bitter failure.

Choosing to follow the professional path was not the only major decision taken by the Wednesday board in the spring of 1887. For several years they had used Bramall Lane and other grounds such as those at Myrtle Road and Sheaf House to play their games. But why, they mused, should their successes - Wednesday won the Sheffield Challenge Cup six times between 1877 and 1888 - benefit someone else's coffers? So they upped sticks and invested the small fortune of £5,000 into erecting a new purpose built home along Queen's Road. Christening it Olive Grove - a sweet sounding name which evokes images of orchards and rural life - the ground was in reality a reclaimed boggy field plonked slap bang in the middle of the Midland Railway line, garden allotments and rows of red-brick cottages. Cinder terraces were punctuated by one tin grandstand with capacity for a thousand fans - quite a luxury in those days - and across its roof, emblazoned in large blue and white letters and advertising the team for miles around, were the words 'Sheffield Wednesday Football Club'.

Wednesday FC were now in full control of their destiny having four years earlier divorced their founders, the Wednesday Cricket Club. This band of merry cricketing men first got together in 1820 and took their name from the day of the week on which they habitually played their cricket matches. It was on 4th September, 1867 that the club's members gathered at the Adelphi Hotel on Arundel Street - where the Crucible Theatre, scene of snooker's World Championships, now stands - and, over a few pints, agreed to form a football team to keep the cricketing fraternity together during the winter break. After the parting of the ways in 1883, Wednesday CC slipped into a prolonged decline, finally disbanding in 1925. The Adelphi, incidentally, was a favoured watering hole of many of Sheffield's sporting luminaries and was a regular venue for Sheffield FA meetings. It was also the birthplace, on 8th January, 1863, of Yorkshire County Cricket Club. The landlord at the time was Harry Sampson, an old-time cricketer considered good enough to play for the United England XI and who still holds a bizarre world record for the highest individual score made on ice: 162 for Wednesday against Sheffield Town in February 1841.

Billy Mosforth, not surprisingly, scored the first goal at Olive Grove in a 4-4 draw with Blackburn Rovers. Within two years the great wage hunter was back at Bramall Lane. His best days were behind him but, always the supreme opportunist, he grabbed the chance of one last big pay day by signing for a brand new professional football team, Sheffield United.

Sheffield United Football Club came about as a direct result of the FA Cup semi final between Preston North End and West Bromwich Albion at Bramall Lane on 16th March, 1889. The match, refereed by JC Clegg, produced a Sheffield record attendance of 22,688 and generated receipts of around £570 - enough to buy three or four terraced houses. This convinced some members of the Sheffield United Cricket Club that football could financially underpin the less profitable summer game. Six days after the semi-final, Charles Stokes who, coincidentally, was a co-founder of Wednesday FC, proposed at a committee meeting held in the offices of the club secretary Joseph Wolstinholm at 10 Norfolk Row that the cricket club should form its own football team and, moreover, that it should be run as a semi-professional unit. Given Sheffield's historic stance against the 'evil' of professionalism, it is no surprise that his proposal was not universally welcomed. All the same, the motion carried by the slimmest of margins, a single vote, with Charles Clegg decisively offering unexpected support. An inauspicious start to life, perhaps, but Sheffield United Football Club had nevertheless gasped its first few breaths.

Across town Wednesday were settling in nicely at Olive Grove. In 1889/90 they were crowned champions of the inaugural Football Alliance League, a 12-team competition launched by their president John Holmes, a convert to professionalism, after his application for Wednesday to join the Football League was rejected. Two years later the FAL merged with its big brother and effectively became Division Two in an enlarged Football League. Wednesday, no doubt benefiting from Holmes's connections, were fast-tracked into the top flight while United had to settle for a berth in the second tier.

A fine season was on the verge of going stratospheric when the Wednesday team ran out at The Oval on 29th March, 1890 to compete in their first ever FA Cup Final. Swifts, Accrington, Notts County and Bolton had all been dispatched in earlier rounds but, ominously, their opponents in the decider were Blackburn Rovers, an outstanding side with a strong Cup pedigree who had walloped them 5-1 when the two last met in the competition in 1882. What should have been a jolly day out in the razzle-dazzle of London became a horrible nightmare for the Yorkshire contingent. Under the rapt gaze of the whole football nation, and with *The Times* proudly declaring, 'The Cup Final has now assumed the dignity and importance of an International match', Wednesday folded like a rickety house of cards. 'Sheffield are beaten already,' claimed Mr Gregson, Secretary of the Lancashire Association, before kick-off. 'They are down in the dumps and sitting in their dressing-room quiet as mice. They look frightened.'

Blackburn, in contrast, oozed confidence and no wonder. They had won the FA Cup three times on the trot between 1884 and 1886 and teemed with Scottish 'professors' and international players. With ten local lads in their line-up, Wednesday looked like a bunch of terrified kids going to war. Shell-shocked by a barrage of Blackburn attacks, their own arsenal was exposed as a pile of damp squibs; it was like trying to combat cannon fire with snowballs. When the flak stopped flying the depressing score line in this distinctly one-sided Battle of the Roses read: Blackburn Rovers 6 Sheffield Wednesday 1. Billy Townley blitzed the first FA Cup Final hat-trick but pity poor Jim Smith, the Wednesday keeper. On only one other occasion in the long tradition of

FA Cup finals has a custodian had the ignominy of picking the ball out of his net as many times as he did.

A gloom settled upon the club. From heroes the previous season, Wednesday, playing in their iconic blue and white stripes for the first time, went to zeroes in 1890/91, picking up the FAL wooden spoon. Amidst the melancholy, however, one bright shaft of light lit up Olive Grove in the run up to Christmas. Sheffield United, the new kid on the block, knocked on Wednesday's door and asked if they wanted to come out to play and so, on 15th December, 1890, the Steel City derby began. For the record, some 10,000 hardy souls braved the bitter cold at Olive Grove, JC Clegg refereed the match and the hosts emerged the victors by two goals to one.

The following October, United exacted revenge, ripping up the form book to crush Wednesday 5-0 at Bramall Lane and prompting some wags to circulate 'funeral cards' in the town bearing the lamentation:

> In Loving Remembrance of the Sheffield Wednesday Football Team who were safely put to rest on Monday October 26th at Bramall Lane

Mickey-taking and good natured banter spilled over into the workplace, fuelling a passionate rivalry that has intensified down the years, sometimes boiling over into vitriol, hate and even violence. But whilst derby matches captured the fans' imaginations and admittance to the money-spinning Football League in 1892 kept the bank manager happy, Wednesday coveted more than anything the FA Cup. A whole new team, overseen by Arthur Dickinson, Wednesday's longest serving and most successful manager (1891-1920), was built to mount a renewed assault. After falling at the semi-final hurdle in both 1894 and '95 they stumbled over it in 1896, beating Bolton in a replay to reach their second Cup Final.

The venue had changed since their last appearance, from The Oval to the cavernous bowl of Crystal Palace, as indeed had the FA Cup itself. In a sensational robbery, the old trophy had been stolen in an overnight smash and grab job while it was on display in a Birmingham shop window the previous September. The Cup was lost forever. Red faced, the FA considered spending the £200 insurance money on commissioning a replacement made of gold but in the end they opted for frugality and a silver replica costing one-tenth the price.

Mercifully, Wednesday's opponents were different too, the might of Blackburn Rovers being replaced by a run of the mill Wolverhampton Wanderers team which had struggled all season to stay in Division One. It was now or never if Sheffield Wednesday were to become the first Yorkshire side to get their hands on the FA Cup.

Wednesday had a useful team, ably captained by right back Jack Earp and marshalled from centre half by Tommy Crawshaw, a tough-tackling, home grown talent who played ten times for England in an era when caps were as precious as gold dust. In the 2-3-5 formation the centre half was not the defensive clogger he became but the midfield linchpin on which the fortunes of a team turned, the man who smoothly linked defence with attack. Often he was his side's best player but the sparkling jewel in Wednesday's blue and white crown was not Crawshaw, wonderful though he was, but 'Flying' Fred Spiksley, an exciting successor to Mosforth at outside left. Snatched from Gainsborough Trinity in 1891 from under the noses of an indignant Accrington, he represented Wednesday brilliantly for twelve years. Possessing all the poise and thundering pace of a thoroughbred racehorse - as a kid he harboured dreams of becoming a jockey - Spiksley dribbled the ball faster than most players could sprint without it. He was, noted Ernest Needham, the Sheffield United captain, someone who could, 'play the combination game to perfection'. He scored five goals in seven matches for England, including two against Scotland in 1893 when Charles Clegg was the referee.

Although he never fell head over heels in love with the game - a football match was, he said, like, 'a descent into the bear pit' - Spiksley racked up 114 goals in 321 appearances, none more vital than the brace he scored in the 1896 Final. The first came barely thirty seconds into the game, a tap-in following a swift run and pass from his left winger Harry Davis. Wolves soon equalized after an uncharacteristic mistake by Crawshaw but, on 18 minutes, Spiksley pounced again to score the deciding goal and what a corker it was. Hammering home a loose ball, he hit it with such venom that it rebounded out of the net before the Wolves keeper Bill Tennant had time to react. Thinking the ball must have hit the woodwork Tennant hoofed it up field and is supposed to have asked Earp at the final whistle, without any discernible sign of tongue in cheek, 'When do we replay?'

Proudly holding the new trophy aloft, Earp erased the horrid memories of 1890. The victory should have spurred Wednesday on but an insipid defence of the Cup - they were knocked out by Nottingham Forest in the first round of the 1896/97 competition - triggered an alarming nosedive which ended in 1899 with the club crashing out of Division One and losing their Olive Grove home.

How Sheffield United fans must have howled with glee to see their foes in such dire straits but it was no laughing matter for the Wednesday board. They had spent hard earned cash building Olive Grove but the crux of the matter was they did not own their mudbath. It belonged to the

Duke of Norfolk, who had granted Sheffield Wednesday a perilously short lease. When it came up for renewal the club discovered, to their horror, that the peer was not such a football fan after all. The Midland Railway wanted to expand their line and in its way was Olive Grove's tin stand. The Duke duly obliged and kicked Wednesday off his land. Suddenly homeless, the board sanctioned an urgent share issue to fund the construction of a new ground. Five thousand pounds was raised, a very sizeable sum at such short notice, and it was wisely spent on *buying* a ten-acre site in Owlerton, an undeveloped district on the northern fringes of the city and from which the club takes its modern nickname, the Owls. The old tin grandstand at Olive Grove was dismantled, carted across town and reassembled as the Owlerton stadium went up over the summer. The location was not ideal. It was a long way from the club's traditional fan base and poorly served by public transport, yet the Wednesday faithful remained loyal, trudging the three or four miles every other Saturday to watch the blue and whites play. Adversity galvanised everyone at the club and no one exemplified the rolling up of sleeves and digging in mentality better than Crawshaw, the new club captain. In 1899/1900 he triumphantly led his men to the Division Two title at the first time of asking and without dropping a single point at their new home.

The wheel of fortune was spinning Sheffield Wednesday's way again. A fresh team, full of Yorkshire grit, grew up around the formidable half back trio of Crawshaw, Bob Ferrier and Harry Ruddlesdin. There was Harry Chapman too, a cunning inside right who was kept out of the England team only by the great Steve Bloomer. His brother Herbert later left an indelible mark as a manager on Huddersfield Town and Arsenal. Then there was Scottish international forward Andrew Wilson who followed the track from the Clyde to the Sheaf first trodden by James Lang a quarter of a century before. A true Owls legend, Wilson scored 216 goals in 545 appearances, both club records that are unlikely ever to be broken and he was top scorer six times. Supplanting Spiksley as crowd favourite, Wilson enjoyed a Wednesday career that was as long as the Pennines, playing on until after the First World War. Curiously, Spiksley briefly toured the music halls with Fred Karno's *Football Sketch* when he retired, earning £7 10s a week - better wages than he had ever received as a player.

This Wednesday side could not be accused of reckless abandon but, unashamedly, they were hard to break down. Blending an abundance of hard graft with a never-say-die spirit they went head to head with heavyweights Sunderland and Aston Villa to land the 1902/03 League Championship by a single point in one of the tightest title races of all time. In late March, they defeated Sunderland, the reigning champions, 1-0 at Roker Park, Wilson scoring the crucial goal. Their reward was to be pelted with stones by irate home fans as they left the pitch.

Wednesday retained the title in 1903/04, their miserly defence once again to the fore. Keeper Jack Lyall conceded a mere 28 goals but at the other end of the pitch a shot-shy attack accumulated just 48 goals - one less than relegated Liverpool. Wednesday's dour approach may have bored the pants and braces off their own fans at times but winning can be as powerful a drug as entertainment. For a long while they were gunning for the double until their clam-like defence inexplicably opened up in the FA Cup semi-final to gift Manchester City, their closest challengers in the League, a 3-0 victory. Even so, it had been a momentous year and the club celebrated it in style with a sumptuous banquet at the old Masonic Hall, dining on mock turtle soup, pigeon, roast sirloin beef, York ham and cheeses and bottles of vintage sherry, claret wine and champagne. Wednesday's golden vein continued with the capture of their second FA Cup in 1907, the holders Everton being beaten 2-1 in, 'an undistinguished match,' according to Geoffrey Green in *The Official History of the FA Cup*, 'with the ball too much in the air and fouls rather plentiful.' Route one football was evidently up and running. Wednesday's goals were scored by James 'Tadger' Stewart and George Simpson who headed in the winner at the back post with four minutes to go. Chapman, meanwhile, twice pulled up to flick a dislodged knee cartilage back into place. With no substitutes back then he had little option but to bravely carry on playing.

The victory was particularly sweet for Crawshaw, the only survivor from the class of '96. A splendid career came to an end in 1908 after his 465th appearance for the club, fittingly a 2-0 victory in the Steel City derby. As Wednesday's imposing midfield broke up so too did their grip on silverware. Although they remained a decent enough side, they did not make another serious tilt for either the Championship or the FA Cup before the Great War, a relatively straitened period in which perhaps the most notable moment came in 1914 when the Owlerton stadium was renamed Hillsborough. It had been a turbulent ride getting there but the Owls had at last a permanent roost of their own.

6

Who Ate All The Pies?

OVER THE years a host of lively characters have lit up Yorkshire football but of them all one quite literally stands out from the crowd: twenty-stone, pot-bellied man-mountain, William 'Fatty' Foulke.

The colossal custodian of the Sheffield United goal in the 1890s, Foulke is reputed to be the heaviest player ever to grace the professional game. He was soccer's prototype cult figure, hero-worshipped and ridiculed in equal measure on the terraces for his great size and eccentric behaviour. The antics of this larger-than-life entertainer have spawned numerous tales; some pure myth, others embellished. Two of the most colourful surround his renowned bad temper and famous love of food.

Imagine for a moment 'Fatty', towering well above six feet tall and completely naked, rampaging about in a foul rage, wanting nothing more than to turn the referee's guts to garters. So spare a thought for Tom Kirkham, the diminutive official in charge of the 1902 FA Cup Final at Crystal Palace who had the audacity to allow a late equalizer by Southampton to stand. His decision, hotly disputed by Foulke as being miles offside, robbed United of a second FA Cup triumph in three years, at least for another week. With the injustice of it all boiling away inside him, Foulke apparently clambered from his post-match bath and without bothering to change furiously set about confronting the ref about his blunder. JT Howcroft, one of the linesmen and an eyewitness to the bizarre saga, later recalled seeing, 'FJ Wall, the secretary of the Football Association, pleading with Foulke, who was in his birthday suit, to go back to his dressing-room, but Big Bill was out for blood.' Luckily, Kirkham caught wind of his impending doom and in a wise act of self-preservation barricaded himself inside his dressing cubicle. Whether the bolt on the door would have held out for long against his assailant's formidable frame is doubtful so he must have been eternally grateful when a posse of FA officials calmed the big man down and prevented him from doing any harm.

Turning the clock back to 1899 we come to the morning of the FA Cup semi-final between Sheffield United and Liverpool. Foulke, recuperating from a torn hamstring, was excused training. While his colleagues traipsed off for a brisk training walk he sneaked down to the hotel dining room and tucked into breakfast. Trouble was he didn't stop at his own. With such a gargantuan appetite to satisfy and no-one around to restrain him, he is said to have polished off the other ten breakfasts earmarked for his team-mates. Not that his Desperate Dan cravings hampered his style too much because after three replays, including a 4-4 thriller at Bolton, United won a place in the Final.

Foulke's feeding frenzy is said to have inspired the 'Who ate all the pies?' song which football fans to this day chant at portly members of the opposition, although this is probably an urban myth. The catcalls were nothing to Fatty who quipped, 'I don't care what they call me, as long as they don't call me late for lunch!' Everything about the former colliery worker was oversized: height, girth, appetite, even his sense of humour: 'I can't train today,' he once told his manager, with a twinkle in his eye and Irish international Peter Boyle strapped across his Herculean shoulders, 'I've got a painful boil on me back!' He once snapped a crossbar in two by idly swinging from it, bringing the United-Wednesday derby he was playing in to a standstill. In another game he stormed off the pitch in a fit of pique, claiming his defence was not trying hard enough. And if he disputed a penalty decision then he was as likely to glower at the referee with ill-disguised malice as attempt to make a save.

Penalty kicks were introduced in 1891 and, up until 1902, the penalty area stretched the full width of the pitch. Goalkeepers were allowed to pick the ball up anywhere in their own half, clearly an advantage, but conversely they were not afforded the mafia-like protection that modern day goalies receive from referees. 'Fatty' may have been big but he still came in for some rough treatment from burly forwards not averse to kicking lumps off him. Sometimes Foulke got his own back, chucking miscreants into the back of the net or sitting on them until he squeezed out an apology.

The impression of Foulke so far is of a bad-tempered, cake-scoffing, referee-threatening lummox but that camouflages the man behind the legend. Good enough to be capped by England - against Wales, at Bramall Lane, in 1897 - for opposing forwards it was like trying to score past an elephant in pantaloons, except this one was surprisingly agile, capable of pulling off spectacular saves and possessing a sledgehammer punch-out that could easily have decked Bob Fitzsimmons, then Britain's world heavyweight boxing champion. Why he was not an England regular is a bit of a mystery. Perhaps the FA thought him far too bulky to be considered a 'proper' international. Maybe they couldn't handle his temper and unconventional manner. Whatever the reason, many good judges of the time lauded Willie Foulke as the greatest goalkeeper alive.

Born a Shropshire lad but raised in Derbyshire, Foulke signed for United as a teenager from Blackwell Colliery in 1894. He joined a talented squad at Bramall Lane, the pick of the bunch being pint-sized skipper Ernest Needham, a box-to-box midfielder known as 'Nudger' on account of his unerring ability to knock opponents off the ball. Able to defend and attack with equal aplomb, Needham's brilliant performances at left half were rewarded with 16 England caps, a record for a Sheffield United player, while his club tally of 554 appearances marks him out as one of the greatest footballers to pull on the red and white stripes. Nor were his sporting talents confined to soccer; a first-class cricket career for Derbyshire yielded seven centuries and more than 6,500 runs between 1901 and 1912.

Together 'Fatty' and 'Nudger' helped transform Sheffield United from professional football's nervous new boys into steely-hearted champions. In 1897/98, the year before Sheffield Wednesday's world crumbled, United became Yorkshire's first League champions. They lost just five games all season and Foulke conceded a measly 31 goals. Attendances at Bramall Lane averaged over 11,500, putting United in the top five best supported teams in the country. Not bad going for a club that a decade beforehand did not exist.

A poor defence of their title - United finished in 16th spot in 1898/99, one place above relegated Bolton Wanderers and Sheffield Wednesday - was more than compensated for by a brilliant run in the FA Cup. Following their epic duel with Liverpool in the semis, United faced Derby County, the pre-match favourites, in the Final at Crystal Palace. Among the crowd of more than 73,000 were such dignitaries as Charles and William Clegg, the latter having followed in their father's footsteps as Lord Mayor of Sheffield; Cecil Rhodes, the South African diamonds mogul and Lord Rosebery, a former Liberal Prime Minister. In a barnstorming display United snuffed out the threat of England's most celebrated forward, Steve Bloomer, before going on a second half goal spree. Bennett, Priest, Beers and Almond all hit the back of the net as United trounced Derby 4-1 to lift the Cup for the first time.

Shortly afterwards, the Sheffield United Cricket & Football Club Ltd, wary of suffering a similar fate to the one that had befallen Sheffield Wednesday, arranged to purchase Bramall Lane from their chief landlord, the Duke of Norfolk. With their future secured, United went head-to-head with reigning champions Aston Villa in a pulsating race for the 1899/1900 League title, pulling up short by just two points. It was of cold comfort to know that their tally of 48 points would have won the Championship in any previous season.

The next year, United's League form again deserted them. Once more they found solace in the FA Cup, powering through to their second final. This time their opponents were Tottenham Hotspur of the Southern League whose presence helped to swell the attendance at Crystal Palace to an unprecedented 114,815. Shoehorned into every conceivable inch of terracing, fans cheered and sang to such deafening effect that the ground rang like church bells. United braved the white hot atmosphere generated by the partisan 'home' crowd and took the tie to a replay after Bennett scored a suspect second equalizer, with no complaints this time from Foulke. But in the re-match at a windswept and piercingly cold Burnden Park Bolton, United were outclassed by a rampant Spurs side that ran out winners by three goals to one.

Both the final and the replay featured right back Harry Thickett, another huge man and as tough as old boots, who played despite the sudden death of his wife. Such a stiff upper lip attitude was commonplace and, as if to prove the wretched point, Walter 'Cocky' Bennett, an aggressive wingman who linked up with Thickett on the right, returned to coal mining at the end of his football career, only to perish in an underground accident at Denaby Colliery in 1908, aged 33.

With that sobering thought in mind, we come full circle to the contentious 1902 FA Cup Final. C.B. Fry, Edwardian cricket's premier amateur batsman and Southampton's right back, reported in the *Southern Echo* that, 'the outstanding feature of the match was the grand goalkeeping of Foulke.' In the replay a week later, again at Crystal Palace, Willie once more took the plaudits, *The Athletic News* hailing him as 'invincible'. At the other end of the pitch centre-forward George Hedley and outside right Billy Barnes, deputising for Bennett who was injured, scored the decisive goals which gave United a 2-1 victory and their third trophy in five years.

The side fielded by the Blades is notable for the inclusion of Alf Common, a chunky, moustachioed inside forward of rare talent who midway through the 1904/05 season became embroiled in a transfer sensation that shook the football world. Claiming he was homesick, Common was allowed to return to Sunderland, his hometown club. Almost immediately, however, he joined relegation-threatened Middlesbrough for a record-breaking £1,000. United were incensed, not least because the price-tag was double the amount they had received. The size of the transfer fee provoked widespread appal with *The Times* thundering: 'The game is heading for financial ruin which is exactly what was forecast when professionalism was first allowed to pollute the sport.' And would you believe it, Common's 'Boro debut not only came at Bramall Lane but involved scoring the only goal of the match. A less popular man could not be found in Sheffield that night.

Such shenanigans were all in the future though when Needham collected the FA Cup from Lady Beatrice Villiers and made a succinct acceptance speech: 'We lost it, so it's fitting that we should win it back.' Few present would have imagined that the river of silver United had been navigating these past few years would so quickly dry up and that 'Nudger' would never get his hands on another trophy.

United went close to reclaiming the title the next season, finishing three points behind Sheffield Wednesday but, in hindsight, the 1902 FA Cup Final was the swansong for many players, including Foulke. His growing inability to get his bulk down to low shots was starting to be cruelly exposed and he was becoming a target for criticism from disgruntled fans. A reprimand was published in one match programme, stuffily informing the taunt boys that, 'a large staff of detectives has been engaged to catch the delinquents and it will go hard with the wrongdoers.' It made little difference. After keeping guard in 340 competitive matches, Foulke was dropped and in 1905 was offloaded to a brand new London club, Chelsea. Within a year, however, he was back in Yorkshire with Bradford City, another fledgling outfit, where he remained until injury forced his retirement from football in November 1907.

Foulke's ampleness was now nudging twenty five stones. He became, in the time-honoured tradition, a publican but a police raid and subsequent conviction for illegal gambling put paid to that career. The happy-go-lucky ex-footballer did not become, as is sometimes reported, a penniless beat-the-goalie sideshow on Blackpool's Golden Mile. He was, in fact, a rather well heeled, gregarious man about town who liked a drink. On 1st May, 1916, as the Great War raged across the slaughterhouses of the Western front, William 'Fatty' Foulke died, age 42, of cirrhosis of the liver at a Sheffield nursing home. It was a sad end to an engaging life, one remembered fondly by Tom Bott, a Sheffield United director: 'Professionals in those days could be quite a handful, but I never had a minute's trouble with Foulke. A wonderful chap. He was intelligent, a good talker, and a marvel for keeping his pecker up when things were running against the team.'

7

The Boxing Parson

A HOLY Trinity of cricket, industry and religion was the catalyst for many a Yorkshire football club being formed. The impact of the first two has been touched upon already, so it is to the last we now cast our eye. Faith began exerting an influence upon the game in the mid-1870s when church congregations started to mix prayer with play. Churchgoers across England founded famous football clubs like Aston Villa (1874), Bolton Wanderers (1874), Everton (1878), Wolverhampton Wanderers (1879) and Southampton (1885). Their connection with the Church of England gave them a social respectability which helped to popularise the game in such areas. Stirring hymns like *Glory, Glory, Hallelujah!*, *When The Saints Go Marching In* and *Abide With Me* found their way onto the terraces, anthemic tunes which rallied teams to the cause. And Praise Be! In the tough coal mining town of Barnsley religion helped gain football a toehold in 1887 when the Reverend Tiverton Preedy arrived in town.

Sounding for all the world like a character out of a Dickens novel, the Rev Preedy was not your typical man of the cloth. True, he was a devout Christian who spent his adult life selflessly spreading the Word of God amongst the poor and needy. But he was also a talented pianist, a brave fighter - one newspaper dubbed him 'The Boxing Parson' on account of his pugilistic skills - and a devoted fan of Association football. He was the driving force behind Barnsley St Peter's, a team which grew up to be Barnsley FC.

How Preedy, a sporty young son of a Norfolk land agent, came to be working in the deprived parish of St Peter's in Barnsley is not entirely clear. What is apparent was his prejudice against the game of rugby which at the time held strong sway in the town. While a buoyant nation celebrated Queen Victoria's Golden Jubilee, Preedy, with all the zeal of the reforming missionary that he was, conjured up, as he put it, 'an Association club such as the Rugbyites will not crush out!' He subscribed to the Victorian ethos of muscular Christianity: keep the body fit and healthy and an otherwise sinful mind will surely follow. He believed that football could be used as a vehicle to drive faith and hope into the harsh lives of ordinary working men. Barnsley, which was ungraciously described by John Wesley, the Methodist minister, in the previous century as, 'a place famous for all manner of wickedness', was not somewhere for the fainthearted. Undeterred, Preedy gained the trust and friendship of his poor community and won the gratitude too of the town's mayor who in later years praised him for having, 'undoubtedly elevated the working class and given them higher aims to work for.'

Preedy's influence on Barnsley St Peter's can not be overstated. A born organiser with a huge appetite for work, he was founder, player, manager, treasurer, recruitment officer, match arranger and PR man all rolled into one enthusiastic bundle of energy. Little wonder the club became known as 'Preedy's Team'. Formed on 6th September 1887, they played their first fixture a fortnight later against Manor House, a team from nearby Worsborough Bridge. Wearing a natty blue and maroon number, they won 4-1, a promising start in anyone's books. Preedy applauded his team for, 'playing honest, robust and straightforward football' but he was stinging in his criticism of those perennial crowd problems: bad behaviour and coarse language. In an open letter to the local press during the 1888/89 season he warned: 'If we allow the football field to degenerate simply into a resort for people who will not conduct themselves aright, we shall lose the support of those people who encourage football for the game's sake, and who are its only true supporters.'

Despite his misgivings, Preedy had big plans for his club. Standing a shade under five-and-a-half feet, he may not have been the most physically imposing of men but he was as tenacious as a Yorkshire terrier. He wished for a better stage for his team to perform upon than the makeshift pitch next to St Peter's. From the church gates he spied the very spot, across Doncaster Road and over the railway line in the open fields of Oakwell. Several times he applied for consent to use the land. Every time he was turned down. His incessant badgering, however, wore down the landlords who also happened to own the adjacent Barnsley Brewery. Permission was granted on the proviso that Preedy and his players 'behaved themselves', a convenient get-out-of-jail card should the teetotal missionary became a troublesome thorn in their brewing sides.

In due course the Oakwell Ground familiar to all Tykes fans was built, but at the time it was little more than a spartan home from where plans were hatched to break into the professional ranks of the Football League. To bankroll his grand ambition Preedy introduced an admission charge of three pence and soon enough Barnsley St Peter's were on their way. In 1890 they entered the amateur Sheffield & District League; in 1893 and '94 they won the Barnsley Charity Cup - a competition Preedy helped to instigate - and in 1895 they were admitted into the Midland League. 'Preedy's Team' were now just one leap away from the Football League.

In 1897, the club took the considerable decision to drop its religious overtone and became simply Barnsley FC. A year later their application to join the big boys in the Football League was rubberstamped. To celebrate the news a brand new kit was designed consisting of red shirts and white shorts, a combination that has remained ever since. Barnsley's first foray in Division Two was tentative - they finished the season in 11th place - although on 28th January, 1899 they set a club scoring record that still stands, thrashing Loughborough Town 9-0.

In little more than a decade Barnsley had risen from obscurity to the Football League, seeing off rugby in the process and turning attendances of a few dozen Congregationalists into a couple of thousand ardent fans. Sadly, Rev Preedy watched his offspring reach those giddy heights from afar. In 1893, his day job took him southwards to Islington to minister the down and outs in what *The Sportsman* described as, 'one of the most unlovely spots in London'. There was no viable space for Preedy to introduce football to his new parishioners so instead he set up a boxing-cum-wrestling ring in the crypt under the All Saints Mission. His venture soon churned out champions, including boxers Matt Wells and Terry Allen and wrestler George Mackenzie, the latter representing Great Britain in five Olympic Games from 1908. It was here, in Islington, that

Preedy earned his 'Boxing Parson' tag for his habit of wearing a dog collar when sparring in recreational bouts or combating drunkards in what could be a dangerous part of the capital.

Barnsley FC, not surprisingly given their rapid rise to the top, found life in the Football League tough going and rarely ventured beyond mid-table. They were not alone. Rotherham Town, winners of the Midland League in 1892 and 1893, lasted just three seasons in the heat of Division Two and at the turn of the century Doncaster Rovers, also twice Midland League champions (1897, 1899), had an equally short taste of the Football League before being voted out in 1905 after they picked up a paltry eight points from 34 games.

In the capital, the Rev Preedy's love for Barnsley burned as bright as ever. No one was more pleased than he when they earned a reputation as relentless cup-fighters. Punching well above their weight they scrapped, kicked and tackled their way past more celebrated opponents to reach the FA Cup Final in both 1910 and 1912. 'Battling Barnsley' the press christened them, and their objective was simple: stop the other team from scoring. In those two drawn-out campaigns an almost watertight defence leaked just eight goals in 21 ties, stingy stats which make even the Sheffield Wednesday team of the Edwardian period seem positively cavalier.

At the heart of Barnsley's workman-like team was local boy George Utley, a powerful left half noted for his long throws. Born into a family of coal miners and foundry workers, he was the very embodiment of his side's rugged, uncompromising style. In February 1913, he became the only Tykes player ever to represent England when he was capped against Ireland in Belfast. Coincidentally, Tommy Boyle, Barnsley's centre-half in the 1910 Final, played in the same match, although by then he was with Burnley. England lost 2-1, their first defeat in 32 matches against the Irish and Utley, echoing the fate suffered by Charles Clegg many years before, was dropped never to be recalled. Later that year he was sold by Barnsley to Sheffield United for £2,000, a huge fee that must have made *The Times* apoplectic. Mindful of his own worth, Utley brokered an impressive package as part of the deal: a long-term contract, the team captaincy, tenancy of a local sports shop, and the guarantee of a benefit which in due course yielded £1,000, the equivalent of almost five years wages.

During the 1909/10 Cup run, Utley and Co. dumped out Everton, the 1906 winners, in the semi final to set up a mouth-watering meeting with three times League champions Newcastle United. Nobody outside South Yorkshire gave the little David's of Barnsley any chance against the Geordie Goliaths. But in a grim game at Crystal Palace - 'there were too many fouls,' records Geoffrey Green, 'and the players spent most of the time appealing, with their arms uplifted to the sky' - Barnsley shook their high-and-mighty opponents to the core. Inside forward Harry Tufnell got on the end of a cross from Wilf Bartrop to open the scoring and then they doggedly held on to their lead until seven minutes from time when Newcastle finally carved a way through Barnsley's red rock defence to equalize.

Barnsley's gritty tactics upset Newcastle's slick rhythm but in the replay at Goodison Park, the Magpies fought fire with fire. In an extremely physical encounter, Fred Mearns, the Barnsley goalkeeper, was laid out early on and right back Dicky Downs, kicked black and blue, had to be taken off for treatment. 'Dirty Newcastle', cried out the Tykes fans in the 69,000 crowd as Barnsley's brave fight ended in a 2-0 defeat.

A day trip to London was, for most Yorkshire folk, an

unaffordable and impractical luxury. But when one of their football teams won a place in the FA Cup Final it was an entirely different matter. All the stops were pulled out and supporters poured into the 'big smoke' in their thousands, carried in on crowded steam trains and a wave of good hope. Wearing rosettes and home-made hats in their club colours, fans brought with them mascots - Barnsley had Amos the donkey - and a carnival atmosphere. Plenty of beer was drunk, there was laughter and song and the playing of brass instruments. Everyone was up for a good time. Yet these rough-and-ready hordes from the industrial North were eyed with suspicion, even disdain, by parts of London society. 'Why can't they be neighbourly? They stare at us like we were pot-cats', complained one Barnsley follower after his big day out in 1910. Most Londoners viewed northerners as nothing worse than harmless 'loonies', but to toffee-nosed socialites they were unintelligent savages dressed in peaked caps, ill-fitting suits and big boots. 'It is rather awful,' wrote one stuck-up journalist in *The Graphic* a week after Bradford City appeared in the 1911 Final, 'to think that these loafers who invaded London have become decadent before becoming civilised.'

'Battling Barnsley' were at the hub of such patronizing snobbery the very next year when they caught cup fever again. Their gruelling march to Crystal Palace involved ten matches and many replays. In the Fourth Round they slogged through three goalless draws and 420 minutes of robust play to overcome Yorkshire neighbours Bradford City, the cup holders. In the last four Barnsley needed a replay to overcome Swindon and in the final they chalked up yet another 0-0 draw, this time against First Division West Bromwich Albion.

The replay at Bramall Lane was watched by 38,555

people, a healthy turnout for a Wednesday afternoon. Phantom funerals must have popped up all over Barnsley that day. Predictably, the contest remained locked at 0-0 and went into extra-time. With barely two minutes left on the clock it was still goalless. And then Barnsley launched a dramatic last gasp attack. Reports differ on whether it was Utley or Glendinning who broke up a West Brom move but all concur that the ball was punched through to Tufnell who dashed off like a whippet. '[He] broke away on his own, and getting clear of the backs, made no mistake,' reported the *Barnsley Chronicle*. 'Pearson [the Albion keeper] ran out, but Tufnell steadied himself and got the ball into the net amid scenes of tremendous excitement!' Bramall Lane erupted in an ear-splitting roar that told the rest of Yorkshire that little old Barnsley had won the coveted silverware.

Cheering them on in the crowd was none other than the Rev Tiverton Preedy who had journeyed north especially for the match. He stayed on for the celebratory banquet at the Clarence Hotel and, to a marvellous ovation, was presented with the match ball as a token of the esteem in which he was still held by the club. Preedy gave a rousing acceptance speech: 'I was not astonished. We set out to win the Cup, and meant to win it ... Now see to it that we get into the First Division next year. If you can not do it next year, see that you do it the next ... Be determined not to rest until you are at the top of the tree.' His charges manfully took up the challenge, finishing fourth, fifth and third respectively in the next three seasons. But just as it was on the threshold of being realised, Preedy's dream was snuffed out by the most terrible of wars.

8

Rugby Conversion

ON HIS arrival in Barnsley, the Reverend Preedy discovered the winter sport of choice in the mining town was not Association football, despite its proximity to Sheffield, but rugby. 'Rugger was the game up to then,' Preedy later recalled, 'and the new style met with strenuous opposition. The Press, the people, everyone seemed to be against us. But we fought on.' Indeed they did and steadily their unshakeable determination won over the townsfolk.

But as the nineteenth century grew old, soccer remained the poor relation in many parts of Yorkshire. While Sheffield, Barnsley, Rotherham, Doncaster and York championed the round ball game, the Pennine mill towns and Humber docklands were stubborn in their uptake. These were major rugby heartlands, more so than Barnsley ever was, and their conversion to the football faith proved a long and difficult task.

In 1863, former pupils of Bramham College founded Bradford Football Club, later joining Bradford Cricket Club at Park Avenue, a ground rated at the time as one of the loveliest in England. Two years later, Reverend Scott instigated Hull FC and, by the early 1880s, the likes of Huddersfield, Leeds, Wakefield Trinity, Halifax, Batley, Hull Kingston Rovers and Hunslet were all up and running. Then there was Manningham FC, a second rugby club from Bradford, formed in 1876. A decade later the club part-bought, part-leased a former quarry site on the steep hillside along Manningham Lane, fashioned it into an 18,000-capacity arena and christened it Valley Parade after its lofty vantage point.

Rugby fans could not have imagined that Manningham and Bradford would one day turn traitor, swapping the oval ball for the round one, when they entered a new competition, the Yorkshire Challenge Cup, in 1877. 'T'owd Tin Pot' attracted big crowds. In 1883/84 more than 100,000 spectators poured through the turnstiles to watch the first round matches alone and the semi-final between Bradford and Batley attracted a crowd of 15,000. 'It will be noticed that the Yorkshire monster attendances are far in excess of those of the metropolis with its millions of inhabitants', crowed one local reporter, clearly revelling in taking a swipe at the FA Cup Final which could only muster 4,000 spectators in the same year. In 1885, some 20,000 supporters crammed into the Park Avenue ground for a cup tie between Bradford and Hull and, by 1887, the *Yorkshire Post* was confidently declaring that a million people followed rugby in the Land of Broad Acres.

The rivers Aire and Calder, Colne and Humber acted like natural barriers, successfully rebuffing the advances of soccer. As early as 1877, missionaries from the Sheffield FA tried to entice rugby fans in Leeds with a Boxing Day exhibition match at the Holbeck Recreation Ground but the locals were having none of it. The following year Sheffield-born Sam Gilbert, a cricket professional at Hunslet Cricket Club, founded Hunslet AFC, but a lack of interest and money brought about its downfall as early as 1883. The Football Association themselves were next to have a go, staging the 1882 FA Cup semi-final tie between Wednesday and Blackburn Rovers at Fartown, the home ground of Huddersfield Rugby Club, a bold but futile attempt to promote the game in the epicentre of Yorkshire rugby's heartland.

Soccer was like an infatuated teenage girl though. No matter how many times rugby gave her the brush off, she just kept coming back for more. By the end of the century enough amateur Association football teams had popped up in Bradford and Leeds, Huddersfield and Hull to warrant the creation of District Associations and competitions. In 1894, the West Yorkshire League was formed followed two years later by the West Yorkshire Cup which Hunslet AFC, resurrected by employees of Leeds Steelworks, won four times on the trot (1897-1900).

Yet let us not kid ourselves. Rugby still ruled the roost in the West and East Ridings. In 1895, the sport cranked up a notch when representatives from twenty-two leading clubs in Yorkshire, Lancashire and Cheshire met at the George Hotel in Huddersfield and resolved to resign from the Rugby Football Union and set up a rebel Northern Union. 'The Great Split', as history records the acrimonious fall out, was sparked off by northern clubs compensating players for loss of wages - so called broken time payments - which was a practice that clearly flouted amateur rules. In a virtual carbon copy of the tug-o-war that nearly tore Association football apart a decade beforehand, rugby was pulled this way and that by advocates of professionalism on the one side and guardians of supposed amateur values on the other. Except this time there was no pacifying figure of the stature of Charles Alcock to reconcile the two feuding factions. The London-based Rugby Football Union banned its member clubs from playing against their Northern Union counterparts and that was that. The quarrelling camps went their separate ways and slowly but surely two distinct codes emerged, Northern Union re-branding itself as Rugby League in 1922.

The professional era gave extra oomph in the rugby loving areas of Yorkshire. Free to employ the best players, irrespective of their social background, clubs pulled in bigger crowds than ever before. The Challenge Cup Final between Batley and Bradford in 1898, for example, attracted an attendance just shy of 28,000, a figure which rose to 29,500 in 1901 and then to 32,500 in 1903, a Headingley record.

On the surface, professional rugby appeared to be thriving but an extraordinary chain of events in Bradford during the winter of 1902/03 showed that underneath all was not well. Reports emerged that Manningham, founder members of the Northern Union and inaugural champions and Yorkshire League winners in 1896, were on the brink of going bust. Professionalism had offered clubs tantalising financial rewards but only if wages and running costs were carefully managed against gate money, a balancing act that Manningham failed to achieve. Only the proceeds from an end-of-season archery competition saved them from immediate bankruptcy.

Enter Scotsman James Whyte, a sub-editor of the *Bradford Observer* and vice-president of the Bradford & District FA Convinced that the Wool City could support a top class football team and buoyed by the recent achievements of Sheffield United and Sheffield Wednesday, he entered into secret and fruitful negotiations with the Manningham committee in January 1903 to convert the club from rugby to 'a game that would pay', as its president Alfred Ayrton would later say. Moreover, an agreement was reached to change the club's name from Manningham FC to the all encompassing Bradford City Association Football Club.

Whyte headed a four-man delegation that travelled to Covent Garden, London on 25th May, 1903 to persuade the League Management Committee to accept their prospective club into the Football League. Given that Bradford City had never played a game and did not have sufficient players yet to make up a first team, their application was audacious at best, outstandingly foolish at worst. Yet remarkably they succeeded - and handsomely too - polling 30 out of 35 votes to dislodge Doncaster Rovers from the Second Division.

There can be no denying that Bradford City was fast tracked. It had long been a source of frustration that while small towns like Burton, Gainsborough and Glossop supported professional football teams, Bradford, Leeds and Hull, three of the largest conurbations in the country, did not. The LMC must have been as eager as young pups when the Bradford deputation arrived on their doorstop offering them the chance of gaining a leg up in the West Riding. Four days later, 'the greatest football scoop ever known' was ratified by the Manningham membership at the club's AGM who voted 75-34 in favour of changing codes after a highly passionate debate.

Valley Parade hosted its first League game - City versus Gainsborough Trinity in front of 11,000 fans - on 5th September, 1903. A month later the Football League chose the ground to host a representative match between an English League XI and an Irish League XI, a promotional campaign that attracted an estimated 20,000 spectators. The Paraders finished the 1903/04 season creditably in tenth place and posted a small profit of £39, a somewhat disappointing sum considering the average attendance at

Valley Parade of nearly 10,000 compared favourably with that at Owlerton (12,600) and Bramall Lane (15,800).

Manningham's supporters had stayed loyal, persuaded perhaps by the common view that soccer was a faster, more attacking and simply more entertaining game to watch than rugby. Northern Union had become boring, bogged down by too many scrimmages and a dearth of tries. Attendances consequently fell. When Bradford beat Salford 5-0 in the 1906 Challenge Cup Final, they did so in front of less than 16,000 spectators, half what the Headingley gate had been three years before and nowhere near the huge crowd of 75,609 that watched the FA Cup Final that season. In a desperate attempt to make rugby more appealing, Northern Union officials pushed through two significant rule changes; the play-the-ball replaced scrums and the number of players per team was reduced from 15 to 13 to open up play. The measures reinvigorated the sport but they were too little too late to keep football at bay.

Having invaded one fortress, soccer laid siege to the other bastions of Yorkshire rugby. 'Leeds can and ought to have a status in this pastime,' the *Leeds Mercury* told its readers. 'The Association game is proving itself week by week to be a sport which in its appeal to human interest has no rival except cricket … The strides it is making suggest that sooner or later soccer will capture the whole of Yorkshire.'

The *Mercury* was spot on with its prediction. Hull City and Leeds City came into being in 1904, the former moving to a ground on Anlaby Road, opposite Hull Cricket Club, after a brief period sharing The Boulevard with Hull FC (the rugby side apparently had no qualms about sharing its stage with football), the latter buying the Old Peacock Ground on Elland Road from Holbeck Rugby Club for £4,500. Within a year both teams were admitted to the Football League in an enlarged 20-club Second Division. Meanwhile, soccer devotees in Halifax founded Halifax Town at a meeting in The Saddle Hotel in May 1911. Ten years later, following a move to The Shay, the team became founder members of Division Three North.

Even in Huddersfield, in the very heart of Northern Union, soccer made its mark. Heavily backed by the Crowther brothers, four extremely wealthy woollen mill owners, Huddersfield Town was launched in August 1908 to great fanfare. Renowned football ground architect and engineer Archibald Leitch was employed to turn recreation fields on Leeds Road into a stadium capable of holding 34,000 spectators. There was little surprise when Town joined their Yorkshire comrades in Division Two, replacing Grimsby Town in 1910. The Football Association did its bit too, awarding Valley Parade the 1904 FA Amateur Cup Final (won by Sheffield FC), Park Avenue an England-Ireland International match in 1909 and Elland Road the 1910 FA Cup Semi-Final between Barnsley and Everton.

Sandwiched in between this flurry of activity was an episode known to rugby followers in Bradford as 'The Great Betrayal'. In April 1907, having seen the positive impact that changing codes had had upon Manningham/Bradford City, Mr Briggs, the dominating chairman of Bradford FC, used his influence to coerce the committee into abandoning Rugby football for Association football. The decision was highly controversial, partly because Bradford FC were a successful team - Yorkshire League Champions (1900, 01), Northern Rugby League Champions (1904), Challenge Cup Winners (1906) - and partly because Briggs ran roughshod over the membership's majority wish for the club to stick with rugby. The Wool City suddenly faced having no major rugby club although when the clamour died down the void was filled by a new outfit, Bradford Northern. There was an outcry in the town but Briggs ignored the public protests and applied for the club to be admitted to the Football League as Bradford Park Avenue. In 1908, after spending a season bizarrely competing in the Southern League, they were duly accepted into Division Two.

It took a long time for the defences to be breached but once Bradford City clambered over them, the Pennine mill towns and Humber docklands took to football in remarkably swift time. But it was not all plain sailing, far from it in fact. Hull City, wearing their iconic amber and black striped shirts, performed well enough, finishing in the top five of Division Two four times between 1906 and 1911 and agonisingly missing out on promotion in 1909/10 by 0.29 of a goal, after they lost 3-0 to promotion rivals Oldham Athletic on the final day of the season. Incidentally, Hull's star man during this period was skipper and Cambridge graduate E Gordon Wright, a talented winger who held the rare distinction of winning a full England cap (against Wales in 1906) and an Olympic gold medal (for Great Britain at the 1912 Stockholm Games).

If missing out on promotion was a heavy blow to the gut for Hull, then Huddersfield Town and Leeds City must have felt their spleens had ruptured. As early as 1912, both clubs were declared bankrupt. Far from packing out their stadiums, Leeds Road and Elland Road became rattling mausoleums for overstretched aspirations. In the 1911/12 season, City's crowds tumbled to below 5,000, Town's to as low as 3,000 as both sides finished in the bottom four of Division Two. Leeds would have gone under sooner had it not been for their chairman Norris Hepworth, a prosperous wholesale clothier, propping them up with a personal investment of £15,000, the equivalent of about a million pounds in today's money. To think that Manningham's committee ever thought that soccer was a 'game that would pay'. Fortunately for West Riding football, neither Leeds City nor Huddersfield Town were lost forever. Liquidation cleared their heavy debts and allowed their assets and club names to be hoovered up by other parties.

There was better news for Bradford Park Avenue. A proposal to amalgamate the city's football teams was firmly rejected by Bradford City but they justified their betrayal of rugby by reaching the quarter-finals of the FA Cup in 1913, gaining promotion to Division One in 1914 and finishing just five points behind champions Everton in 1915. The 1914/15 season gave rise to the first all-Bradford derby in the Football League, City grabbing local bragging rights by winning the match 3-2 in front of a bumper Valley Parade crowd of 29,802.

And so the story comes back to Bradford City. Of all the clubs that sprouted up in Yorkshire after 1900, it was the one from Manningham that enjoyed the most tangible success before the First World War. Under the canny guidance of Scotsman and former player Peter O'Rourke, City stormed to the Second Division title in 1907/08, walloping the likes of Chesterfield Town 8-1 and Gainsborough Trinity 7-1 along the way. Top scorer with 21 goals was bustling centre-forward Frank O'Rourke (no relation to the manager) whose shoot-on-sight policy bagged him five hat-tricks and a long standing club record 88 League goals between April 1907 and March 1914.

On clinching promotion, City engaged Leitch to overhaul Valley Parade into a 40,000-capacity stadium worthy of Division One football. The Kop end was built, existing terraces and stands modernised, extra turnstiles installed, the pitch and changing rooms repositioned, all for the princely sum of £9,958. The renovations spurred the Bantams on to new heights. In 1910/11 they finished in fifth place, the club's best ever League showing, set a Valley Parade attendance record of 39,146 for an FA Cup quarter-final tie with Burnley and, to cap it all, overcame illustrious Newcastle United to win the Cup, still the club's only major trophy to date.

Captained by Scottish international inside right Jimmy Speirs, the side that season was pretty special. In goal was Mark Mellors, who kept a clean sheet in 13 successive FA Cup ties (1910-12), a record for the competition. George Robinson, a tall and slim right half, played in City's first League game at Grimsby Town in 1903 and went on to make a then club record 343 appearances. Peter Logan, City's longest serving player (1908-24), was a charismatic forward and the darling of the Valley Parade crowds. Frank O'Rourke churned out the goals and then there was Dickie Bond, arguably the best of the lot, who was regarded as the finest outside right in the country in his pomp. Unhappily, Bond missed Bradford's big day out in London because he was serving a ban for using 'improper language' during a match at Woolwich Arsenal.

The world around was moving on a pace in 1911. The country had a Liberal Prime Minister, Herbert Asquith, born in Morley, and a new monarch, King George V. The motorcar and the biplane were the marvels of the age. Fashionable men wore straw boaters. Suffragettes campaigned for women's votes. A new political movement, the Labour Party, was on the rise. And Scott of the Antarctic and the *Titanic* were about to set out on their ill-fated voyages. Meanwhile on the football pitch the face of the game was changing, quite literally. Bushy beards and waxed moustaches were out, clean cut shaves were in. Shorts were close fitting and knee-length, shirts laced-up at the collar. Goalkeepers were now restricted to handling the ball inside the penalty area, which itself had been reduced in 1901 from the width of the pitch to an 18-yard box and, across the land, 2-3-5 was the undisputed team formation.

The sun shone as the Bradford team ran out at Crystal Palace for the FA Cup Final on 22nd April, 1911. The match, however, was dull, so dull in fact - it ended in another 0-0 bore draw - that one national tabloid screamed: 'English Cup Final Fiasco'. The replay at Old Trafford the following Wednesday afternoon tempted ten thousand Bradford fans to skip work and make the short trip across the Pennines. Imagine their joy when, in the 15th minute, Speirs, one of a record eight Scotsmen in the team, headed in the decisive goal in a packed goalmouth, although some reports attribute O'Rourke with supplying the final touch. The victory certainly vindicated Manningham's historic decision to chuck rugby for soccer.

In Bradford, a brass band and hundreds of cheering supporters packed the railway station platforms to welcome home the triumphant City party that evening. The new king sent a congratulatory telegram and the Cup was proudly put on display at the Victoria Hotel for all to view. Admirers would have seen a brand new trophy commissioned by the FA, a fluted silver urn with lughole handles standing on an ebony plinth. If any team can ever say their name was on the Cup then it surely must be Bradford City for the smiths who crafted this third incarnation were Messrs Fattorini and Sons ... of Bradford.

9

In Memoriam

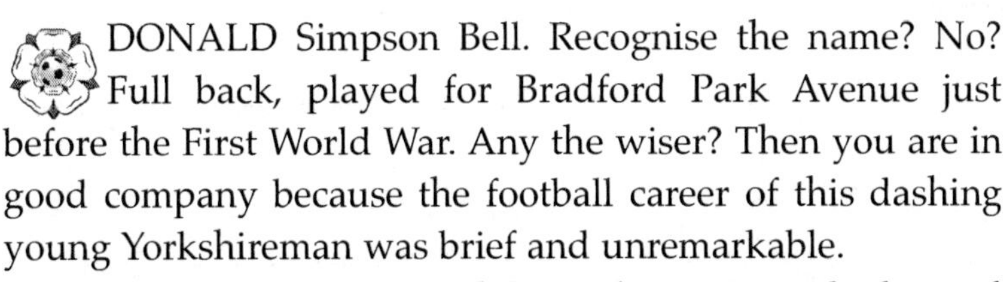

DONALD Simpson Bell. Recognise the name? No? Full back, played for Bradford Park Avenue just before the First World War. Any the wiser? Then you are in good company because the football career of this dashing young Yorkshireman was brief and unremarkable.

Born in Harrogate on 3rd December, 1890 and educated at the town's grammar school and at Westminster College, London, Donny, as he was known, occasionally turned out during his student days as an amateur for Crystal Palace, Bishop Auckland and Newcastle United. After completing his studies he returned home to Yorkshire to take up a teaching post at Starbeck School. To bolster his modest weekly salary of £2 10s he signed on as a professional footballer with Park Avenue. Never more than a capable if athletic defender, Bell's Football League debut came against Wolves, at Molineux, on 13th April, 1913. The following season he was a member of the squad that jubilantly won promotion as runners-up in Division Two. But that was about the sum of it all, a handful of matches. No silverware, no international caps, no money-spinning move to a big time club.

So what merits Bell a place in the history of Yorkshire football? The answer lies not on the playing fields of Bradford but on the shell-torn killing fields of the Somme in north-east France. For Bell was a war hero, reputedly the first English professional footballer to volunteer for active service and certainly the only one during the whole bloody conflict to be decorated with the Victoria Cross, the highest award for gallantry in the face of the enemy. In November 1914, after gaining permission from the Bradford directors to terminate his contract, he enlisted with the West Yorkshire Regiment as a private. Rapidly working his way up through the ranks, in June 1915, shortly after marrying his sweetheart, Rhoda Bonson, he was commissioned as a Second Lieutenant into the 9th Battalion of the Yorkshire Regiment, also known as the Green Howards.

Cometh the hour, cometh the man, the old saying goes, and at 18:00 hours on 5th July, 1916 it was 2nd Lt. Bell who stuffed his pockets with hand grenades and led a daring three man attack on a German machine-gun position at a place called Horse Shoe Trench. The *London Gazette* later paid glowing tribute for the way he, 'rushed across the open under very heavy fire and attacked the machine gun, shooting the firer with his revolver, and destroying gun and personnel with bombs. This very brave act saved many [British] lives and ensured the success of the attack.'

Little wonder Bell was awarded the Victoria Cross. But rather than revelling in his 'supreme act of gallantry' - assuming that anyone ever did revel in the desperate conditions of the trenches on the Western Front - the footballer-turned-officer was a reluctant hero. He wrote humbly to his mother: 'I must confess that it was the biggest fluke alive and I did nothing. I only chucked the bomb and it did the trick.'

Five days later, Donny was dead, killed in action in the village of Contalmaison, 'performing a very similar act of bravery'. The spot where he fell was named 'Bell's Redoubt' in his honour. 'He knew no fear. He had the courage of a lion,' recalled one of his brother-in-arms. '[He] was ready to risk his life many times over if only he could lessen the risk to his men and brother officers.'

Back home in Blighty, the heroically tragic story of Second Lieutenant Donald Simpson Bell, VC, made for uncomfortable reading at the Football Association and the Football League. When Britain went to war with Germany on 4th August, 1914 the impending football season's fixtures were not cancelled. The jingoistic and widespread view was that the might of the British Empire would easily bash the Bosch and the troops would be home by Christmas. So what was the point, mused Charles Clegg and his fellow administrators, of disrupting the soccer season?

Such blind faith in the country's military capabilities - which had hardly improved since the Boer War (1899-1902), itself an unexpectedly protracted conflict in far off South Africa - was woefully misplaced. Within a few weeks the British Expeditionary Force had been decimated. Christmas Day 1914 was marked not by triumphant parades of a victorious army but by an impromptu and surreal football match between English and German soldiers in 'No Man's Land' during an all too brief lull in the fighting.

An urgent call-to-arms was issued by Lord Kitchener, the Minister for War, under the tagline 'Your Country Needs You'. Ferried along on a tidal wave of patriotism, ordinary young men like Donald Bell volunteered in their tens of thousands to fight for King and Country. They banded together in 'Pals' Battalions and marched off to war, side by side, blissfully unaware that they could so easily be, 'two years in the making and ten minutes in the destroying' as one Leeds Pal gravely put it after seeing his platoon all but obliterated on the Somme.

And still professional football played on. The sport's authorities insisted that they had the backing of the War Office, but public opinion - which lionized the amateur Rugby Football Union for nobly and immediately suspending its fixture list until such time as the war was won - turned against the working man's game. Association football stood accused of cowardice, of letting the country down, of aiding the German military machine. Clubs attempted to put a gloss on their tarnished reputations by organising charity matches in aid of the War Fund and offering stadiums for drill practice and as recruitment centres. In his tome *The Ball is Round: A Global History of Football*, David Goldblatt states that by the end of 1914 as many as, 'two thousand players out of around 5,000 professionals' in Britain had joined their peers on the frontline. That did not stop *The Times* from savagely putting the boot into the People's Game: 'We view with indignation and alarm the persistence of association football clubs in doing their best for the enemy ... There is no excuse for diverting from the front thousands of athletes in order to feast the eyes of crowds of inactive spectators, who are either unfit to fight or else unfit to be fought for.'

As more and more men enlisted in the army, so the 'crowds of inactive spectators' collapsed during the second half of the 1914/15 season. Gates at Valley Parade plummeted from a high of nearly 30,000 for the Bradford derby in October to 5,000 for the game against Liverpool in March. Those at Elland Road more than halved to a low of 4,000 for the visit of Nottingham Forest in early April. Crowds at Leeds Road slumped to less than 5,000 and at

Bramall Lane and Hillsborough average attendances fell by a quarter on the previous season.

Even the FA Cup Final did not escape the downturn. Switched from London to murky Manchester - partly because Crystal Palace had been requisitioned by the Admiralty, partly over fears that it could otherwise be the target of a German zeppelin air raid - the season's showcase finale between Sheffield United and Chelsea on 24th April, 1915 was watched by, as Geoffrey Green put it, 'a drab and silent crowd' of 49,557, the lowest figure for a final in twenty years. The Old Trafford terraces were lined with so many men dressed in battle kit that the match assumed a lasting sobriquet, the 'Khaki Cup Final'. On a foggy afternoon United ran out comfortable 3-0 victors and so got their hands on the FA Cup for a third time. Jimmy Simmons, a nephew of the great Bill Foulke, opened the scoring, Stanley Fazackerley added a second and Joe Kitchen arrowed in the third two minutes from time after a tremendous 40-yard solo effort reminiscent of Harry Tufnell's for Barnsley three years earlier. At 5ft 7$\frac{1}{2}$ins Kitchen was a diminutive but highly productive centre forward who notched up over a hundred non-wartime goals for the Blades and was top scorer for the club on five occasions.

Sheffield's victory was a hollow one, its unimportance brought into sharp relief by the death of Gerald Kirk, a former centre-half for Bradford City and Leeds City (1905-08) and a Second Lieutenant in the King's Own Royal Lancaster Regiment, who was killed in action in Flanders on the same day as the Final. Lord Derby captured the mood of the nation when at the finish he presented the Cup to George Utley, late of 'Battling Barnsley', now captain of Sheffield United: 'You have played with one another and against one another for the Cup. It is now the duty of everyone to join with each other and play a sterner game for England.'

At last, the Football Association and the Football League saw sense and closed down professional football. The FA Cup and the League Championship trophy were locked away and contracts suspended. Professional players effectively became amateurs, forbidden to profit from the game while lives continued to be lost on foreign shores. Organised football did not die a death, however. The War Office, ignoring the wrath of *The Times* and other detractors, regarded the game as a vital way of maintaining morale among soldiers home on leave and workers labouring in reserved industries like coal mining. Fuel for transport was scarce, so regional wartime leagues were set up in place of a national competition. The Midland Section brought together, for the first and only time, all of Yorkshire's principal soccer clubs: Sheffield Wednesday, Sheffield United, Bradford City, Bradford Park Avenue, Barnsley, Huddersfield Town, Hull City, Leeds City and Rotherham County.

Released from their contractual obligations, footballers who did not volunteer for - or were not commandeered to join - the frontline, or were stationed at barracks nearby, were free to 'guest' for any football club they liked. Yorkshire clubs were compelled by choice and by circumstance to hire their services. Leeds City, in particular, took advantage of the system, strengthening their depleted squad with England internationals Clem Stephenson from Aston Villa, Charlie Buchan of Sunderland, and Franny Walden from Tottenham. Also drafted in were Newcastle defender Billy Hampson, a future manager of Leeds United, and Notts County centre forward Jack Peart, a man who boasted an unenviable reputation as the 'most injured man in football' - which included a broken leg in 1910 when on the books of Sheffield United.

An outstanding exception to the guest rule was Hull

City's David 'Magical' Mercer, an outside right who from his debut at the fag end of the 1913/14 season, made 218 consecutive appearances for The Tigers, a run which included all of Hull's 142 wartime games. When peacetime returned he joined Sheffield United, winning an FA Cup winners' medal in 1925 and two England caps (1922-23).

The acquisition of 'guest' players would come back to haunt Leeds City at the end of the 1914-18 War, but for now they did the trick. From being perennial also-rans in Division Two, the club was buffed and polished into sparkling champions. Forty-one wins in 58 matches gave City back-to-back titles in 1916/17 and 1917/18, during which time they scored an avalanche of goals, the bulk coming from the boots of Peart (45), Arthur Price (32), a *bona fide* City player, and Stephenson (23). Leeds' supremacy was confirmed when in a Champion of Champions fixture they beat Stoke City, winners of the Lancashire Section, 2-1 on aggregate in May 1918. And in the following year they went to within an ace of completing a title treble, a 4-0 home defeat by Notts Forest, the champions elect, late in the season proving decisive.

It is poignant, to say the least, that as Leeds City entered this golden period so a couple of their pre-war stars, half back Evelyn Lintott and inside forward Jimmy Speirs, were mown down during two of the most infamous engagements in the whole war. Speirs was Bradford City's goal scoring skipper in the 1911 FA Cup Final but in December 1912 he dropped down a division and joined Leeds for £1,400. During his six years at Valley Parade and Elland Road he accumulated 65 goals in 174 appearances. Almost as soon as the last ball of the 1914/15 season was kicked he enlisted with the Queen's Own Cameron Highlanders and in April 1917 won the Military Medal at Arras on the France-Belgium border for an unrecorded act of bravery in the field.

Promoted to sergeant, the 31-year-old was wounded and presumed missing in action at the Battle of Passchendaele, a three month conflict which claimed 310,000 Allied casualties. The *Bradford Daily Telegraph* reported that Sgt Speirs had been, 'hit in the thigh during an advance, and [had] managed to crawl into a shell-hole. There he was attended to for a short time, but the Cameron Highlanders did not return from their raid that way, so he was not seen again.' His body was never recovered.

Lintott, a schoolteacher like Bell who, unlike him, remained an amateur throughout his football career, joined the Leeds Pals as a Lieutenant in September 1914, two months *before* Bell enlisted as the first professional footballer. Lintott was a decent midfielder who won seven England caps, four of them while on the books of Bradford City who he joined from QPR for £1,000 in 1908, a deal which dug the London club out of a financial hole. Missing out on the Bantams' FA Cup triumph, he moved to Leeds City shortly afterwards and stayed at Elland Road until duty called. On the first day of the Battle of the Somme on 1st July, 1916 he was shot, one of a staggering 58,000 casualties sustained by British Forces in the first twenty-four hours of fighting. 'Tragically, Lt Lintott was killed leading his platoon of the 15th West Yorkshire Regiment, The Leeds Pals, over the top,' read a letter published in the *Yorkshire Post*. 'He led his men with great dash and when hit the first time declined to take the count. Instead, he drew his revolver and called for further effort. Again he was hit but struggled on but a third shot finally bowled him over.' His body, like that of Sgt Speirs, was never found.

Another member of Bradford City's golden team, Bob Torrance, also perished. At the start of the war, he worked in a munitions factory before joining the Royal Field Artillery as a Gunner. He was killed, near Ypres, on 24th April, 1918 when the field hospital in which he was recuperating after being badly wounded was destroyed by shelling. Hailing from Kirkintilloch in Scotland, Torrance won renown as a footballer for a magnificent performance at centre half against Newcastle in the FA Cup Final replay, after he was drafted in as a replacement for the injured William Gildea.

Another high profile Yorkshire footballer to fall was Wilfred Bartrop, outside-right for the 'Battling Barnsley' teams of 1910 and 1912. He was, to draw on the title of his biography, 'swifter than an arrow' down the wing, tormenting defenders in over 150 games for the Tykes before moving to First Division Liverpool in 1914. Another Gunner in the RFA, he was killed at Warcoing, Belgium on 7th November, 1918 just four days before the Armistice.

Whilst hundreds of thousands of Tommies were killed or injured, others were captured and spent at least part of the interregnum as prisoners of war. Into this group falls an unlikely victim, ex-Sheffield Wednesday crowd favourite Fred Spiksley. In his forties, he would have been considered too old to fight but he happened to be in Germany when war broke out, working as a coach for FC Nuremburg. Interned at Ruhleben, a detention camp in the Spandau district of Berlin, he was a fellow POW of the great Steve Bloomer who had also been coaching in the country, with Britannia Berlin 92, when Kaiser Bill began his sabre rattling. After the war, Spiksley worked in Spain, the USA and Mexico and coached Fulham before returning to Germany where he led his old team Nuremburg to the German Championship in 1927.

The guns finally fell silent on 11th November, 1918. The Great War was over, but at what cost? One million soldiers from the British Empire were dead, a further two million wounded, the flower of a generation crushed by four long years of carnage. As shell-shocked survivors drifted home they fished around for rods of familiarity on to which they could hook themselves. One of them was football. To the rank and file, the game was a comforting reminder of a time before horror and a reassurance that they could start rebuilding battered lives. Just as attendances had plunged post-Christmas 1914, so they began to rise again after the Armistice. Indicative of the upsurge was the Leeds City v Nottingham Forest match at Elland Road on 15th February 1919, which attracted 11,000 supporters, a significantly better turnout than the 2,000 for City's home game against Rotherham County the previous October. After four dark and desperate years organised football was on its way back.

The precise number of Yorkshire footballers who died or were wounded in the First World War - amateurs and professionals, reserves and first teamers, players from works teams, pub teams, church teams and a myriad of minor league sides - is unlikely ever to be known, but the Roll of Honour probably runs into several thousands. In 2000, a monument made of Yorkstone and jointly paid for by the Green Howards and the Professional Footballers' Association was erected at Bell's Redoubt in memory of Second Lieutenant Donald Bell, VC, and his Yorkshire Regiment comrades who lost their lives during the Battle of the Somme. To paraphrase the war poet Rupert Brooke, it is one corner of a foreign field that will be forever Yorkshire.

Scandal

THE FIGHTING over, official football competitions came back with a bang for the 1919/20 season. After four long years out in the wilderness the FA Cup was given a good spit and polish, the hiatus on professionalism lifted and the Football League, bigger and better than ever before, welcomed four new combatants: Coventry City, West Ham United, South Shields and Rotherham County.

While Rotherham celebrated, elsewhere in Yorkshire such jubilation was substituted by a strong stench of scandal. In neighbouring Barnsley, the Reverend Preedy's dream of seeing his beloved Barnsley FC reach the First Division was crushed by an extraordinary decision from the Football League Management Committee and the ruthless ambition and skulduggery of the scheming chairman of Arsenal, Sir Henry Norris, MP.

Norris's counterpart at Barnsley Football Club, John Rose (1908-33), had presided over the club's rise to prominence before the War and expected them to be handed one of the two extra vacancies up for grabs in the top flight. Barnsley had, after all, finished the last official season in third place in Division Two. Promotion should have been theirs by right. The LMC, however, had other plans. Whereas champions Derby County and runners-up Preston North End - two famous old names who had fallen on hard times - were accorded safe passage, little Barnsley were told to scrap it out via the ballot box for the one remaining place. The competition for votes was stiff, the other candidates being Tottenham Hotspur, anchored at the bottom of the First Division, and four clubs who had finished below the Reds in Division Two in the last season of full competition in 1915; Wolves, Birmingham City, Hull City and, most significantly as events turned out, Arsenal. Having had their automatic route to the top blocked, Barnsley were about to be shunted off the road completely by the red and white juggernaut from North London.

In retrospect, the whole affair can be seen for what it truly was: a rigged game of football poker in which Barnsley were dealt a bum hand and Norris, a thin faced, white-haired property tycoon with a sharp business brain, held an ace up his sleeve. Norris was a working-class lad made good who had more connections than Clapham Junction. He was knighted and given the rank of colonel for his efforts as a military recruitment officer during the Great War, became a Conservative MP in 1918, was a prominent face in the Freemasons - rising to become Grand Deacon of the United Grand Lodge of England - and was closely acquainted with the Archbishop of Canterbury.

Norris originally made his mark in football as a director of Fulham (1903-19), but subsequently used his vast personal fortune to buy up shares in Arsenal, becoming its majority stakeholder in 1910 at a time when the club was crippled by debt. Norris poured over £80,000 into building Highbury Stadium - another football ground designed by Archibald

Leitch - in 1913. Six years later and desperate for a return on his heavy investment, the 'Honourable' Member of Parliament was prepared to stop at nothing to achieve promotion. 'I have never met his equal for logic, invective and ruthlessness against all who opposed him,' was the cool assessment of Arsenal's own manager, Leslie Knighton, who was briefly caretaker-manager of Huddersfield Town in April 1912.

Utilising his political skills and, it would seem, his purse, Norris is alleged to have bribed or in some way manipulated other member clubs to vote for Arsenal. Dodgy dealings or not - the accusations were never proven but later events lent credence to them - the Norris ticket was publicly backed by two of the most influential men in football at the time; JAH Catton, the distinguished editor of *Athletic News*, and, more potently, 'Honest' John McKenna, founder of Liverpool FC and President of the Football League. The pair believed that Arsenal deserved to go up because they were the Football League's first members from the south of England and had incurred financial difficulties during the War, as though no other club had suffered such hardships. It was a flimsy argument. Was it mere coincidence that McKenna and Catton were on more than nodding terms with Norris, two powerful friends in high places whose support gave the property magnate's campaign a distinct advantage over Barnsley's?

The pendulum swung away from South Yorkshire and towards North London. The result of the ballot was announced on 10th March, 1919 at a meeting held at the Grand Hotel, Manchester and it was decisive: Arsenal 18 votes, Tottenham 8, Barnsley 5, the rest collecting one or two apiece.

Barnsley had been conned out of promotion by the underhand tricks of a man of high standing but low scruples. Norris's financial impropriety was finally exposed in 1927 when the *Daily Mail* revealed that he had made illicit payments to Sunderland's Charlie Buchan to induce the most famous footballer of the day to move to Highbury in 1925. The FA launched an investigation which not only substantiated the tabloid's claims but also revealed that Norris had embezzled club funds. The Arsenal chairman hit back, suing the Association and the newspaper for libel; he lost. The governing body exacted swift revenge, banning the knight errant from ever working in football again.

The outcome was of cold comfort to the staff and supporters of Barnsley. By the time Norris fell from grace, Arsenal were on the verge of greatness and Barnsley had turned into perennial strugglers. The Reds had one more go at promotion in 1921/22 but Stoke City, who won their last game of the season 3-0, beat them to it on goal average, by a mere 0.07 of a goal. Barnsley's aspirations had once again taken an almighty hit and it took them another 75 years to recover from it, Danny Wilson finally delivering the Tykes unto the Promised Land of the top division in 1997.

Barnsley were the unfortunate and unwitting victims of a wily politician's unbridled ambition but, 15 miles to the north, Leeds City pressed the self destruct button in what became known as 'The Leeds City Scandal', which ended with the club being kicked out of existence.

Few people spotted the black clouds gathering over Elland Road when City kicked off the 1919/20 season beside the seaside, at Blackpool on 30th August. Hopes of promotion were sky-high after their successes during the War, even if the squad had been weakened by the loss of Jimmy Speirs and Evelyn Lintott to German bullets and the return of celebrity 'guest' players to their pre-war contracted clubs. Supporters were heartened, though, by the return from his own wartime duties of Billy McLeod, a sharp shooting centre forward who rifled in 171 goals in 289 League games for Leeds and was top scorer in nine successive seasons, both club records. Now aged 32, he was a little ring rusty but the consensus was he still had 'it', that his eye for goal would spearhead the promotion charge and more than compensate for Jack Peart returning to Notts County.

Bought from Lincoln City for just £25 in June 1906, McLeod made his debut away at Wolves in November that year, in sad circumstances. He filled the shirt vacated by David 'Soldier' Wilson who died of a heart attack during a home game against Burnley the previous month. Wilson had fought with The Black Watch regiment in the Boer War, hence his nickname, and the gallant trooper's sudden death in the players' tunnel shocked the world of football, his passing being described by one commentator as, 'a national calamity'.

McLeod's firepower on the pitch was augmented by the tactical genius of a rising star whose deeds as a manager would touch galactic heights - Herbert Chapman. Born on 19th January, 1878 in Kiveton Park, near Rotherham, the son of a coal miner, Chapman was a journeyman inside forward who lacked the ability of his younger brother Harry Chapman, the celebrated Sheffield Wednesday forward. But, as a manager, he was by far the superior. Cutting his teeth with unfashionable Northampton Town, who he guided to the Southern League championship in 1908/09, he arrived at Leeds in May 1912 in the wake of their financial ills. Never short on confidence, his first act at Elland Road was to predict that he would lead City into Division One.

Chapman blended the strategic thinking and leadership qualities of a Roman general with the showmanship of PT Barnum or Buffalo Bill. In his playing days he sported flashy yellow football boots. His teams were precision built, as befitted a man who studied mining engineering at Sheffield Technical College. They were efficient and effective, fluid yet robust, all cogs and oil and timing. England international forward Harold Fleming once remarked to him, 'You have something more than a team; you have a machine.'

With a glint in his eye that suggested he was always one step ahead of the game, Chapman guided Leeds to within two points of promotion in 1914, doubled the average gate at Elland Road to 16,000 and turned the club from a loss making concern into a profitable organisation. Everything seemed to be in place for a promotion push in 1919/20 but Leeds made a stuttering start to the new season, winning just three of their opening seven games despite McLeod instantly finding his shooting range with six goals. By the end of September, City sat in mid-table but their on-field problems were nothing compared to what was going on behind closed doors in the Elland Road boardroom. The storm that had been brewing suddenly hit with a fury. At its eye were tales of corruption and blackmail and four characters whose dubious actions brought Leeds City to its knees; George Cripps, Joseph Connor, Charlie Copeland and James Bromley.

Cripps, a schoolteacher by profession, had been Chapman's right-hand man before the war. Connor was club chairman, having headed a syndicate which took control of Leeds City from the official Receiver in August 1914; Copeland a run of the mill full back and Bromley a city solicitor.

The winds of discontent first whipped up in 1916, when Chapman temporarily vacated his manager-secretary post to join a local munitions factory to assist the war effort. Cripps took over the reins but soon got into a pickle over the club's books prompting Connor, who accused the academic of gross incompetence, to bring in an accountant's clerk to sort out the mess. Cripps was confined to team affairs. But whereas Chapman was as popular with his squad as fish and chips are in Whitby - 'He was a lovely man and a great manager for the players,' was the glowing assessment of goalkeeper Willis Walker - Cripps was disliked intensely.

City skipper John Hampson even wrote to the directors on one occasion informing them that if the acting boss travelled with the team for an away game in Nottingham they would go on strike, a course of action averted only by the personal intervention and calming influence of Connor.

There was immense relief all round when Chapman returned to Elland Road in 1918 to resume control of day to day affairs and Cripps was demoted to his previous role of assistant. But, with a wartime record that stood up to close scrutiny - he was in charge when City won successive Midland Section titles in 1916/17 and 1917/18 - Cripps was not prepared to be walked over. He belligerently informed Connor that he would sue for wrongful dismissal and engaged Bromley to act on his behalf. He then played a trump card, notifying the solicitor that he had obtained knowledge of excessive and forbidden payments made to 'guest' players during the War and informed him that he wanted £400 from Leeds to hold his tongue.

Connor, who was also President of the West Riding FA, knew how combustible Cripps' information would be if it ever made it into the public domain. The club would be burnt at the stake. So, in January 1919, a secret deal was thrashed out. Bromley handed over all potentially incriminating documents that were in Cripps' possession in return for a £55 pay-off, a figure well short of his client's original demand but one which was nevertheless accepted. All parties gave their word that they would never speak to anyone about the matter; it was a secret that would remain under lock and key.

Leeds had weathered the storm, or so it seemed. However, in the summer of 1919, Charlie Copeland, an unspectacular fringe player, huffed and puffed for a big pay rise and blew the Elland Road house down when he was denied. The club directors baulked at his inflation-busting, 'double-your-money' demand to be paid the new maximum wage of £6 a week. Instead they offered him £3 10s and not a penny more. Disgruntled, Copeland chucked a ticking time bomb into the negotiations. He too knew about the illegal payments made to players during the War and, what was more, was prepared to report City to the Football Association and the Football League, so would the board care to reconsider their offer?

Copeland was holding a gun to the club's head but Connor called his bluff and released the defender on a free transfer to Division Two newcomers Coventry City. The Leeds chairman had seriously misread the situation and Copeland promptly carried out his threat, placing the matter in the hands of his solicitor ... none other than James Bromley.

The situation had suddenly got a whole lot worse. Connor was furious, suspecting Bromley of being a whistleblower although the lawyer strenuously denied breaking his vow of silence. How Copeland stumbled across his evidence did not matter; the Football Association and Football League were bound to act. A joint commission was set up, chaired by FA Chairman, Charles Clegg. City officials were summoned to Manchester on 26th September, 1919 to answer the charges but when the club's representative, Alderman W (later Sir William) Clarke was asked to present the club's books for inspection, he replied that he was unable to do so. Clegg, as scrupulous and officious as ever, was not prepared to stand for such rot and nonsense and ordered Leeds either to produce the documents within the next ten days or else face the consequences of their defiance.

Two days before the deadline, McLeod struck a hat-trick in a 4-2 win away at Wolves. Unbeknown to him, they would be the last goals he would score in the blue and gold of Leeds City. On their way home to Yorkshire, the Leeds team gave several people a lift in their charabanc. Among them was their old colleague Charlie Copeland, a rat aboard a sinking ship whose spite would, by the month's end, deprive his travelling companions and former team-mates of their livelihoods.

The day of reckoning the 6th October, 1919 came and went without any communication from Leeds. Maybe Connor and his fellow directors were trying to protect their own skins - the documentation was likely to implicate them - or perhaps they felt a misguided loyalty towards the mystery 'guest' players at the heart of the payments scandal.

Whatever the reasons, silence implied guilt and the joint commission acted swiftly and severely. Connor and three fellow directors were banned for life from working in football as was Herbert Chapman who, according to some sources, burned the incriminating evidence at his home before quitting the club - a highly improbable scenario.

Leeds City was expelled from the Football League, John McKenna announcing, 'We will have no nonsense. The football stable must be cleansed.' Fine words from a man who had supported Sir Henry Norris and admitted some years later that, 'Perhaps others have escaped being found guilty of malpractices'. The club was formally wound up by an FA order, Charles Clegg declaring simply that Leeds City FC had, 'ceased to exist'. The Lord Mayor of Leeds, Alderman Joseph Henry, having openly rebuked the Association and the Football League for, 'punishing the public' over City's demise, rang Clegg in a last ditch effort to keep the club alive. He was given short shrift. 'My Lord Mayor,' replied the Sheffield stickler, 'do you think you have the right to talk to me after your public outburst?' And that was that, no reconsideration, no review, nothing. City's playing record was inherited by Burslem Port Vale, who went on to finish the season in thirteenth place.

When the sensational news of 'The Leeds City Scandal'

hit the back pages it was voraciously gobbled up by readers who were by turn shocked, indignant, dumbstruck and enthralled by the revelations of corruption and blackmail. And there was still more to come. The League Management Committee organised a humiliating auction of the City players at the Hotel Metropole in Leeds on 17th October, arguing that it was the quickest and best way for the players to secure alternative employment. The auction was widely condemned, Ivan Sharpe of the *Yorkshire Evening News*, a journalist of high renown who had sparkled on the left wing for Leeds City before the Great War, likening it to, 'Selling flesh and blood!'

The mood in the auction room was sombre as the players waited for their 'lot' to come up. Billy McLeod, unsurprisingly, commanded the highest fee, £1,250 from First Division Notts County. Club captain John Hampson (Aston Villa), Wales international full back Harold Millership (Rotherham County) and outside left Simpson Bainbridge (Preston North End) all went for a grand each. The whole 22-man squad was snapped up for the bargain price of £10,150. Ten of the players joined clubs operating in Division One while four (George Stephenson, Billy Kirton, William Ashurst and William Pease) went on to play for England.

'The Leeds City Scandal' robbed England's third most populous city of its professional football club and cut short the career of a dynamic and brilliant young manager. That is, perhaps, where the whole sorry saga should have ended but there were more twists and turns to come before this particular tale ran its course.

11

The Team That Herbert Built

'HE SHOULD have been prime minister,' wrote Cliff Bastin, the Arsenal and England winger, about the man who defined the role of the modern team manager. He had, Bastin added, 'an aura of greatness' about him. In those few words is revealed the very essence of the 'outstanding football personality' of his age, a chubby and jovial Yorkshireman who in the 1920s and '30s dominated the sport's increasingly high-rise skyline. He was just as wondrous too, uniquely guiding two clubs with no previous pedigree, Huddersfield Town and Arsenal, to League Championship and FA Cup glory. The Colossus in question is Herbert Chapman.

Furious at being thrown out of the game for his alleged role in 'The Leeds City Scandal', Chapman successfully appealed against his lifetime ban on the grounds that he was managing a munitions factory when the illegal payments were said to have been made. His reputation, if not exactly in tatters, was frayed around the edges. It took a brave gamble by the Huddersfield Town board in September 1920 to pluck Chapman from his duties as industrial manager at an oil and coke firm in Selby and install him as secretary at Leeds Road. Brave, yes, but also brilliant.

An inspirational and charismatic leader who commanded immense loyalty and devotion from his players, there was something Churchillian about the 'Boss'. Chapman turned out to be Town's best ever signing. Promoted to manager the following March, he saved the club from relegation in 1921, guided them to a famous victory in the 1922 FA Cup Final, and masterminded the first two legs of an historic League Championship treble (1924-25-26) before he was attracted away by the bright lights of London.

Transforming a small woollen town football club from a carthorse into a thoroughbred was a prodigious achievement, akin to a pit pony winning the Grand National. What makes Huddersfield's success even more remarkable is that before Chapman arrived, the club was one step away from being lost forever.

In October 1919, Town sold their popular centre-forward Jack Cock to Chelsea for £2,500, fuelling rumours that the club was in the grips of a financial crisis. Odds of 100-1 against the Grim Reaper visiting Leeds Road were offered and, on 6th November, one newspaper report under the sensational headline 'Town Club Dead' bluntly declared, 'The Huddersfield Town Association Football Club, so far as this town is concerned, is to all intents and purposes extinct.'

The curious choice of the phrase 'so far as this town is concerned' was explained the following evening when a lively crowd packed the YMCA Hall on Albion Street in Leeds. Out of the wreckage of Leeds City quickly emerged a new professional outfit, Leeds United, also based at Elland Road, and its supporters, of which the city's Lord Mayor,

Alderman Joseph Henry, was one, gathered to listen to an extraordinary proposal from Huddersfield Town's sugar daddy, Hilton Crowther. Disenchanted by Town's poor performances and even poorer pulling power - rugby remained the main attraction in the town and attendances at Leeds Road hovered disappointingly around the 4,000 mark - Crowther believed that the commercial heart of the West Riding offered far more potential. He was, he told a rapt audience, prepared to sacrifice his ailing club and move operations 'lock, stock and barrel' to Elland Road.

The planned amalgamation was greeted with enthusiasm, not least because it entailed Crowther's wealth. There was one major stumbling block, however. Crowther did not have the approval of his fellow Huddersfield directors. If he felt confident that the merger would meet with little opposition in his home town then he was wildly off the mark. The public reacted angrily, pillorying Hilton Crowther as a Judas. If his plotting had come to fruition then in magnitude it would have rivalled 'The Great Betrayal' of Bradford rugby before the war.

Determined that their soccer team should not go down without a fight, Huddersfield's hardcore supporters held demonstrations and petitioned the local workforce for cash donations and for them to attend matches. The *Huddersfield Examiner* gave printed voice to outraged fans and local dignitaries were encouraged to become shareholders to boost the club's coffers.

Alas, all the feverish campaigning was to no avail. Hilton Crowther and his brother Stonor were fed up with chucking good money after bad in the vain hope of building up a footballing Titan and hit Huddersfield Town with a triple whammy. First, Hilton demanded the immediate repayment of his £25,000 investment. Then, Stonor sued Town for £10,000 in unpaid loans and interest. And finally, the

Football League ordered the club to stump up the money by the end of the year or be forcibly unified with Leeds United. There was no way that Huddersfield Town could conjure up such vast sums at such short notice, not when they were already teetering on the edge of economic ruin. The local community tried its best, digging deep to raise more than £9,000 but, as the dreaded deadline loomed, it was clear to everyone that the club's brave fight was almost at an end.

That the knockout punch never came was thanks to the sluggish machinations of the High Court. Stonor Crowther's law suit was adjourned until the New Year, giving Huddersfield Town crucial time to beseech the Football League to reconsider their decision and to successfully persuade Stonor to drop his legal action in favour of an out-of-court settlement comprising £6,000 in cash, shares in the club and a place on the board.

Against all the odds, Huddersfield Town was saved. Hilton Crowther, his controversial plan in effect wrecked by his own brother, switched allegiances anyway, taking over as chairman of Leeds United in December 1919. He brought with him Town's secretary-manager Arthur Fairclough, a Barnsley man who had guided his hometown club to FA Cup victory in 1912.

Leeds United, looking suspiciously like Huddersfield in a kit of blue and white striped shirts and white shorts, were invited to play in the Midland League for the 1919/20 season. If Crowther thought his fresh new club would soon replace his dying old one in Division Two, then again he was much mistaken. After enduring their tumultuous winter of discontent, Huddersfield Town, under the steadying stewardship of former Hull City boss Ambrose Langley, miraculously won promotion and reached the FA Cup Final.

It was a breathtaking turnaround. Gates at Leeds Road ballooned; 27,000 for a top of the table clash with Spurs;

28,000 for the promotion clincher against Stoke City in April; 47,500, the most spectators the ground had ever held, against Liverpool in the Fourth Round of the knock out competition. The goals flowed too, Sammy Taylor, a replacement for Jack Cock up front, hitting 35 in the League to set a new club individual scoring record.

If gaining promotion was one in the eye for Hilton Crowther, then the brilliant Cup run was reward for the fans who had stuck by them through their dark times. There was no shame in losing 1-0 to a star-studded Aston Villa side in the Final at Stamford Bridge. Villa boasted an enviable heritage, six times champions of the Football League and, with victory here, six times winners of the FA Cup too. In a wonderful twist to his own rags-to-riches season, 23-year-old Billy Kirton, one of the players auctioned off in the great Leeds City sale, scored the game's solitary goal in extra time.

Alongside Kirton at inside left was a stocky and clever playmaker from the North-East, Clem Stephenson. Criticized by some judges for being too slow and the sole reason why he gained only one England cap, Stephenson's forte was not fast moving legs but a quick and alert brain, his passes being described as, 'sweet as stolen kisses'. Signing Clem was Herbert Chapman's top priority on succeeding Langley as manager at Huddersfield on the latter's resignation in March 1921. Detractors said the £4,000 move was proof that Stephenson was past it but Chapman knew better. The 31-year-old brought experience, guile, creative spark and a cool head to the relegation dog fight in which the 'Terriers' had become embroiled during the 1920/21 season. Chapman and Stephenson, the general and his trusty captain, marshalled the team so adroitly in the final month of the campaign that Huddersfield won seven of their last ten fixtures and effected a great escape that was worthy of Harry Houdini himself.

That late run was the catalyst for unimagined success. The next year they won the FA Cup, a drab Final with Preston North End being settled for the first time by a penalty. When Billy Smith, a tall and agile outside left who played in more games (574) for Town than anyone else, scoring 126 goals, was brutally chopped down on the edge of the box after a long dribble, he picked himself up, dusted himself down and followed his skipper's simple advice, 'Just shove it in the net', slamming the ball home from the spot. A victory parade through the streets of Huddersfield was attended by some 30,000 cheering well-wishers, a resounding confirmation that the rugby loving town had finally taken soccer to its heart too.

If the 'Roaring Twenties' were epitomised by the exhilarating, danger-packed sport of motor racing then Chapman's Huddersfield side could be said to be like the Bentley sports cars that roared to triumph after triumph at Le Mans; powerful yet classy, high octane but robust and, above all, winners. Chapman has often been accused of buying success - he splashed out £26,000 on David Jack, Alex James and Ted Drake alone when he was manager of moneybags Arsenal - but at Huddersfield the purse strings were drawn tight. He was forced to scour the football landscape for raw talent, utilising gut instinct and a practised eye to unearth players on the cheap who he believed could be fashioned into top grade footballers.

Goalkeeper Ted Taylor was brought in from Oldham Athletic; Roy Goodall, a brilliant tough-tackling right back who played in 440 games for Town, from Dronfield; fellow full back Sam Wadsworth via Nelson; David Steele, a tireless wing half, prized out of Bristol Rovers; inside forward George Cook from Rotherham County and George Brown, a prolific centre forward known as 'Bomber' for his booming shots who became Huddersfield's all-time top scorer with

159 goals in 229 appearances, from the coal pits of Mickley Colliery in County Durham. Under Chapman's tutelage all but Cook went on to play for their country, Goodall skippering England 13 times in a splendid international career.

Together with the likes of centre half Tommy Wilson (500 appearances, 1919-30) and half back Billy Watson - two players inherited from the Langley era and veterans of the 1920 Cup Final - this inexpensively assembled but well drilled team concluded the first phase of their unprecedented hat-trick of titles in dramatic fashion. Sitting in second place going into the last day of the 1923/24 season, Huddersfield had to win and hope that leaders Cardiff City slipped up against Birmingham for them to have any chance of capturing the Championship. Surprisingly, Cardiff obliged, drawing the game 0-0 after Len Davies, crippled by nerves, crucially missed a late penalty. Meanwhile at Leeds Road, Town beat Nottingham Forest 3-0 to finish level on points with the Welshmen. The toast of the town that night was George Cook whose all-important third goal squeezed Town's goal average up a fraction to beat Cardiff to the title by just 0.024 of a goal - a thrilling climax to an amazing season.

An old foe now returned, Hilton Crowther, who having pumped another £54,000 of his fortune into getting Leeds United promoted, must have felt rather smug when a heaving crowd of nearly 42,000 crammed into Elland Road on 27th September, 1924 to watch the two feuding clubs lock horns for the first time in the League. Even at the height of their fame Huddersfield lacked mass support, the average gate at Leeds Road never breaking through the 20,000 mark, a situation which was exacerbated by high unemployment.

Nevertheless, neither Crowther's Leeds United nor any other big city football club could match Huddersfield

Town's prowess on the pitch. After a wobbly start to their title defence comprising six wins and four defeats in the opening 16 fixtures, Stephenson missing half of them through injury, Town lost just once from mid-November 1924 to be crowned champions for the second year running.

In the close season, Chapman was allowed the extravagance of forking out £5,000 on a young outside right from Aberdeen, Alex Jackson. If Stephenson was Huddersfield's efficient project manager, implementing his boss's tactical instructions to perfection and effortlessly linking defence with attack, then Jackson, 'The Flying Scotsman', adventurous and lightening quick, a lithe panther on the wing, was the bums-on-seats entertainer. 'In his day there was probably no greater match winner,' wrote Geoffrey Green. 'He was a genius for snatching goals from unexpected positions.' Jackson won 14 Scotland caps during his five years in Yorkshire and scored a famous hat-trick all from headers - no mean feat for someone who was only five feet seven inches tall - for the so-called 'Wembley Wizards' in a 5-1 humbling of England in 1928.

The Jackson deal was undoubtedly one of Herbert Chapman's best pieces of business for Huddersfield Town. It was also his last. On 10th June, 1925 he quit the club, swapping the grit of Yorkshire for the glitz of London when Arsenal's controversial chairman and Barnsley's nemesis, Sir Henry Norris, offered to double his salary to £2,000 a year - this at a time when the maximum wage for a professional footballer was £8 per week. Chapman's departure was keenly felt. 'He knew when to blow you up and when to blow you down, when to be the Big Boss and when to be the Family Friend,' recalled Jackson. 'He was a genius and that's the fact of it.'

As Chapman set about building up a dynasty at Highbury, the one he left behind did not crumble as might have been expected. In the summer of 1925, the offside law was amended to encourage more attacking play and Huddersfield responded splendidly, scoring 92 goals of which Brown hit 35 to equal Taylor's club record. They positively romped to their hat-trick title, pushing, as fate would have it, Chapman's Arsenal into second place.

Huddersfield Town were *the* team of the 1920s but imagine just how great posterity would have remembered them had they also captured the 'double' in 1927/28. Scotsman John Chaplin was now in charge and Stephenson, at the grand old age of 38, was still pulling the strings on the pitch. Town scored a whopping 111 goals, the Jackson-Brown-Smith combination racking up 80 of them. Sensing another historic season, the fans flooded into Leeds Road, sending the gate soaring beyond 50,000 on three occasions.

In late March, however, the wheels came off the bandwagon. A trio of punishing, if ultimately successful, duels with Sheffield United in the Cup semi final took their toll on an ageing team. At the same time, Town stumbled to five defeats in the League allowing Everton - for whom 'Dixie' Dean scored a record-breaking 60 goals - to overhaul them at the top of Division One. Then, in the Cup decider at the new Empire Stadium in Wembley, the favourites were left scarred and empty handed by un-fancied Blackburn Rovers who scored within sixty seconds of kick-off and then tackled the life out of Huddersfield's celebrated but jaded forward line to win the Roses clash 3-1.

Stephenson, after notching up 50 goals in 275 appearances, swapped his football boots for the managerial hot seat at Leeds Road. In 1930, he took what was still essentially a Herbert Chapman team to another FA Cup Final where their opponents were ... Arsenal. Stephenson versus Chapman; captain against general; kings of the 1920s facing the crown princes of the 1930s. Clem tried his best but he was outwitted by his old mentor, his team outplayed by a side whose fulcrum was the baggy-shorted midfield genius Alex James. As the giant *Graf Zeppelin* airship floated menacingly over Wembley, Arsenal eased to a 2-0 victory to win their first major trophy. The baton of power had been handed on.

Tasked with rebuilding his team, Stephenson guided a remodelled Huddersfield Town to five top-six finishes in the 1930s but he was unable to put any further silverware in the trophy cabinet. The closest the 'Terriers' came to another title was in 1933/34 when they were runners-up behind Arsenal, who else. The season was overshadowed, however, by the tragic death, at the age of 55, of Herbert Chapman who succumbed to pneumonia on the morning of 6th January, 1934. At the time Arsenal were well on the way to winning a third Championship in four seasons and midway through emulating Huddersfield's title treble.

There has never been anyone quite like Chapman. He had that indefinable X-factor and was light years ahead of his time, advocating the use of floodlights (which had, of course, been trialled at Bramall Lane many years before), white balls, numbered shirts, all-weather pitches, BBC broadcasts, physios and exercise regimes. He redefined the role of the football manager too, wresting team selection from the hands of club directors, overseeing the coaching of his players and demanding physical fitness and high standards of behaviour at all times.

Most significantly, perhaps, Chapman revolutionised how the game itself was played. Since the 1880s, the 2-3-5 pyramid had been the tried and trusted system but when the offside law was amended in 1925 - ruling an attacker to be onside if there are two opponents rather than three between him and the goal - Chapman developed an innovative 3-4-3 system that became the tactical blueprint for the next generation. Known as the 'WM' formation, it dragged the centre-half back into defence to become a 'stopper' and the inside-forwards deeper into midfield. Its success relied upon stubborn defence, swift counter-attacks, slick passing, wingers who could cut inside and shoot at goal rather than just hugging the touchline and a clever midfield maestro able to orchestrate everything, someone very much in the mould of a Stephenson or a James.

In 1938, as Hitler and his Nazi thugs planned their domination of Europe, Chapman's protégé, Clem Stephenson, treated Huddersfield fans to one last hurrah in the FA Cup. There was an uncanny sense of deja-vu in the Final, the first to be shown live on BBC television, to a viewing audience of 10,000. Just as in 1922, their opponents were Preston North End. Proceedings were dreary, the score was 1-0 and the match decided by a controversial penalty, except this time the spot kick went the other way. In the final minute of extra-time, England centre-half Alex Young clattered into Preston's George Mutch on the edge of the penalty area. 'Outside the box!' screamed the ranks of Huddersfield fans on the terraces but the referee was having none of it and pointed to the spot. And, just like Billy Smith had 16 years before, Mutch groggily picked himself off the floor and hammered the ball into the net, off the underside of the bar.

It was a cruel way to lose but how many Huddersfield fans present at Wembley that day and who bewailed the injustice of it all stopped to think how lucky they were even to be there. Had Hilton Crowther got his way in 1919, then there would have been no Huddersfield Town to support and football fans in the Colne Valley would never have been treated to the magnificent deeds of the team that Herbert built.

12

Good Old Days

YORKSHIRE football reached its zenith in the inter-war years. These were the good old days of hardly a season going by without one or other of the county's teams challenging for the title or the Cup, of bumper crowds and mammoth score lines and of gritty Yorkshiremen forming the backbone of the England team.

The ascendancy of Yorkshire teams coincided with an expansion in the game's popularity and exposure. The Football League doubled in size after the First World War with Divisions Three (South) and (North) - of which Halifax Town were founder members - being grafted on by August 1921. Football pools offered the public the chance to win thousands of pounds for a penny stake. New technologies - first wireless radio and then black and white television - hurled the game out of stadiums and into the front parlours of millions of homes and Yorkshire clubs were in the thick of the action from the very start. Sheffield United took part in the first live radio football commentary to be broadcast by the BBC, a 1-1 draw with Herbert Chapman's Arsenal at Highbury on 22nd January, 1927. To help listeners visualise proceedings, the *Radio Times* printed a diagram of a pitch split into eight numbered squares and to which the commentators referred when describing passages of play. The 1930 FA Cup Final between Huddersfield Town and Arsenal was covered on wireless in real time for the first time and Huddersfield took centre stage again in 1938 when their dramatic last-minute defeat by Preston North End in the FA Cup Final was the first to be shown in its entirety on TV, albeit to a limited viewing audience of around 10,000.

Leading players became household names, ranking alongside stars of the silver screen in terms of celebrity but without the glamorous Hollywood lifestyle to match. Their fame was exploited by various companies eager to sell their products. The Sheffield United FA Cup Final team of 1936 was photographed eating breakfast, rather woodenly, under the tagline, 'Shredded Wheat again in the Cup Final News!' and two years later the Huddersfield team that reached Wembley were apparently fond users of Watermen's Pens - useful, no doubt, for signing all those autographs. A generation of lads grew up idolising these footballers, reading all about their exploits in *Boy's Own Paper* and Charlie Buchan's *Football Monthly*, collecting their portraits on cigarette cards given to them by their chain-smoking dads and pretending to be them when kicking a battered old leather ball about with their mates in grimy streets.

The bard of Bradford, JB Priestley, waxed lyrical when he said: 'To think of football as merely 22 hirelings kicking a ball is to say that a violin is wood and cat-gut, Hamlet so much ink and paper. It is conflict and art.' Yet it was in the years immediately after the end of the First World War that soccer lost its flair, its art and the offside law was to blame. Newcastle United full back Bill McCracken perfected a cunning trap which exploited an inherent problem with the three-man offside rule. Rather than remaining square with his fellow back, McCracken ventured near the halfway line, the intention being to catch out forwards who were too quick off the mark. Then, even if an attacker did spring the trap they still had to cover half the pitch and beat another defender before having a shot at goal. McCracken's system was brilliantly effective and many other clubs quickly followed suit which had the effect of strangling free-flowing football.

The game's authorities took decisive action. On the eve of the 1925/26 season, the offside law was amended to allow an attacking player to remain onside if only two opponents lay between him and the goal. It was the shot in the arm that the game needed. Overnight the output of goals in the Football League rocketed by more than 40 percent from 2.6 per game to 3.7. Matches became faster, more fluid. Defenders struggled to adapt and in the confusion forwards helped themselves to a feast of goals. Sheffield United, Sheffield Wednesday, Barnsley, Hull City, Bradford City and Bradford PA all piled their plate high, scoring, at some time or other, 100 or more goals in a League campaign. Indeed, Park Avenue topped the century in three successive seasons (1925-28), a feat that has been surpassed on only one occasion by Wolves, who rattled in a hundred goals in four consecutive campaigns in the late 50s.

Fantastical scores, more suited to Sunday pub leagues than professional football, abounded. Bradford City opened the 1928/29 season with an 11-1 trouncing of Rotherham United. Sheffield United put 10 past Burnley in the same campaign. Barnsley beat Fulham 8-4 at home in 1928 and Accrington Stanley 9-0 away in 1934. Huddersfield stuffed Blackpool 10-1 in 1930 and Leeds United thrashed Leicester City 8-0 in 1934. Let us spare a thought for the poor goalies who endured such ritual humiliation, in particular Halifax Town's rookie keeper Stan Milton who had a hellish debut away at Stockport County on 6th January, 1934. After 45 minutes he had let in two goals. Not good but not disastrous either. However, whatever the manager said at half-time must have put the willies up him because at the final whistle a dispirited Milton had picked the ball out of his net a further eleven times in an embarrassing 13-0 defeat. Suffice to say, he never made the grade.

The goal glut continued right up until the Second World War. Clubs were either too slow to implement Herbert Chapman's counteractive 3-4-3 formation or lacked the required personnel to make it function effectively. A notable exception was Hull City who had one of the best defensive records in the League; then again they were managed by Bill McCracken. Not that the fans cared. They loved the thundering centre forwards who dished up what they craved most - goals, goals, and yet more goals.

George Brown netted 35 times for Huddersfield Town in the first year of the amended offside law. Scotsman Tom Jennings also scored 35, for Leeds United in 1926/27, although, amazingly, they were not enough to prevent his team from being relegated to Division Two. Abe Blight struck 31 times for Third Division (North) champions Barnsley in 1933/34 and in the same year Albert Valentine posted 34 goals for Halifax. Hull City's Bill McNaughton plundered 41 goals in 1932/33, Sheffield United's Irish international Jimmy Dunne scored the same number in 1930/31 and Dunne's successor, Ephraim 'Jock' Dodds, a bull of a man, headed the Second Division scoring charts with 34 in 1935/36. Then there was Harry Johnson who reigned supreme at Bramall Lane in the 1920s. A part-time amateur, during the week he worked as a metallurgist at Hadfield Steelworks. The son of 'Old Harry' Johnson, who shared in all of the Blades' major triumphs at the turn of the century and played six times for England, 'Young Harry' hit the first Steel City derby hat-trick in 1928 and is the club's all-time leading scorer with 205 League goals. He took his tally to 307 with Mansfield Town in the early Thirties thereby joining the exclusive 300 Goals Club, fellow members of which include the illustrious triumvirate of Steve Bloomer, 'Dixie' Dean and Jimmy Greaves.

At Elland Road, Jennings shared centre forward duties with Charlie Keetley who between 1928 and 1934 scored 110 goals for Leeds at the extraordinary rate of two every three games. The youngest of a brood of, ironically, 11 Derbyshire brothers, football positively coursed through Keetley's blood. Seven of his siblings were also top-class footballers and four of them - Frank, Harold, Joe and Tom - played professionally for Doncaster Rovers. Of the quartet Tom was a Donny legend, accumulating 180 League goals in just six seasons at Belle Vue, including a double hat-trick in a 7-4 win against Ashington in 1929; a feat which Frank emulated for Lincoln City in a 9-1 thrashing of Halifax Town in January 1932 and all inside 21 minutes to boot.

Many of the stadiums in which these local heroes performed were modernised, revamped and extended after the War. From being the equivalents of parochial churches they became vast cathedrals, capable of holding 50, 60 or even 70,000 disciples. The steep cinder terraces at such grounds as Elland Road, Hillsborough and Valley Parade were christened 'Spion Kop' after a hilltop in South Africa upon which an infamous battle took place during the Second Boer War (1899-1902).

Crowds, cloth-capped, noisy and ribald, could be huge. Sheffield United drew 59,000 for a Sheffield derby in 1928 and 68,000 for the clash with Leeds in 1936. Leeds got 57,000 against Arsenal in 1932; Barnsley attracted 40,000 for a match against Stoke City in 1936; Doncaster versus Barnsley was seen by 34,000; York City had 28,000 against Huddersfield in 1938. And just under 73,000 - the biggest football crowd ever to assemble in Yorkshire - watched Sheffield Wednesday draw 2-2 with Manchester City in the FA Cup in 1934. Many of the above set lasting club records which have as much chance now of being broken as Ilkley Moor has of becoming a part of Lancashire.

The country, however, was in a parlous state. Post-war economic gloom gave way to the Great Depression of 1929 which in turn spawned mass unemployment. Yorkshire, with her heavy industries of coal mining, textiles and steel production, was particularly hard hit. The majority of football supporters could not afford to watch more than a handful of games each season and, consequently, those they attended were often major matches like FA Cup ties, local derbies or Boxing Day fixtures. The result was a wild fluctuation in the size of crowds. Huddersfield Town, for example, drew a gate of 67,037 for a sixth round Cup clash with Arsenal in 1932; six week later they attracted just 3,000 for a First Division game against Manchester City. In February 1934, Hillsborough rocked and rolled to its record turnout of 72,841 but nine days later echoed to the voices of 6,500 hardy souls for a Sheffield Wednesday-Leeds match.

Such volatility made for severe cash flow problems. Halifax Town constantly struggled to stay afloat. A run to the FA Cup fifth round in 1932/33 and an unexpected promotion challenge in 1934/35 generated rare profits which were used to alleviate their debts. Creditors sued for unpaid bills, players went without wages. That the club survived was in no small part down to a loyal band of supporters who launched SOS ('Soccer On Shay') initiatives in the textile town, raising enough funds to keep their heads just above water.

Bradford City also went close to going under after suffering two relegations in five years. From playing the likes of Huddersfield, Newcastle and Liverpool they now faced Halifax, Durham and Southport. Players were not paid, an embargo was placed on new signings and liquidation was avoided only by an influx of cash from directors and supporters' organisations at the eleventh hour. But what a difference a year makes. In 1928/29, City racked up 128 goals - a new League scoring record - as they blazed their way to the Third Division (North) title. The average gate at Valley Parade was 18,500, yielding sufficient receipts to drag the club out of its financial mire.

Elsewhere in the Ridings, there was far greater success. Huddersfield Town, of course, conquered all before them in the 1920s. In 1925 Sheffield United became the first Yorkshire side to play at the brand new Wembley Stadium, which had opened to great fanfare two years before and was said to be, 'as big as the Biblical city of Jericho'. They beat Cardiff City 1-0 to win the Cup for a fourth time, outside left Fred Tunstall, from Darfield, scoring the goal after half an hour. Man of the match was skipper Billy Gillespie, a prematurely balding and brilliant inside left from Ireland who missed the club's previous Cup triumph in 1915 with a broken leg. 'No player on view trapped the ball so surely, retained it with such good judgement, and exhibited such power and precision in sending it either to the left or right wing or more delicately down the middle,' purred Ivan Sharpe, by now editor of *Athletic News*. United returned to Wembley in 1936, as a Second Division side, and put in a plucky display against mighty Arsenal. Dodds even managed to rattle the bar. It was late in the second half that Ted Drake, the Gunners' own bulldozing centre-forward, hammered home a shot to record a slender 1-0 victory.

Hull City, Barnsley and Doncaster Rovers - who were

readmitted to the Football League in 1923 - were champions of Division Three (North) in consecutive seasons (1933-34-35), and Leeds reached the dizzy heights of fifth place in Division One in 1929/30, their best showing before Don Revie's golden team of the late Sixties. Outside the Football League, Mexborough (1926) and Scarborough (1930) both won the Midland League, the Seasiders also reaching the third round of the FA Cup in 1931 and 1938. York City, whose best showing in the Midland league was sixth in 1924/25 and 1926/27, surprisingly won election to Division Three (North) in 1929 at the expense of Ashington. Formed in March 1922, as the successor of a defunct club of the same name and moving to Bootham Crescent from a ground in Fulfordgate ten years later, York scored well over 100 goals in that final non-league campaign with Scottish striker Jimmy Cowie bagging 56 of them. The Minstermen struggled in the Football League, however, losing far more games than they won before the Second World War, thrice conceding more than 90 goals in a season and suffering their biggest ever defeat, 12-0 away, at Chester on 1st February, 1936.

Further down the football pyramid, Selby Town impressed winning the Yorkshire League - a competition founded after the Great War to cater for an eclectic mix of the county's reserve, semi-pro and amateur sides - on four occasions (1933-35-36-37) and the West Riding Challenge Cup in 1935 and 1936. Leeds-based Yorkshire Amateurs, who briefly played at Elland Road in between the demise of Leeds City and the rise of Leeds United, had a season to remember in 1931/32, reaching the first round proper of the FA Cup going out to Carlisle United 3-1, and the semi-finals of the FA Amateur Cup, losing 2-1 to Marine. That trophy was instigated in 1893 in the wake of professionalism being legalised and at the proposal of those bastions of amateur ideals, Sheffield FC. Eleven years later 'The Club' won the tournament themselves, beating Ealing 3-1 in the Final at Bradford before a crowd of 6,000.

Back in the professional world, the best side in Yorkshire after Huddersfield Town was Sheffield Wednesday who, before Arsenal got the game in a headlock in the Thirties, won back-to-back titles in 1929 and 1930. On the second occasion they claimed the championship with ten points to spare, the largest winning margin for nearly 40 years. They went close to performing the coveted 'double' too but were knocked out in the Cup semi final by Huddersfield. A third Yorkshire club, Hull City, who were relegated from Division Two on goal difference that season, also reached the last-four stage, scalping Manchester City and Newcastle en route and holding Arsenal to a 2-2 draw at Elland Road before being gunned down in the replay by the eventual winners.

Wednesday's return to the limelight bore uncanny parallels with Huddersfield's emergence as a northern powerhouse. Champions of Division Two in 1926, they avoided relegation in 1927/28 by taking 17 points from their last ten games and then purchased an inventive inside forward, aged 32, from Tottenham who was supposedly past his best and had far fewer England caps, with five, than his talents deserved. Jimmy Seed became the driving force behind their triumphs. A rugged ex-miner from County Durham, he was made team captain, an appropriate post for someone whose middle name was Marshall.

Unlike their goal-shy predecessors from 1903-04, this winning Wednesday team was full of verve and vigour and attacked at every conceivable opportunity. In each of Seed's five years at Hillsborough they averaged over 100 League and Cup goals, centre-forward Jack Allen claiming 33 in both championship winning years. Allen later won the FA Cup with Newcastle, scoring the goals that gave his boyhood heroes a surprise 2-1 victory over Arsenal in the 1932 Final. At around the same time Seed, his knee ligaments perished, retired from the game. He carried his Midas touch into management, however, transforming Charlton Athletic from Third Division plodders into First Division runners-up in 1937 and Cup winners ten years later.

Sheffield Wednesday, as they were now officially christened, remained a force to be reckoned with. Four times they finished third (1931-32-33-35) and in the last of those years won the Cup for a third time, defeating West Bromwich Albion 4-2 in a thriller. The central figure around whom the team now revolved was Ronnie Starling, a slightly built inside forward snapped up from Newcastle United for £3,250 in June 1932. More schemer than scorer, his mind was always racing ahead to the next move. He teased opponents with what Geoffrey Green described as, 'that same impudent "fluttering" of the foot over the ball' that Arsenal's midfield imp Alex James displayed. Starling was on song at Wembley but the plaudits went to Wednesday's free-scoring outside left Ellis Rimmer who scored twice in a breathtaking climax to seal victory and keep up a splendid record of scoring in every round.

Rimmer also bagged a brace on his England debut, the first of four caps, in a 5-2 victory over Scotland in April 1930. He lined up alongside team-mates Bill Marsden, Alf Strange and Ernie Blenkinsop plus Huddersfield Town's Roy Goodall. It was not uncommon between the wars for England to call up four, five, even six players from Yorkshire clubs. Goodall, a tough tackling right back, and Blenkinsop, a stylish, intelligent left back, were a defensive marriage made in heaven. They went together like beef and Yorkshire pudding; one without the other for England was just unthinkable. Between 1926 and 1933 they won a combined

51 caps and when in tandem tasted defeat on only one occasion, a 2-0 loss against the Scots at Hampden Park, Glasgow in March 1931, before a huge and intimidating crowd of 129,810.

Leeds United served England well too, providing the national team with their formidable half back line of Willis Edwards, Ernie Hart and Wilf 'Iron Man' Copping, later of Arsenal, he of the bone busting tackles and brooding gangster looks. Yorkshire representation was still strong - Sproston (Leeds), Willingham and Young (Huddersfield), Robinson (Sheffield Wed) - when, during a European tour in the summer of 1938, England thumped Germany 6-3 in Berlin against a backdrop of swastikas. The match is infamous for the shameful way in which the English players were ordered to perform the Nazi salute during the pre-match ceremonies. One cannot imagine Sir Charles Clegg, had he been alive and in the Football Association party, indulging Herr Hitler and his fascist regime so blithely.

The Twenties and Thirties were, in so many ways, good old days for Yorkshire football, but the storm clouds of war were once more gathering and things would never be the same again.

13

Carry On Football

ON 30th SEPTEMBER, 1938 Prime Minister Neville Chamberlain stepped off an aeroplane at Heston Aerodrome, London, fluttered a flimsy piece of paper in the air and proudly proclaimed: 'Peace with honour ... peace for our time'. But Adolf Hitler had hoodwinked him in Munich as adroitly as the England team were duped into saluting the Nazis less than five months before in Berlin.

A year later and Hitler invaded Poland, thereby showing utter contempt for the terms of the Munich agreement which had aimed to limit his expansionist plans. On Sunday 3rd September 1939, Chamberlain, his policy of appeasement having clearly failed, went to the airwaves and solemnly announced to an anxious nation, 'I have to tell you now ... this country is at war with Germany'.

Three matches into the season, competitive soccer was terminated with immediate effect. The Football Association and Football League had no intention of being pilloried as they had been at the start of the 1914-18 hostilities. For a second time in a generation, the League Championship trophy and the FA Cup went into hiding. The War Office, however, as in the previous world war, wanted organised football to continue in some shape or form as a morale booster for men stationed on the Home Front. Ten regional wartime leagues and a nationwide War Cup were hastily arranged to fill the void. The *Yorkshire Post* prophesised matches, 'would be played at a slower pace' but hoped that the wartime game, 'would afford the chance for players to show greater accuracy and introduce experimental movements'. Some hope. The standard of football proved extremely patchy with the *Post* itself describing one game between Halifax and Leeds as of, 'a level usually associated with the village green'.

The 'new' season kicked off in October 1939 and that it was ever completed is a minor miracle. Teams were depleted by conscription, fuel for travelling was in short supply, matches were confined to Saturdays and public holidays and the number of spectators was limited by the Home Office to 8,000 or half the capacity of the ground, whichever was lower. But, football played on through the chaos.

Most matches attracted far fewer supporters than the new maximum. Huddersfield Town, for instance, had six crowds numbering several hundred in the first two years of hostilities. In such reduced circumstances it was not surprising that many clubs, hamstrung by high running costs and low income, struggled to make ends meet. Bradford Park Avenue posted a £1,763 loss in the first year of the war. The situation was exacerbated by professional players continuing to receive match fees - attitudes had changed since the Great War - although the maximum rate of 30 shillings was well below pre-war levels.

By the early months of 1940, some 150 professional footballers had joined HM Forces. Squads were stripped back to their barest bones and so local youngsters were drafted in to add some flesh. A handful of them went on to enjoy notable post-war careers; Jimmy Glazzard and Vic Metcalfe (Huddersfield Town), Willie Watson (Huddersfield/ Sunderland), Eddie Shimwell (Sheffield United/Blackpool), Wally Ardron (Rotherham United/Nottingham Forest), George Robledo (Barnsley/Newcastle), Joe Harvey (Bradford City/Newcastle) and, sounding like an extra from *Last of the Summer Wine,* Redfern Froggatt (Sheffield Wednesday). The cream of the crop, though, was a boy from Bradford who happened to be the most naturally gifted footballer of his generation - Len Shackleton.

Born on 3rd May, 1922, 'Shack' - a plain-speaking Yorkshireman who liked to entertain the public but scorned authority- was the natural heir to Billy Mosforth. In his autobiography *Clown Prince of Soccer* - a title that captured both the slapstick and the majesty of his play - he famously included a chapter entitled, 'The Average Director's Knowledge of Football'. The page was left blank. Such disdain for the establishment, allied to a disinclination to conform, cost him a bagful of international caps. One selector refused to pick him on the grounds that, 'we play at Wembley Stadium, not the London Palladium'. His five appearances in an England shirt (1948-54) was scant reward for one of the game's all-time great inside forwards. His football career began inauspiciously, Arsenal axing him from their ground-staff in 1939 for being too small and skinny. He returned home, bulked up as a Bevin Boy in the mines at Fryston Colliery near Castleford and, on Christmas Day 1940, signed professional forms for Bradford Park Avenue. To celebrate he played for them against Leeds at Elland Road that morning and then turned out as a guest for rivals Bradford City at Huddersfield in the afternoon, scoring in a 4-3 victory. He never looked back.

'Shack' was a true *Boys' Own* hero, a showman who illuminated the football field with dazzling ball skills, breathtaking body swerves and a keen eye for goal. Occasionally he was downright rubbish, other times he showboated but more often than not he was magnificent. His natural talent and the small matter of 166 goals in 202 wartime appearances for Park Avenue attracted the attentions of Newcastle United who paid the princely sum of £13,000 for him in October 1946. In a sensational debut, he scored a double hat-trick in a 13-0 demolition of Newport County but, sixteen months later following a clash with management, he was sold to archrivals Sunderland for a British record transfer fee of £20,500. He racked up more than a hundred goals in 348 games for Sunderland and the Roker Roar in turn bellowed its appreciation for the flamboyant Bradfordian who played the game with a touch of arrogance, a dash of comedy and plenty of style.

Giving youth a fling was one thing but wartime soccer would have folded had it not been for the return of 'guest' players. Starting XIs were often not finalised until the last minute as clubs attempted to sweet-talk commanding officers of nearby barracks into releasing any decent footballers who happened to be stationed there. The results were sometimes comical, as Jack Rollin relates in *Soccer at War: 1939-45*:

> Leeds United heard that Chelsea's much sought-after winger Alf Hanson was billeted at Harrogate and the wheels were set in motion to have a taxi collect him for the match with York on 21 November 1942. Despite arriving ten minutes after the start, he took his place on the vacant right wing. A portly figure, not what was expected in appearance - they had the wrong man. The newcomer was an Irishman called Stanley Anson.

The deployment of 'guests' made for some very interesting team sheets. The town of Aldershot, for example, was the traditional home of the British Army and that enabled its small time football team to field some big names including Tommy Lawton, Joe Mercer, Denis Compton, Stan Cullis and Bert Sproston, who Leeds sold to Spurs for £9,500 in 1938. Yorkshire clubs could also call on the services of some of the game's biggest stars. Huddersfield Town attracted Sunderland captain Raich Carter and Blackpool's Stan Mortensen for a handful of games, Doncaster Rovers fielded pre-war England international players Cliff Britton, of Everton, and Freddie Steele from Stoke City. Arsenal goalkeeper George Swindin, who turned pro with Bradford City in 1934, turned out again for the Bantams and also for Leeds United.

Another keeper, Sam Bartram of Charlton Athletic, a strapping ex-miner turned RAF Sergeant-Instructor, was a hugely popular guest player for York City. Brave, agile and widely regarded as the finest No.1 never to play for England, Bartram was an almost permanent fixture between the sticks at Bootham Crescent during the latter half of the war. He was an integral member of the York team that reached the semi-finals of the League North Cup in 1942/43, the second leg of which, against Sheffield Wednesday on 24th April, 1943, attracted a record wartime Bootham Crescent gate of 16,350. Three goals down from the first leg at Hillsborough, City earned a creditable 1-1 draw thanks to a spot kick by local boy George Lee who thus became the first player to score 100 goals for the club. A talented left winger, Lee later joined First Division West Brom and won a Cup winners' medal in 1954. Bartram too won that silverware, with Charlton, managed by Jimmy Seed, in 1947.

In real battle, among a host of heroes, Wilf Copping, who

rejoined Leeds from Arsenal in March 1939, served as a Company Sergeant Major in North Africa, Eric Stephenson, a cultured inside left, also of Leeds and England, became a major in the Gurkha Rifles and Sheffield United playmaker Jimmy Hagan rose to the rank of major in the Physical Training Corps.

As the first wartime season drew to a close - with Huddersfield Town convincing champions of the North-East League, losing just once and scoring 54 goals in 20 matches - it became abundantly clear that the military campaign on mainland Europe was not going well. Tens of thousands of allied troops were evacuated from the beaches of Dunkirk, an inglorious retreat by the British Army which signalled the end of the so-called 'Phoney War' and the beginning of the Battle of Britain. Britannia put on her tin hat and prepared for invasion. What she desperately wanted in her hour of need was an inspirational war leader. He duly arrived in the roly-poly shape of Winston Churchill who replaced Chamberlain as Prime Minister on 10th May, 1940.

Football might have been seen as a trifling and expendable frivolity but Churchill, though no keen fan himself, understood the vital role the game had to play in keeping spirits up among the rank and file and so he gave his seal of approval for it to carry on regardless. The myriad of regional Divisions were scrapped and replaced by two cumbersome Leagues, North and South, each comprising more than 30 clubs. The champions would, for the first and last time, be decided by goal average.

Sheffield, a crucible of armaments production, suffered the full force of the Blitz in December 1940. Ten bombs hit Bramall Lane, demolishing half the John Street Stand and turning the pitch into a cratered lunar landscape. Bootham Crescent suffered damage when incendiaries landed on houses at the Shipton Street End during a night raid in April

1942. Hull City fared even worse, their ground on Anlaby Road ruined to such an extent that they had to withdraw from all football competition until 1944. The city of Hull suffered incredibly. Routinely targeted because of its vital importance as a port, no other place outside of London was bombarded as intensely as it was between May 1941 and July 1943.

Amid all the shelling, football soldiered on. Barnsley were the leading Yorkshire club in 1940/41, their long-winded mathematical average of 1.775 putting them in fourth place in the North Regional League. Unlike Bradford City, Leeds United, Doncaster Rovers and Halifax Town, all of whom relied heavily upon guest players, Barnsley put out a remarkably settled team for the duration of the war. In common with that of Rotherham United, the bulk of their squad went down the coal mines, a protected industry, rather than see active service. Other professional footballers either opted for, or were obliged to take on, essential war work. England international half back Ken Willingham became a fitter and turner in a munitions works. His Huddersfield team-mate Reg Mountford acted as an Air Raid Precautions Control Officer. Halifax's full back Harold Jackson became an Air Ministry inspector for an engineering firm and Len Shackleton, before going down the pit, was employed by GEC on aircraft wireless.

It was all change again for football in 1941/42. The North Regional League was split into two separate competitions, one operating up to Christmas, the next from then until May. The national War Cup was replaced by regional League South and League North cups which were played for on a home-and-away basis.

Blackpool, with Stanley Matthews - the 'Wizard of Dribble' - now in their ranks, dominated proceedings in the North. Yorkshire sides hardly got a look in, although

Sheffield Wednesday reached the League North Cup Final in May 1943 where they were beaten 4-3 on aggregate by the seasiders. By then, the threat of a German invasion had receded and with it the restrictions on football attendances were relaxed. Crowds started to boom again. The second leg of the final at Hillsborough was watched by 47,657, a wartime record for the ground. Opening the scoring for Blackpool with a thundering 30-yard free-kick was former Sheffield United favourite Jock Dodds who joined the Tangerines in March 1939 for £10,500. A masterly marksman during his time at Bramall Lane in the Thirties, he churned out more wartime goals, 253 - 227 of them for Blackpool - than any other player.

Dodds also garnered nine goals for Scotland. Rather remarkably, international fixtures between England, Scotland and Wales carried on throughout the war years although Yorkshire representatives were rather thin on the ground. Willingham added six unofficial appearances to the 12 England caps he won before Hitler annexed Poland. Bradford full back Jimmy Stephen played five times for Scotland, Leeds United winger Aubrey Powell on four occasions for Wales. Only Jimmy Hagan, who notched up 13 goals in 16 internationals for England, excelled.

Slightly built, similar to Shackleton, Hagan was, unlike the brash boy from Bradford, an unobtrusive and unselfish team player who adapted his game to the needs of his colleagues. He reached his international peak on 16th October, 1943 when, from his berth in the middle of a mouth watering forward line of Matthews-Carter-Lawton-Hagan-Compton, he scored twice in an 8-0 dismantling of Scotland in front of 60,000 fans at Maine Road. Lawton called him, 'a master craftsman' while to his club colleague Joe Shaw, who holds the Sheffield United record for League appearances with 631, he was, 'a wonderful footballer, one of the best I ever saw. His ball control was extraordinary … some of his passing was unbelievable, and many of the goals he scored were fabulous, so stunning they took your breath away.'

Yet Hagan won only one official England cap, against Denmark in 1948. His unswerving loyalty to a struggling Sheffield United side for whom he scored 116 goals in 361 games, injuries, loss of form at inopportune times and the emergence of inside forwards of the calibre of Shackleton, Mortensen and Wilf Mannion severely curtailed his international career. But to the Bramall Lane faithful he was, and always will be, a hero who endeared himself still further by refusing to join Wednesday in 1951 after the board had agreed to sell him for what would have been a new record fee of £32,250.

Huddersfield Town ended the War as they started it, as champions. On 23rd December, 1944 they beat Newcastle United 4-1 in front of a season's best gate at Leeds Road of 17,253 to pip Derby County to top spot in the North Regional League (1st). The stars of the side were Glazzard, Watson, Willingham, fellow half back Eddie Boot and centre forward Albert 'Billy' Price who plundered 40 goals that season and nigh on 200 in all for Town at the astonishing rate of one every game.

On 8th May, 1945 came the news that everyone had been hoping and praying for - Hitler was dead and Germany had surrendered. Fighting continued in Asia for another three months until the Second World War was finally over.

Britain lost more than 90,000 civilian lives and some 265,000 combatants. Yorkshire football did not escape the bloodshed. Major Eric Stephenson was killed in action in Burma in 1944. In dedication to him, and other servicemen and women who lost their lives, a memorial stained glass window was erected in Lidgett Park Methodist Church in Leeds. Gunner Glynn Jones, educated at Doncaster

Grammar School and a guest player for Rovers, died when his Lancaster bomber was shot down during a disastrous raid on Nuremburg in March 1944. GAC Reynolds, a popular player for York City, died in an RAF hospital in August 1944 from injuries he sustained in Normandy the previous month. His team-mate Leonard Milner, a left-footed midfielder, was also killed in northern France, in July 1944. Sheffield United inside forward Harry Hampson, the first man from the club to enlist with the Army, died after he contracted an illness in 1942. Barnsley outside right George Bullock perished in June 1943 while serving as a rating in the Royal Navy. Another Barnsley player, Tom Robinson, lost a leg in the D-Day landings. The Roll of Honour gained an illustrious postscript when ex-Huddersfield Town legend Alex Jackson, who was still serving in the British Army, was killed in a road accident in Egypt in November 1946.

14

The Millers' Tale

ROTHERHAM UNITED, the Merry Millers of Millmoor, never had much to cheer about. A couple of appearances in the FA Cup third Round and a best placing of sixth in Division Three (North) in 1938 were not exactly the stuff of legend. Every now and again they cast off their customary mediocrity to put in an unexpected display of excellence, such as in January 1930 when they humbled Accrington Stanley 8-1. But against these rare events must be set half-a-dozen bottom-six finishes and a litany of heavy losses, culminating in an 11-1 thrashing by Bradford City at Valley Parade on the opening day of the 1928/29 season. Rotherham's masochistic supporters had to endure plenty of punishment for their fleeting days in the sun.

Then, in the first peacetime football season after the War in 1945/46, Rotherham United were suddenly the toast of the town. They did the double of sorts, pipping Darlington to the Third Division North (East) title and defeating Chester 5-4 on aggregate in the Final of a one-off Third

Division North Cup. Two trophies in one season, the Millers' demob-happy fans pinched themselves. And were United good enough to keep the dream alive when a full football programme resumed the next season? The answer was a resounding yes.

In the post-war age of austerity, rationing and bomb sites, Rotherham United were the talk not only of South Yorkshire but the whole country. Over the next decade they put Rotherham on the map, winning more games and scoring more goals than any other White Rose side. Eight of the squad made over 200 Football League appearances for the club and in Wally Ardron they possessed one of the best centre-forwards outside the First Division. After steadily climbing the rungs of the league ladder, they agonisingly missed out on promotion to the top division on goal average in 1955.

Glory was on the near horizon in the summer of 1946 but it was clear that the club had assembled a constellation of star attractions. Albert Wilson, a summer signing from Mansfield Town, sparkled on the right wing. Jack Shaw and Gladstone Guest, two wily inside forwards who gave the club great service, plotted up front. Ardron, as strong as the steel the town was renowned for and a lethal marksman in wartime football, lead the line with aplomb. The defence and midfield, in contrast, relied more on shovel loads of Yorkshire grit than on Fancy Dan football. At right back, Jack Selkirk was redoubtable; Horace Williams was a tough tackling centre-half; his namesake Danny and Jack Edwards - nicknamed 'Nutty' for his penchant for peanuts - were the engine room, twin turbo half-backs who could run all day and made the rest of the team tick. The side brimmed over with working class heroes who supplemented their low football wages by toiling away in the pits during the week.

Confidence was sky-high going into the 1946/47 season,

as one might expect from a swaggering bunch of young chaps whose average age was 25 and had just collected two trophies. They got off to a cracking start, winning 11 of their opening 14 fixtures in Division Three (North). Ardron scored eleven goals, including four in a 5-1 drubbing of Crewe Alexandra at Millmoor in October. The goals and victories just kept on coming, trouble was, so too did neighbours Doncaster Rovers. The season quickly developed into a two horse race but it was the men from Doncaster, a town more renowned for the running of the St. Leger than for its football, who galloped into the lead. On 26th April, 1947, United inflicted one of only three defeats suffered by Donny, winning a thrilling local derby 3-2 in front of 20,247 at Millmoor but it was not enough. In an extended season that ran into June because of a big winter freeze, Rovers outgunned United on all fronts, winning more matches (33 to 29), scoring more goals (123 to 114) and setting a new points' record (72) to clinch the sole promotion place. Doncaster centre forward Clarrie Jordan was prolific, grabbing 42 goals to Ardron's 38 as both men set individual scoring records for their respective clubs.

It was rotten luck for Rotherham to come up against such formidable opponents, nevertheless, it had been a memorable year. Home attendances averaged over 13,000, up by 6,000 on 1938/39, as Millmoor turned into a South Yorkshire Fort Knox, all but impregnable. An incredible home record read; played 21, won 20, drawn 1, lost 0, goals for 81, goals against 19. Oldham Athletic were routed 8-0, Halifax Town and York City both 6-1. In the FA Cup a 3-0 loss at Wolverhampton Wanderers in the third round was sweetened by the words of Stan Cullis, the Wolves and England centre half, who declared that Rotherham had played better football than at least ten of the teams he had faced in the First Division that year.

There has probably never been a more aptly named

football team than Rotherham United. Formed in May 1925, they were the result of Rotherham County and Rotherham Town, two financially strapped clubs struggling to survive, uniting together as one viable semi-professional outfit. County came into existence in 1877 as Thornhill FC, won the Midland League four times on the trot between 1912 and 1915 and gained election to the Football League in 1919. Town, formed in 1899 and long-time members of the Midland League, succeeded another club of the same name, who in the mid-1890s had three unsuccessful seasons in Division Two before abruptly folding. The roots of both Rotherham Town clubs go further back, to 1878 and the strangely named Lunar Rovers, so called, according to local legend, because its patrons played matches by moonlight.

'These are momentous days for Rotherham football,' read a rallying cry in one of County's last match programmes adding, with prophetic foresight, that Rotherham United would be, 'a strong and virile body and with a determination to realise high ambitions … and given the support of the public, success will be met with.' United took over County's membership of Division Three (North) and moved into their old home of Millmoor, an unlovely ground surrounded by railway tracks and huge scrap yards.

Adopting their now iconic Arsenal-style red shirts with white sleeves, Rotherham made another strong challenge for promotion in 1947/48. In a nerve jangling climax to the season, a crowd of over 20,000 squeezed into Millmoor to watch them slug it out with promotion rivals Lincoln City. United were in red-hot form. One more victory and Second Division football would be guaranteed. But, as the weight of expectation pressed down on them like ten tons of local coal, Rotherham buckled. The visitors scored twice inside the first nine minutes and then defended stoutly for a 2-0 win. The Millers missed out on promotion by a single point.

It was an open secret that Ardron, who bagged another 30 goals, wanted to move to a bigger club but the week before the 1948/49 season was due to begin he re-signed for United. With their talismanic forward staying and a talented and handsome young winger called Jack Grainger - a crowd favourite in the making - ready to be blooded, there was a strong feeling that United could take that one step further and be crowned champions. But for the third year in a row they ended up as bridesmaids, beaten this time to the promotion altar by Hull City. Crucially, United lost 3-2 to the Tigers in a top of the table clash on Christmas Day at Boothferry Park, a new ground which had opened in August 1946 as a replacement for Hull's old war-torn stadium on Anlaby Road. The gate was staggering for a Third Division game - 49,655. Hull City enjoyed a marvellous season all round. Under the stewardship of silver haired player-manager and ex-England inside forward Raich Carter, the team played a brand of skilful, attacking football which reaped not only the title but an FA Cup run that only ended in the quarter finals with a narrow 1-0 defeat by the holders, Manchester United.

Ardron played his full part in Rotherham's promotion challenge, racking up another 30 League goals to head the club scoring charts for the eighth season running. But the time had finally come for him to leave Millmoor for pastures new. In the close season he joined relegated Nottingham Forest in Division Three (South) for £10,000. The transfer seemed good business for a 30-year-old who had cost United £750 but Ardron remained a clinical finisher and in 1951 scored 36 goals to help Forest get back into Division Two.

Rotherham prepared for life after Wally. There was plenty of cash in the kitty - the accounts were in the black for the eighth successive year - but precious little of it was spent on buying a decent replacement and Horace Williams was pressed into service as an emergency centre forward. Rotherham slipped to sixth in the League, attendances dwindled to below 8,000 and fans accused the club of not actually wanting to go up. There was unrest in the dressing room too. Gladstone Guest, top scorer in 1949/50 with 18 goals and a firm favourite of the vocal fans who stood in the Tivoli End, rocked the board by putting in a transfer request. Danny Williams held out on signing a new contract and Grainger was reported to be the subject of a £20,000 bid from an anonymous club.

And yet, in spite of the disquiet, Rotherham finally won promotion in 1951 as the champions of Division Three (North) and they did it in style. Their game plan was refreshingly simple - attack, attack, and attack again. It produced 31 wins and 103 goals over half of which came from the shooting boots of Shaw (37), who was converted into a centre forward with startling success, and Guest (23), who put to bed all thoughts of a move elsewhere.

While the nation celebrated the Festival of Britain in the summer of 1951, every Merry Miller waited anxiously, excitedly, jubilantly for their Second Division odyssey to begin. There were some fallen giants with illustrious histories knocking about. Sheffield Wednesday, Sheffield United, Blackburn Rovers and Everton all had trophy cabinets echoing with the prizes of past glories. It was a tough division to be in but Rotherham were not fazed. Thanks to their potent attack, which made up for a rather leaky defence, by the start of December they proudly sat on top of Division Two. A dazzling 5-3 win at Hillsborough, watched by some 10,000 Millers fans in a crowd of 54,846, had the national newspapers eulogising, as Gerry Somerton reveals in his club biography *Now We Are United*:

> 'Wednesday were played out of the game. [Rotherham] would have given First Division teams a fright,' wrote the *Daily Mirror*.

> 'I goggled with surprise at them, what a combination,' cooed the *Daily Mail*.

> 'In a feast of goal conscious football Rotherham gave their neighbours a rare lesson in the finer arts of soccer team work,' extolled *The People*.

The Rotherham public lapped it up. Millmoor was packed to the rafters every other week. But the exhilarating ride they had all been enjoying suddenly ran out of fuel. In a winter of discontent, the goals dried up and just one more victory came their way before the start of March. Having begun the season in fertile form, Shaw hit the back of the net only six more times. The alarming decline was arrested, eventually, but United finished a season that had augured well closer in points to bottom club QPR than to champions Wednesday.

The sharks began to circle. There were rumours that promoted Wednesday were about to snap up Grainger, the wonder kid. The really surprising news, however, was the announcement that, after two decades of devoted service as player and manager, Reg Freeman was quitting Millmoor for Bramall Lane. Freeman had created a wonderful camaraderie within the squad and had been instrumental in putting the club on a sound financial footing. As if to emphasize what they had lost, he steered Sheffield United back to the First Division at the first time of asking.

Grainger, who stayed at Rotherham, began the 1952/53 season as a temporary replacement for Shaw, who was injured, while a 22-year-old discovery from Upton Colliery, Len White, covered for him on the right flank. The League campaign did not reach the heights of the previous year but in the Cup, Rotherham produced the shock of the season when they beat the holders Newcastle United 3-1 at St James's Park in the fourth round. The hero was Grainger who helped himself to a second half brace to set up the stunning victory. So impressed were the Magpies by his display that they offered a record £30,000 for him immediately after the match. It was turned down, but they came back with a counter offer - if not Grainger, then what about the lad White? That deal was approved and White went on to star alongside Jackie Milburn in the Newcastle side that lifted the FA Cup for a third time in five years in 1955.

It was rough justice for Grainger, an England 'B' international, whose skills merited a grander stage. It was left to his cousin Colin Grainger, an outside left who patrolled the wing for Sheffield United in the mid-1950s, to gain seven full England caps and to play alongside such stars of the game as Wright, Matthews, Edwards and Finney.

Victory over Newcastle propelled Rotherham United into the next round for the first time in their history. Their reward was a lucrative home tie against Aston Villa. Two months beforehand, 25,170 supporters - a record crowd for Millmoor - had crammed into the ground for the derby with Sheffield United and now another full house created a carnival atmosphere in anticipation of a further upset. But the boys from Brum popped Rotherham's party balloon and emerged 3-1 victors.

The FA Cup was something of a Holy Grail for Yorkshire teams in the post-war years, an object they came tantalisingly close to holding without ever doing so. Hull City (1949), Leeds United (1950), Sheffield United (1947, 1952), Sheffield Wednesday (1954) and Huddersfield Town (1955) all reached the quarter or semi finals, as did York City of Division Three (North) who, during the 1954/55 season, tugged at the heartstrings of romantic neutrals everywhere. In a fairytale run to the last four, the giant killers conquered 1953 Cup winners Blackpool and 1951 League champions Tottenham, the latter 3-1 at Bootham Crescent in what is widely regarded as the club's greatest ever performance. In the semis they held Newcastle United, FA Cup winners in 1951 and '52, to a 1-1 draw at Hillsborough, Arthur Bottom - scorer of 39 goals in all competitions that season - equalizing for York. 'It was a great struggle with no quarter asked or given,' remembered Geoffrey Green in *The Official History of the FA Cup*. 'It was 50-50 all the way and York would have won but for a foot or so in the last seconds and a superb interception by Scoular close in front of an open goal.' Sadly, beset by injuries, the Minstermen lost the replay 2-0 at Roker Park and so ended one of the most magical of all Cup stories.

At Rotherham, the old guard that had served the club so well and for so long began to break up. Horace Williams faded away, so too Edwards, while Shaw, after scoring 124 goals in 262 League games, was sold to Sheffield Wednesday. Guest, Grainger, Selkirk, Danny Williams and defender Norman Noble were the only survivors of the old school and all were the wrong side of 30. It was now or never if they were ever going to achieve their ambition of playing top flight football. Rolling back the years, they charged into the 1954/55 season like men possessed, netting 58 goals and picking up 14 victories in the first 24 League matches to storm into the top three. A mini collapse followed but seven wins in seventeen gruelling days in April put them back among the leading pack. The race for promotion could hardly have been tighter, as the table of the time shows:

	P	W	D	L	GA	Pts
1. Luton Town	41	22	8	11	1.604	52
2. Stoke City	41	21	10	10	1.816	52
3. Rotherham United	40	24	4	12	1.419	52
4. Birmingham City	40	21	9	10	1.909	51
5. Leeds United	41	22	7	12	1.288	51

Thousands of Merry Millers swarmed over the Peak District for the game against Port Vale on 30th April, 1955, safe in the knowledge that their team could afford to drop a point and still go up. Again, the tension of the occasion and the rigours of playing so many matches in such a short space of time took their toll. On a gusty day 'Nobby' Noble missed a penalty, Vale scored and Rotherham lost the match 1-0.

Now faced with the impossible task of beating Liverpool 16-0 at Millmoor to overhaul Luton at the top, Rotherham gave it a desperately good go, winning the game 6-1 to go into second place. Their fate now rested in the hands of Doncaster Rovers who took on Birmingham City, two points adrift of the Millers but with a superior goal average, in their last match the following Wednesday night. United fans trooped off to Belle Vue in their droves, hoping beyond hope that Donny could sneak a draw. Alas, it was not to be. Birmingham triumphed 5-1 to take the title. One fluffed penalty and some mathematical equations had denied Rotherham promotion.

The dismantling of the team gathered pace. Selkirk, Noble and Guest, Rotherham's all-time top scorer with 130 goals in 356 League games, dropped into non-league football. Grainger was sold to Lincoln City, his potential never having been truly fulfilled. Danny Williams, the last of the Rotherham stalwarts, soldiered on until March 1959, setting an unsurpassed club appearances record of 459 League games before he retired to the post of coach. By then

Rotherham were just another jobbing Second Division club. Attendances nose-dived, debts racked up and the fame that had rested so easily on the club in the post-war years soon dissipated.

The Millers' Tale was not quite at an end, though. In 1960, Alan Hardaker, secretary of the Football League, initiated a mid-week knockout competition designed to exploit the possibilities of floodlit matches and so was born the League Cup. Intended to be a money-spinner, in fact it received a barrage of criticism for clogging up the fixture list. Some leading First Division teams, Sheffield Wednesday among them, even refused to enter. Few seemed to care for such a pointless 'Mickey Mouse' competition. And yet for Rotherham United the League Cup holds fond memories for it presented them with their first and only appearance in a major cup final.

A new-look team breezed their way through the knockout stages to set up a meeting in the decider with Aston Villa of Division One. Strangely, the final - which for the first six years was played not at Wembley but on a home-and-away basis - was held over until the start of the following season. The first leg at Millmoor took place on the evening of Tuesday, 22nd August, 1961. A good gate of 12,226 cheered when keeper Roy Ironside saved a penalty and then roared when Barry Webster and Alan Kirkham scored to give Rotherham, the huge underdogs, a precious 2-0 cushion. In the return leg at Villa Park a fortnight later, the football was fast and furious. Midway through the second half the home side levelled the aggregate score before Don Weston, a fast running but inconsistent striker who later helped Leeds United win promotion to Division One in 1964, wasted three gilt-edged chances to wrap up matters for Rotherham.

The game went into extra-time. United laid siege to the

Villa goalmouth in search of the winner but, with ten minutes to go, Peter McParland embarked on a counter attack. His shot ricocheted off the underside of the Rotherham bar and into the back of the net: 3-0 on the night, 3-2 on aggregate. Aston Villa became the first winners of the unloved League Cup; Rotherham, rueing missed opportunities, reflected on what might have been.

Younger fans talk of the Ronnie Moore years, dads of a certain age go all dewy-eyed over the memory of that 1961 League Cup final outfit but go and ask granddad about Wally Ardron and Gladstone Guest and Jack Grainger. Now that was a team to make any Miller merry.

15

On Me Head, Son

A NEW BREED of centre forward prowled football's penalty boxes in the 1940s and 50s. Big, brave and Brylcremed, they got their head on the end of crosses, shot on sight at goal and used their strength to cause havoc in opposing goalmouths. Brawn was what mattered, not brains; leave the thinking and the artistry to the midfield playmakers. Fully paid up members of the school of hard knocks, they took no prisoners and asked for no favours. To hoards of fans on the terraces they were Viking warriors and with the advent of shirt numbering a new name was bestowed upon them. Here begins the tradition of the good old fashioned number nine.

In September 1948, a strapping 16-year-old Welsh boy, his chest as wide as Swansea Bay, arrived in Leeds by steam train. Taking stock of the 'dirty old place' about him, he headed off to digs on Beeston Hill, south of the River Aire. His new home overlooked the Leeds United football ground on Elland Road from where this muscular teenager from the

Valleys matured into the greatest No. 9 of his generation. His name was John Charles.

Above six foot and tipping the scales at over 14 stone, Charles was exactly what the Leeds manager, Major Frank Buckley - a veteran of World War One - was looking for. He liked them big, strong and gutsy. A strict disciplinarian, Buckley fed this 'Adonis of a youth' a diet of steak, steak and more steak and very soon Charles, aged 17 years 117 days, was ready to make his Second Division debut against Blackburn Rovers on 23rd April, 1949. Not up front in the goal scorer's shirt, however, but in the middle of defence.

Charles spent the first few years of his professional life as a centre half. Hard but fair - he was never cautioned or sent off in his entire career - his tackles rattled bones without there ever being any intention to inflict hurt upon his opponent. He hit the heights without having to resort to skulduggery. When he left Leeds for Italian giants Juventus in 1957, the Juve fans were so impressed by how he maintained his dignity under severe provocation from defenders who deliberately kicked and thumped him, that they gave him a nickname - *Il Buono Gigante* - the Gentle Giant. Buckley knew he had unearthed a gem. 'No one can take the ball from him; he is so strong and sure of himself ... I honestly don't think he knows how good he is.'

In Charles's first season, 1948/49, 41.2 million people clicked through the turnstiles, an all-time high figure which dwarfs modern attendances. Consider these bumper gates: 19,271 at Bootham Crescent for York City against Rotherham; 37,149 at Belle Vue, a ground record, for Doncaster Rovers against Hull City; 55,019 at Boothferry Park, another ground record, for Hull against Manchester United in the FA Cup - and in each case the home team was in the Third Division.

It was on Easter Saturday, 24th March, 1951 against Manchester City at Maine Road that Charles's career changed course forever. Playing up front as a stopgap for Leeds' regular centre forward Len Browning, who was injured, he made such an impact that from that moment onwards the No.9 shirt was his own. In 1952/53 he found the back of the net 26 times. The next year he scored a club record 42 goals, including five hat-tricks. Many of his goals came from bullet-like headers, a seemingly armour-plated forehead pounding the heavy laced leather balls into the back of the net with exceptional force and accuracy. He was described by his hero Tommy Lawton as, 'a great centre-forward' and favourable comparisons were drawn with pre-war star 'Dixie' Dean. Arsenal submitted a record bid of £40,000 but Leeds turned it down, the club's new manager Raich Carter, lately of Hull City, declaring that, 'John Charles is not, I repeat not, for sale.'

Big John's brilliance lay in his versatility. Who else can say they spent a great part of their international career - 38 Wales caps, 15 goals - in defence while consistently topping the scoring charts at club level? He was two breathtaking players rolled into one. At the back he was imposing, solid and extremely difficult to navigate around. Up front he was explosive, powerful and too hot to handle. A perfectly balanced athlete and a genuinely two footed player, Charles's missile shooting made goalkeepers quake, defenders bounced off him like dodgem cars and so supreme was he in aerial dogfights for the ball that Leeds fans gave their imperious striker a new title - King John.

In 1954/55 Charles was pulled back to centre half to shore up a defence that was leaking goals. The following season, however, the Welsh Dragon breathed fire into the attack once more, netting 29 goals for Leeds as they won promotion back to Division One (they were relegated in 1947 with a woeful 18 points) as runners-up behind champions Sheffield Wednesday.

The best defences in the land were no match for King John who topped the Division One scoring charts with 38 goals in 1956/57. Billed as, 'The World's Greatest Player', glamour clubs in England and from across Europe entered into a frenzied bidding war for his services. Juventus emerged the winners, paying a British record £65,000 to make John Charles, quite literally, worth his weight in gold. Leeds cashed in for a very good reason. Midway through the season the West Stand at Elland Road had caught fire and burned to the ground. The windfall was used to rebuild it and, rather appropriately, is now officially called 'The John Charles Stand'. Leeds team-mate Albert Nightingale could be forgiven for thinking he had walked under a ladder and then trodden on a black cat for, in 1950, he was on Huddersfield Town's books when their main stand at Leeds Road was also destroyed by fire.

After scoring 154 goals in 316 games in the blue and gold of Leeds, King John swapped beer and darts for a luxury lifestyle in Turin. He was given a £10,000 signing-on fee, the equivalent of ten years' wages, a rent free apartment, swish sports cars, hand-crafted suits and silk shirts and a £3,000-per-year salary plus bonuses, which was enormous considering players in England were still yoked to the £20-per-week maximum wage. In return, Juventus expected him to repay their massive investment in full and Charles did not let them down. Voted 'Italian Player of the Year' in 1958, he made a mockery of the stifling catenaccio defences, scoring 93 goals in 150 games during his five-year stay at the *Stadio Comunale* during which time Juventus won three *Serie A* titles and two *Coppa Italias*. They had never seen his like before in Italy. One newspaper described him as, 'a centre-forward completely different from the others ... a new model, unique, unmistakable.' Juve fans simply idolised their *Gigante Buono*.

Charles was at the very height of his fame when Wales qualified for the World Cup for the first and only time in 1958. But he was ruthlessly hacked out of the tournament in Sweden by a brutal Hungary side and forced to watch from the sidelines as his comrades, including his brother Mel, lost 1-0 to the champions elect, Brazil, in the quarter-finals. The decisive goal was scored by a precocious unknown 17-year-old called Pele who in later years remarked, 'If King John had been fit then the 1958 World Cup story might have had a different ending.'

His Italian job complete, John Charles made a sensational return to Leeds United for £53,000 in the summer of 1962. Leeds had slipped into Division Two in 1960 and wanted the 30-year-old to spearhead another promotion charge. The hierarchy saw in him the magnificent No. 9 of seasons past but, in reality, Charles was unfit, lacking pace and scarred by injuries. To put it bluntly, he was past his best and the move was a disaster. Angered by the doubling of ticket prices to fund the costly exercise, Leeds fans boycotted his homecoming, a crowd of only 14,119 turning up at Elland Road for the match against Rotherham United. In the dressing room Charles felt isolated and on the pitch he struggled to readjust to, 'the long-ball style with players scuttling around at 100 miles per hour.' Admitting that he had made, 'the biggest mistake of my career', he played only 11 games and scored three goals before returning to his spiritual home of Italy, joining Roma for £70,000.

While John Charles bestrode the football world like a colossus in the 1950s, elsewhere in Yorkshire other notable No. 9s made their presences well and truly felt. Barnsley discovered Tommy Taylor, a tall and broad-shouldered centre-forward destined to lead the line for Manchester United and England with distinction, working at the local Warncliffe Colliery. Able to play with both feet and a fearsome header of the ball, he made his first-team debut for Barnsley, aged 18, in a 3-1 home win over Grimsby Town on 7th October, 1950. A month later he scored his first hat-trick in a 7-1 hammering of QPR. Behind him in midfield that season was the oddest of couples; Irishman Danny Blanchflower, a £6,000 buy from Glentoran in 1949, and local hero Sid 'Skinner' Normanton. Blanchflower was a deep-thinking tactician and cultured passer of the ball who went on to skipper the Spurs double winning team of 1961. By contrast, 'Skinner' was an unrefined mauler and brawler who loved nothing better than to kick lumps off the opposition. 'Although there were many more skilful and talented than he,' wrote Michael Parkinson, a boyhood fan, in *Sporting Heroes*, 'there was no one who better represented what you were up against if you took on a collier from Barnsley.'

Taylor rattled in 26 goals in 44 games for the Tykes which tempted Man United into tabling a bid of £29,999 for him in March 1953. Matt Busby, not wanting to lumber young Tommy with the tag of being the country's first £30,000 player, gave the extra quid to a tea-lady. The money did not do Barnsley much good, however, for at the end of the season they were relegated to Division Three (North) with a truly awful record that read: Played 42, Won 5, Drawn 8, Lost 29, Goals For 47, Goals Against 108, Points 18.

An integral member of the 'Busby Babes' who won successive League championships, Taylor scored 131 times in 191 games for the Red Devils. Real Madrid's Alfredo Di Stefano hailed him as *Magnifico* and Inter Milan were prepared to break the bank to get their own version of John Charles but Busby rejected all offers. He knew his young striker's worth could not be measured in pound notes. Shortly before the coronation of Queen Elizabeth II in May 1953, Taylor made his England debut against Argentina.

Less than five years later he had 16 goals in 19 international matches to his name and had displaced the celebrated Nat Lofthouse as England's first choice centre forward. Hopes were high that he and Duncan Edwards, his exceptionally talented team-mate at Old Trafford, would be major performers for England at the forthcoming World Cup in Sweden. The pair had the world at their feet but on a freezing cold night in Germany on 6th February, 1958, Taylor and Edwards, along with six team-mates, including Mark Jones, from Wombwell, and Doncaster born David Pegg, perished in the Munich air crash. Taylor was 26 years old.

But for shattering his right leg while playing for England Under-23 against France in October 1956, Doncaster Rovers' 17-year-old starlet Alick Jeffrey might have died in the same disaster. Busby was a huge admirer of the young inside-forward from Rawmarsh with the Elvis Presley looks and had been on the brink of signing him before he sustained his career defining injury. Having made his Rovers debut in 1954 at the ridiculously tender age of 15 years 229 days, the consensus is that had Jeffrey gone to Old Trafford then he would have hindered the progress of a certain Bobby Charlton. 'He bears the stamp of genius,' said Stanley Matthews, a man not known for hyperbole. 'By far the best youngster I have ever seen,' was Jackie Milburn's assessment.

Busby, instead, poached Doncaster's Northern Ireland international keeper Harry Gregg for £23,000, thereby making him the world's most expensive No.1. Gregg survived the Munich horror, heroically dragging team-mates, including Charlton, from the burning wreckage. Poignantly, a few months later he was voted best goalkeeper at the 1958 World Cup.

No one ever thought they would see Alick Jeffrey on a professional football pitch again. But seven years later he staged a remarkable comeback. Still only 24, he showed enough glimpses of his former prowess to suggest that he would have lived up to the forecasts of stardom. Considered by many Donny supporters to be their best ever player, for six wonderful years Jeffrey entertained the Belle Vue crowds. In 1964/65 he scored 36 goals and in 1965/66 added another 22 as Doncaster won the Fourth Division championship. Had things turned out differently, Alick Jeffrey might have spent one sunny summer's afternoon in 1966 dancing round the Wembley pitch holding the World Cup aloft. Then again, he might have died in the snowdrifts of a Munich runway. Such are the twists of fate.

Horrific injury brought to a premature end the career of another wonder kid tipped for big things; Derek Dooley, a tall, ginger haired No. 9 with thighs like pit props. He scored 63 goals in as many games for Sheffield Wednesday, including 46 in 30 League matches, a club record, in the 1951/52 Division Two championship campaign. A rather awkward player, he was not averse to throwing his weight about in the penalty area, gaining a not wholly unwarranted reputation for being a dirty player. Major Buckley considered making an offer to bring the explosive 'Goal Kid' to Elland Road and it is interesting to speculate whether, had he come, John Charles would have remained a centre half for the whole of his career.

The following season the 23-year-old battering ram from Pitsmoor netted another 16 goals in 24 First Division games before breaking his right leg in a sickening collision with Preston North End goalkeeper George Thompson at Deepdale on 14th February, 1953. Not the best of Valentines' Day gifts, worse was to follow. Gangrene set in and, with his life now at stake, the leg had to be amputated. An unfortunate victim of his own rumbustious nature, Dooley was a fully committed player who chased down every loose ball, never shirked a challenge and, when pumping at full throttle, was as dangerous as any centre forward in the country, John Charles included.

The unenviable job of filling Dooley's massive boots in time went to Roy Shiner, a menacing looking attacker who signed from Huddersfield Town in the summer of 1955. Bagging 96 goals in four productive seasons for Wednesday, the unheralded Shiner epitomised the battling, never-say-die attitude of the No. 9 in the Forties and Fifties. Another was ex-miner Clarrie Jordan who joined Sheffield Wednesday from Doncaster for £6,000 plus a player in February 1948. Plagued thereafter by a knee injury - which, ironically, gave Dooley his big chance - Jordan scored just 36 goals for the Owls in seven years before retiring. Around the county; Wally Ardron, Joe Shaw, Alf Patrick, Cec McCormack, Des Frost, Eddie Carr and Norman Moore will be fondly remembered by more senior followers of Rotherham United, York City, Barnsley, Halifax Town, Bradford City and Hull City as wholehearted centre forwards who were prepared to put their bodies where it mattered to get the job done.

One player who did not fit the usual big and burly identikit of the number nine was Sheffield United's aptly named Derek Pace, a nippy little forward who relied more on speed, guile and anticipation to score his goals. More pickpocket than human bludgeon, 'Doc' - a nickname given to him during his National Service in the Medical Corps - may have been a sparrow among eagles but he sure could head the ball and was a master at putting it in the net. Joining United from Aston Villa for £12,000 in December 1957, he became an instant fans' favourite by scoring eight minutes into his debut against Blackburn Rovers at Bramall Lane on Boxing Day and, over the next seven seasons, he went on to score 163 goals in 294 matches, an astonishing strike rate that deserved an England call-up that never came.

Of all the No. 9s operating in Yorkshire in the post-war years the one who came closest to matching Charles's tally of goals for a single club was Huddersfield Town's Jimmy Glazzard. Yet another ex-miner, born in Normanton, he started out as an inside forward during the Second World War but developed into a target man of some renown. In a long career almost exclusively devoted to the Terriers, he hit the back of the net 153 times in 321 League and Cup games. Only George 'Bomber' Brown has scored more goals for the club. When Huddersfield finished 3rd in 1953/54, he topped the Division One scoring charts with 29 goals. Like the rest of his ilk 'Gentleman Jim' was a terrific header of the ball, once scoring four goals in a match with his head, all from crosses delivered by England outside left Vic Metcalfe; another tremendously loyal club servant who made 459 appearances for Town between 1945 and 1958.

Towards the end of his career, Glazzard was sold to Everton for £4,000 after Huddersfield suffered relegation to Division Two in 1956. That November Bill Shankly, a wily, sharp tongued and quick witted collier's son from Ayrshire, took over as manager. The ex-Preston and Scotland wing half was a master of kid psychology. Nor was he often lost for words but he must have been left dumbstruck by his team when they squandered a four goal lead away at Charlton Athletic just before Christmas 1957. After an hour's play, Town were cruising at 5-1 and the Addicks were down to ten men. But in a frenetic last half hour, the Terriers lost their heads completely as Charlton scored six times to win the game. 'Amazing, fantastic, incredible ...' reported one newspaper but you can bet they were not the adjectives used by Shankly in the dressing room.

One player who missed the incredible fight back was Denis Law, a precocious and tetchy teenager from Aberdeen who was once given little hope of making the grade and was described as, 'weak, puny and bespectacled'. Huddersfield fans can but wonder at what might have been had Shankly and Law remained in tandem at Leeds Road. Could they have been the next Chapman and Stephenson, two genius sparks for rekindled success? Shankly subsequently built up a football empire at Anfield and Law, who was sold to Manchester City for £55,000 in March 1960 to finance the erection of floodlights at Leeds Road, became the original King of Old Trafford in Matt Busby's last great Manchester United side.

All these barnstorming No. 9s were - and still are - terrace heroes of the Yorkshire sides they represented but the one who stands out as the complete centre forward and who undertook a real life *Boy's Own* adventure is, of course, John Charles. England captain Billy Wright believed him to be the greatest he ever faced. Fellow Leeds legend Jack Charlton described him as, 'the most effective player I ever saw, the one that made the most difference to the performance of the whole team.' Denis Law rates him as one of the three best No.9s the world has ever seen and Danny Blanchflower thought he could, 'never be as great a footballer' because, 'when he moves into position for a goal chance it is *instinctive*.'

John Charles died, aged 72, in a Dewsbury hospital on 21st February, 2004. The final tribute goes to his former striking partner at Juventus, Omar Sivori: 'When we were at Juve, the two most important people for most Italians were the Pope and *Il Gigante*.' Yes, John Charles, the most majestic of number nine's, was that close to God.

16

The Swindling Sixties

BY 1964, the Sixties were in full psychedelic swing. Beatlemania was sweeping the nation, Sean Connery was suave MI6 agent James Bond, the classic Mini Cooper drove to victory in the Monte Carlo Rally, Mods and Rockers clashed at seaside resorts, Huddersfield's Harold Wilson was Labour Prime Minister and *Match of the Day* aired for the first time, on a new channel, BBC2.

The country was in buoyant mood but for bleary-eyed Sheffield Wednesday fans waking from their slumbers on Sunday, 12th April, 1964, there was incredulity when they read the sensational news that three players, past and present, were implicated in a match fixing scandal. 'TOP SOCCER STARS BRIBED', screamed out the front page headline in *The People*, which went on to exclusively report: 'They agreed to 'fix' a First Division match. They backed Sheffield Wednesday, their own team, to lose against Ipswich, and each won £100 in a betting coup.'

The startling exposé, which harked back to a fixture at

Portman Road on 1st December, 1962 that ended in a 2-0 victory to the home side, lifted the lid on what many people had suspected for some time - that dodgy betting was commonplace among professional players. The shamed Sheffield trio who rocked football to its foundations were all household names; David 'Bronco' Layne, a thundering centre forward and England internationals Tony Kay and Peter Swan.

Swan was a handsome and marvellously composed centre half who passed, tackled and headed the ball with aplomb. He joined the Wednesday staff as a 16-year-old kid in 1952 and played nearly 300 senior games before the scandal broke. Called up by Walter Winterbottom for his England debut against Yugoslavia at Wembley in May 1960, he played in 19 consecutive internationals until a bout of dysentery cost him his place in the run up to the 1962 World Cup in Chile. By April 1964, a recall to the national set up was very much on the cards with England's new boss Alf Ramsey - who, incidentally, was in charge of Ipswich when the illicit betting took place - an open admirer of the tall, elegant stopper from South Elmsall, near Pontefract.

Tony Kay, a hot-headed, flame-haired half back who tackled with the ferocity of a pit bull terrier, had moved to Everton by the time the story hit the news stands. Born in Attercliffe, Sheffield, he made over 200 appearances for his boyhood heroes before switching to the Toffees for a British record £60,000 in December 1962, three weeks after the Ipswich game. He added bite and leadership to a classy Everton side which romped to the League title in 1962/63 and in June 1963, after winning six under-23 caps, he scored on his full England debut in an 8-1 hammering of Switzerland in Basle.

Completing the line-up of suspects, David Layne was rapidly becoming one of the deadliest centre forwards in the business. Another Sheffield man, he was built in the classic big, beefy No.9 mould, with a booming shot and a thumping header. Nicknamed 'Bronco', after Bronco Layne a television cowboy of the day, he belted in 58 goals in 81 matches for Wednesday in a shade under two seasons. His outstanding strike rate had the pundits tipping him for international honours, lofty predictions that were cut short by his untimely demise from the game.

The People accused the threesome of each placing a £50 bet at odds of 2-1 on Ipswich Town winning the winter clash. For a profit of £100 - the equivalent of a week's wages for English football's top earner, Johnny Haynes - they ended up going to gaol, being fined £150 each, receiving lifetime bans from football and having their character ripped to shreds in the courts and by the papers.

So what prompted three football stars at the very top of their game to recklessly risk their careers and livelihoods on a betting scam, and who spilled the beans to *The People*? Before answering those two conundrums it is first necessary to set the scene.

Sheffield Wednesday went into the 1962/63 season with a dream team oozing experience and not a little class, as depicted:

1 Ron Springett
2 Peter Johnson
3 Don Megson
4 Tom McAnearney
5 Peter Swan
6 Tony Kay
7 Alan Finney
8 Johnny Fantham
9 David Layne
10 Colin Dobson
11 Derek Wilkinson

Six of the side clocked up more than 300 appearances in the blue and white stripes including Finney (503), Megson (442) - father of Gary who followed him into the Owls team in the 1980s - and Fantham (435). 'Flying Fantham', another local product, went into the 1962/63 season having tucked away 56 Division One goals in the previous three years. By the end of the decade the clever 'fox in the box' had taken his tally to 167, overtaking Redfern Froggatt (149) as Wednesday's post-war leading marksman.

Meanwhile, Springett was well on his way to becoming Wednesday's most-capped England player. He kept goal in 33 internationals between November 1959 and June 1966 and spent the summer of 1962 in Chile competing in the World Cup where England lost to Brazil in the quarter final. Within the year Springett - whose younger brother, Peter, joined the Owls in 1967 as part of a curious swap deal which took Ron to QPR - was ousted by Gordon Banks, arguably the greatest of all Yorkshire-born footballers, although he never played professionally for any of the county's teams. As understudy to Banks, Springett found himself a non-playing member of the triumphant 1966 England World Cup squad.

As one of the best teams in the land, Sheffield Wednesday were enjoying their most successful period since the days of Ernie Blenkinsop and Ronnie Starling before the war. In the four seasons from 1958/59 to 1961/62 they won promotion from Division Two, finished fifth, second and sixth in Division One, reached the FA Cup semi-final in 1960, where they were knocked out by Blackburn Rovers 2-1 at Maine Road and, in the 1961/62 Inter-Cities Fairs Cup, lost by the odd goal in seven against Spanish giants Barcelona in the last eight.

Prior to this flurry of success, Wednesday spent the Fifties flipping between the top two divisions, winning promotion four times (1950, '52, '56, '59) but suffering demotion on another three occasions (1951, '55, '58) - they were the archetypal yo-yo team. Credit for their rise to the top goes to a Darlington man who, at the time of his recruitment in 1958 from Division Three (North) side Rochdale, was a relatively inexperienced and unknown manager - Harry Catterick.

Not yet forty years old, Catterick was destined to become one of the great club managers with Everton. First though, he whipped a talented but wayward group of youngsters at Hillsborough into an efficient, coordinated unit which cantered to the Second Division Championship in his first season and then took the First Division by storm. Everything was looking rosy in the Hillsborough garden when Wednesday, sitting in second place, travelled to White Hart Lane in April 1961 for a match against the soon to be crowned champions, Tottenham Hotspur. But, on the eve of the top of the table clash, Catterick dropped a bombshell - he was quitting the club.

Frustrated by not having full control of team affairs and by the club's reluctance to spend big money on big name players, he walked out and took over at Everton, a club he played for in the 1940s, leading them to glory in the FA Cup (1966) and League Championship (1962/63, 1969/70). Wednesday fans were dismayed but Catterick left them a team to be proud of, one whose tally of 58 points would have won the Championship in either the preceding or succeeding seasons.

Catterick's replacement was Vic Buckingham, a cerebral and extrovert manager who came with impressive and varied credentials. He managed the 1954 FA Cup winners West Bromwich Albion, coached 1951 FA Amateur Cup winners Pegasus FC and was head manager of Dutch side Ajax Amsterdam. A rather romantic character who believed in the amateur ideal of fair play and had a continental outlook when it came to tactics, Buckingham wanted Wednesday to play with freedom of expression, to be eleven Monets on the pitch rather than the simple yet extremely effective Lowrys they had been under Catterick.

His side produced some of the finest exhibition football ever seen at Hillsborough but such performances were, regrettably, all too infrequent. In 1961/62 an expected title challenge never materialised and Wednesday finished the season ten points and five places behind the champions, Ipswich Town. To add salt to the wound, Sheffield United finished above them in the table. The Wednesday faithful were not impressed and in the latter half of the season attendances slumped to under 20,000 which left the sumptuous 10,000-capacity, all-seater North Stand, built at a cost of £150,000 and unveiled before the first home game of the season, looking like an expensive white elephant.

Buckingham's priority was to bring in a proven goalscorer to take some of the pressure off young Fantham, who had almost single-handedly carried the Wednesday attack in their charge to the top of the football tree. With little money to spend, buying a Jimmy Greaves or a Denis Law was out of the question so Buckingham scoured the lower divisions for up and coming talent. His roving eye came to rest upon a young gun banging in the goals for Fourth Division Bradford City, David Layne.

'Bronco' began his career as a part-timer with Rotherham United and joined Swindon Town for £500 in 1959, a move that barely registered on the radar at the time but which had ramifications in the years to come. He made a mockery of the Millers' decision to sell by netting 28 goals in 41 Third Division (South) games, volcanic form which prompted Bradford City to fork out a club record £6,000 to bring him back to Yorkshire, midway through the 1960/61 campaign. The following year he broke the Bantams' scoring record with 34 League goals. In May 1962, Sheffield Wednesday paid £22,500 for his services, a tidy fee for a player who had never been tested at the highest level.

The 23-year-old settled quickly into his explosive stride;

two goals in the second game of the season (a 3-3 draw at Leicester City), two more each in wins against Arsenal and Birmingham, another brace in a 2-all draw in the Steel City derby at Bramall Lane in front of 42,687 fans, 13 in total by the time the Ipswich game came around.

Before travelling to Portman Road on Saturday, 1st December, 1962, Layne, Kay and Swan placed their suspect bets. The day was bone chillingly raw, the beginning of a winter so harsh that it became known as 'The Big Freeze'. The Football League programme was decimated. The sheer volume of postponed matches necessitated the setting up of the Pools Panel and the backlog of fixtures meant that an elongated season did not finish until the last days of May.

Wednesday duly went down 2-0 on that cold afternoon in December. 'We lost the game fair and square,' insisted Swan in an article in *The Times* in July 2006. He swears they did no wrong and points to the fact that Kay was named man of the match by none other than *The People*. 'The game went like it always did at Ipswich,' he states in his recently published autobiography *Setting The Record Straight*, the inference being that Wednesday always lost on their travels to Suffolk. But that assessment does not stack up. Wednesday met Ipswich at Portman Road on just two occasions after the Second World War and before the fateful match, winning 2-0 in August 1958 and losing 2-1 in March 1962. Although Ipswich Town were the reigning champions, they were struggling to stay up this particular season and eventually avoided relegation by just four points. A home win was, therefore, not the banker that Swan seems to believe it to have been. He maintains his team were just not good enough on the day but candidly concedes that the temptation of earning an extra month's wages might have been too great to resist had they been winning, saying: 'It would have been easy for me to give away a penalty or even score an own goal'.

Swan says he was naïve. Kay gives the impression he was misled. In an interview with *The Observer* in July 2004, Kay recalls: 'Layne approached me before the Ipswich game and said, "What do you reckon today?" I said, "Well, we've never won down here." He said: "Give me £50 and I'll get you twice your money." I thought that was a good deal.'

Indeed it was. Footballers were only just beginning to enjoy the fruits of their labours, the restrictive maximum wage finally being swept away in 1961. Johnny Haynes, the England and Fulham captain, saw his annual pay soar five-fold to £5,000 but most players still took home only a few pounds more than they had before the £20-per-week cap was abolished, so the opportunity to make a bit on the side was sorely tempting.

Kay points the finger at 'Bronco' but Layne was in fact a gofer. The real ringleader in what turned out to be a nationwide betting ring was a man whom Layne met in 1959 when they were both at Swindon Town, Scottish forward Jimmy Gauld. A moderate and well travelled footballer whose stop offs included Everton and Charlton, by December 1962 Gauld's career was over, ended by a broken leg. An apparently chance meeting with his old chum Layne in the stands before a game at Mansfield Town - the last club the 31-year-old Gauld played for - set in motion a devious scheme to rig three games on the same afternoon; Ipswich Town versus Sheffield Wednesday, Lincoln facing Brentford and York City against Oldham. As anticipated, all three matches ended in home wins and the bookmakers were reportedly taken to the cleaners for £35,000.

That 'Bronco' got himself involved is not wholly surprising for, as *The People* went on to reveal, the young Wednesday striker had already taken part in a thrown game for Swindon Town, a 6-1 defeat at Port Vale in the second last game of the 1959/60 season. Layne defends himself, however, arguing that he too was duped by Gauld, as he reveals to respected Sheffield journalist Keith Farnsworth in *Sheffield Football, A History*: 'We were innocents really, and what we did was more bravado than anything ... a bit of foolishness. There was never any question of fixing or throwing a match.'

After the game Layne, Swan and Kay picked up their £100 winnings and carried on as normal with their football lives. 'Bronco' scored 30 goals that season and 28 the next, including, ironically, a hat-trick in a 4-1 away win at Ipswich Town. Swan was an ever present in the Owls defence while Kay was reunited with Harry Catterick at Everton and won a championship winners' medal in 1963. Wednesday's form remained patchy, so much so that Buckingham left the club on 9th April, 1964 after being told his contract would not be renewed. Three days later *The People* went to press with their revelations.

'The Biggest Sports Scandal of the Century' hit the streets the day after Scotland beat England 1-0 at Hampden Park in the Home International Championship. Swan, Kay and Layne were staggered to see their names plastered all over the *The People*'s front page, more so to learn that they had been incriminated by Gauld. In search of one last big payday, the avaricious Scotsman sold his 'kick-and-tell' story for £7,000, secretly recording conversations with various players, including those he had with Layne and Kay, to back up his allegations. With little thought for the consequences, Gauld dropped his former comrades in the you-know-what and what a stink it caused.

The People carried the story for several weeks, their ever widening net catching more and more wrongdoers although none were as high profile as the three Sheffield Wednesday stars. Among the supporting cast were Walter Bingley (Halifax Town), Jack Fountain (York City) and Peter Wragg

Captain and Major: Major Nathaniel Creswick, in military regalia, co-founder and captain of Sheffield FC and the man who sparked the 'Battle of Bramall Lane' in 1862
COURTESY OF SHEFFIELD FC

Man of Hallam: John Charles Shaw, co-founder and captain of Hallam FC, later President of the Sheffield Football Association
COURTESY OF HALLAM FC

Early FA Cup winners: The cult of the cigarette cards. (Left to right) Sheffield Wednesday 1896, Sheffield United 1902, Bradford City 1911, Barnsley 1912.
AUTHOR'S PRIVATE COLLECTION

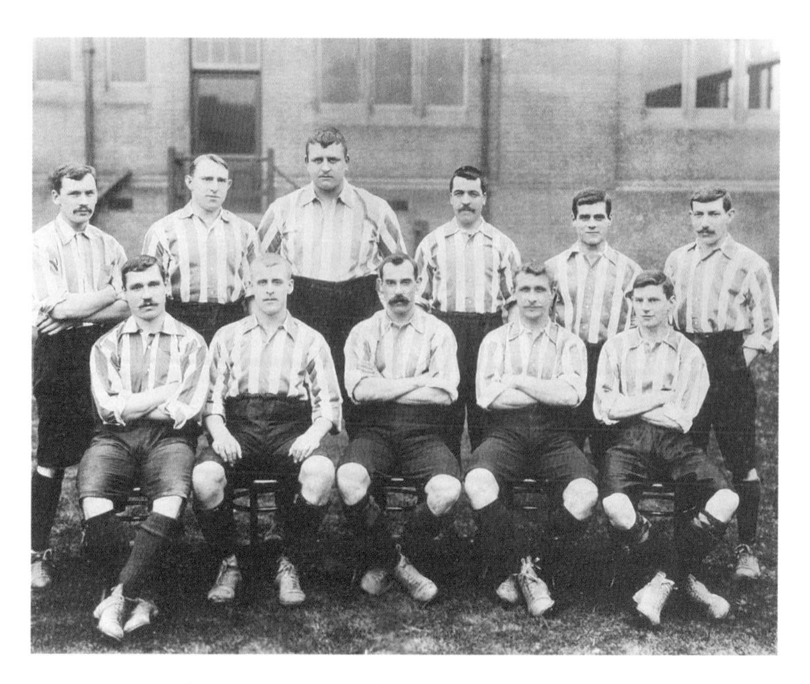

Blades Stunners: Sheffield United, 1901/02 FA Cup winners, featuring the unmistakeable Bill Foulke (back row, third left), skipper Ernest 'Nudger' Needham (back row, furthest right) and Alf Common (front row, second left).
COURTESY OF SHEFFIELD UNITED FC

Chapman's Champs: 'The Boss' Herbert Chapman with his charges at Huddersfield Town, winners of the FA Cup in 1922 and three League titles (1924-25-26)
COURTESY OF ROGER PASHBY, www.homepage.ntlworld.com/roger.pashby

Hip, Hip, Hurrah: Sheffield FC, left,, winners of the FA Amateur Cup in 1904

COURTESY OF SHEFFIELD FC

1857
SHEFFIELD F.C.
THE WORLD'S FIRST FOOTBALL CLUB

By 'Eck It's Cold: The giant killers of York City, shivering in the snow, who came within an ace of reaching the FA Cup Final in 1954/55

Cup fighters: Halifax Town in 1952/53, the season they reached the FA Cup 5th Round before losing 3-0 to Tottenham at The Shay

COURTESY OF JOHNNY MEYNELL, HALIFAX TOWN HISTORIAN

Stars down the ages: Alex Jackson, left, star winger for Huddersfield Town and Scotland in the 1920s

COURTESY OF ROGER PASHBY, www.homepage.ntlworld.com/roger.pashby

Let Me Entertain You: One of the great maverick entertainers of the 1970s, Frank Worthington (Huddersfield), pictured below

©GEORGE HERRINGSHAW www.sporting-heroes.net

O' Footballs And Cricket Balls: Chris Balderstone, right, one of the last sportsmen to combine football with cricket professionally

©GEORGE HERRINGSHAW www.sporting-heroes.net

He Shoots, He Scores: John Charles, above, 'The Gentle Giant', hammering another left-footed shot at goal for Leeds United in the 1950s

©VARLEY PICTURE AGENCY

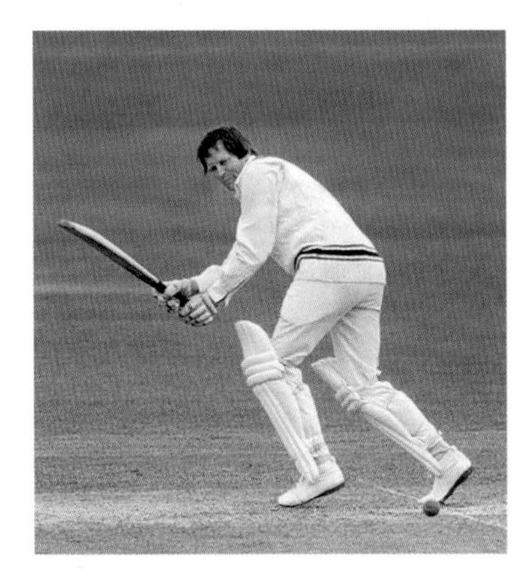

Mr York City: Keith Walwyn, the barnstorming West Indian striker who in six years (1981-87) scored 140 goals for the Minstermen

Shezza of Sheffield: Republic of Ireland midfielder John Sheridan, scorer of the goal which won Sheffield Wednesday the League Cup in 1991

Lane Legend: Brian Deane, scorer of more than a century of goals in three spells for Sheffield United (1988-93, 1997-98, 2005-06)

We Are The Champions: Leeds United captain Gordon Strachan, above, hoists the 1992 League Championship trophy aloft

Bradford's Best: Stuart McCall, above, international midfielder, inspirational skipper, popular manager and all-round modern-day hero of Valley Parade

Rovers Return: Doncaster Rovers' heroes James O'Connor (left) and goal-scorer James Hayter (right) holding the League One Play-Off Trophy after Leeds were defeated 1-0 at Wembley, 2008

HULL CITY A.F.C.
'THE TIGERS'

The Real Thing: Jubilant Hull City players celebrate promotion to the Premier League after winning the Coca-Cola Championship play-off final at Wembley, 2008'
© HULL CITY AFC

(Bradford City) all of whom were on York's books when they played Oldham on 1st December, 1962. Bingley and Fountain had also played for Swindon alongside Gauld and Layne in that thrown match against Port Vale in 1960.

From James Lang receiving a sinecure from a Sheffield Wednesday director to play for the club in the 1870s, to Leeds City officials making illegal payments to guest players during the Great War, to any number of chairmen stuffing an extra shilling or two into the boots of their star players, there has always been some form of underhand dealings in professional football. The extent of the latest corruption, however, appalled the Football Association and they came down with the toughest possible sanctions on the offenders, banning them for life from working in football. The extreme reprimand sent out a strong and clear message to other would-be transgressors that bribes and match-fixing would not be tolerated. The Sheffield Wednesday players lost everything - their livelihoods, their reputations and the game they loved.

That should have marked the end of the whole match-fixing row but the police stepped in and the situation suddenly got a whole lot more serious. Swan, Layne, Kay and a clutch of other players including Gauld, were charged with conspiracy to defraud. 'We didn't think we were committing a criminal act,' says Layne in *Sheffield Football, A History*. 'If anyone had pointed out the implications we would never have done it.'

The court case at Nottingham Assizes reached its conclusion on 26th January, 1965. Nine professional footballers, including Swan, Layne and Kay, were found guilty as charged. The Wednesday trio were each sentenced to four months behind bars, a harsh penalty if we are to believe their protestations that they were just foolish pawns in a complex game, the rules of which they did not fully comprehend. Gauld, the black king who masterminded the betting coup, discovered that colluding with *The People* gave him no protection against the law. He received the heaviest punishment of all - four years behind bars plus £5,000 costs.

The bans were eventually lifted in 1972. Kay never played top class soccer again - he absconded to Spain after selling a counterfeit diamond - but Swan and Layne, now in their mid-30s, were welcomed back to Hillsborough with open arms. Derek Dooley, the ex-Wednesday hero turned manager, had hopes that the presence of the two fading stars would ignite a promotion charge after Wednesday were relegated from Division One in 1970. It was not to be. Although Swan was given a rapturous reception at his homecoming, he made only 17 more appearances while Layne, dogged by knee trouble, made none. At the end of the season they parted company, joining Bury and non-league Matlock Town respectively where their tumultuous and controversial careers came to a gentle close.

Diagnosed in recent years with Alzheimer's disease, Swan knows that he and his team-mates let a lot of people down, not least themselves. The stigma remains and so too does a nagging question. What heights might the three Wednesday players have hit had they stayed on the straight and narrow? Play in an FA Cup Final for one. In 1966, Sheffield Wednesday lost 3-2 to Harry Catterick's Everton at Wembley and there is little doubt that the three of them would have featured in that match. Win the World Cup for another. We can only speculate, but the possibility is strong that Peter Swan, Tony Kay and David 'Bronco' Layne would have beaten Jack Charlton, Nobby Stiles and even hat-trick hero Geoff Hurst to places in the starting XI against West Germany in the 1966 World Cup Final. That they did not is, perhaps, the heaviest price they paid for getting entangled in one of the most infamous betting swindles in sporting history.

17

The Don

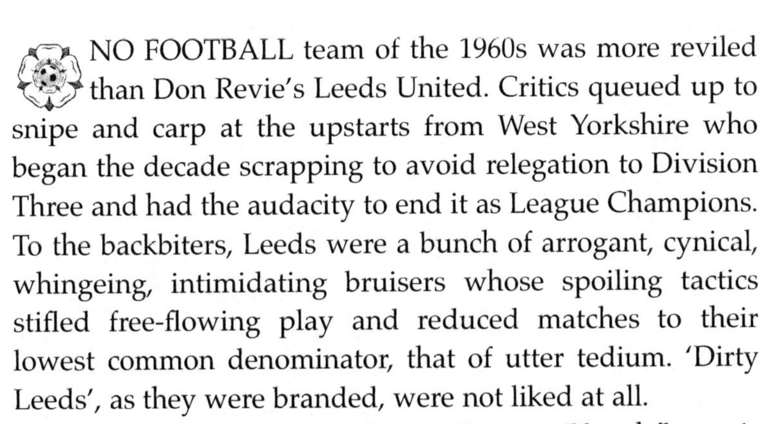

NO FOOTBALL team of the 1960s was more reviled than Don Revie's Leeds United. Critics queued up to snipe and carp at the upstarts from West Yorkshire who began the decade scrapping to avoid relegation to Division Three and had the audacity to end it as League Champions. To the backbiters, Leeds were a bunch of arrogant, cynical, whingeing, intimidating bruisers whose spoiling tactics stifled free-flowing play and reduced matches to their lowest common denominator, that of utter tedium. 'Dirty Leeds', as they were branded, were not liked at all.

Leeds did not subscribe to Danny Blanchflower's carefree view that the game is, 'about doing things in style'. The classy Spurs side which the ex-Barnsley midfielder captained to the double in 1961 was held up as a shining example of the beautiful game. Revie's men were dismissed as northern thugs, über professionals who never stopped chasing or harrying or fouling, tenaciously defended 1-0 leads and took advantage of every trick in the book to influence the course of a match. What is more, they didn't give a damn, a shoulder-shrugging indifference which caused apoplexy among their many detractors.

Born into a working-class family in Middlesbrough on 10th July, 1927, Revie had himself been a clever forward who gained six caps for England, was voted Footballer of the Year in 1955 and won an FA Cup winners' medal with Manchester City in 1956. His functional Leeds side was the embodiment not of his own abilities as a player but of his belief that a tough guy was of more benefit to a team than a stylist, as he revealed to Frank McGhee of the *Sunday Mirror*, in 1969. 'It wasn't much good being useful when you had the ball unless you also had players in the side who could get the ball for you. That's what makes the Norman Hunters ... of this world so valuable. I was never a hard player. I wish I had been. I'd have been of more use to my clubs.'

Revie arrived at Elland Road in 1958 to wind down his playing career. In March 1961, he was offered the manager's job when the Leeds chairman-in-waiting Harry Reynolds realised what a good candidate he was while writing him a reference to support an application for the vacant post at Bournemouth. 'One day, this club will rule in Europe,' Revie confidently predicted. Everybody sniggered. The club had little pedigree and attendances had tumbled to a pitiful 9,000. Ditching Leeds' traditional navy blue and gold colours for an all-white strip made famous by five times European champions, Real Madrid, he declared: 'If you think small then you stay small.' That the roughest brawlers in town were now attired in angelic white was an irony not lost on outsiders.

Revie's towering target seemed impossible when the club only dodged relegation to the Third Division in 1962 by winning their final game of the season. Knowing he had to build a new team from scratch, Revie stripped the squad he inherited of its dead wood. Big Jack Charlton, Scottish left back Willie Bell and a 20-year-old, ginger-haired firebrand from Stirling, Billy Bremner, were the only notable survivors of the cull.

Revie raided the transfer market to plug some of the gaps. In came the likes of Albert Johanneson, a black kid plucked from the ghettoes and apartheid of South Africa and nicknamed 'Black Flash' for the scorching pace he generated down the left flank; young Irishman Johnny Giles, a gifted right winger nicked from Manchester United for £33,000 and 31-year-old ex-Scotland international inside forward Bobby Collins, bought from Everton for £25,000. Aggressive, confrontational, fearless, Collins was ten stone of Celtic menace. Converted into a central midfielder, he became the Regimental Sergeant Major in Operation Leeds, drilling into the team its mean streak and 'win at any cost' attitude.

More significantly for the club's long term future, Revie invested in youth. A crop of talented teenagers with Beatles mop-tops soon graduated from the junior team, including goalkeepers Gary Sprake - an error-prone Wales international who Liverpool fans nicknamed 'Careless Hands' after spectacularly throwing the ball into his own net at Anfield in 1967 - and the more solidly reliable David Harvey; defenders Norman Hunter, Paul Reaney, Paul Madeley and Terry Cooper; midfielder Mick Bates; winger Eddie Gray; forward Jimmy Greenhoff, and attacking midfield man Peter Lorimer, who in a long career set club records as youngest player - his debut against Southampton in September 1962 came at the age of 15 years and 289 days - and highest scorer with 238 goals in two spells, 1962-78 and 1983-86.

As ridiculous as it might sound now, Revie next arranged for Elland Road to be exorcised of an ancient gypsy curse. Highly superstitious, Revie genuinely believed that the club was being held back by a Romany jinx. This peculiar trait of his character was made public in 1970 when Revie admitted on Yorkshire TV that he wore the same lucky blue suit and blue tie for each match, kept some charms in his pockets in the dugout and took the same stroll before every home game. Allied to his somewhat quirky nature was a meticulous bent which manifested itself most famously in the detailed 'dossiers' he had prepared on opponents and in the pre-match games of bingo and carpet bowls he introduced to help his players bond and relax.

Once Elland Road was 'cleansed' of its evil omens, Leeds duly delivered the Second Division Championship in 1964. But their naked aggression, typified by human machetes Collins, Bremner and 'Bites Yer Legs' Hunter, combined with their gamesmanship - arguing with referees, going over the top of the ball, histrionics over minor incidents, stealing yards at free-kicks and throw-ins, feigning injury and time wasting - alienated many neutral supporters. At least the exciting Johanneson, with 15 goals in all competitions, brush-stroked some vibrancy on to what was an otherwise mundane canvass.

Many people within the game would have loved to have seen 'The Mean Machine' make a swift return from whence they came. But with Collins snarling and gnashing from the front - contentiously he was elected Footballer of the Year in 1965 - Leeds gate-crashed the First Division party like a gang of Burberry-clad chavs. Indeed, they went to within a whisker of accomplishing the coveted double, a rare feat which had it been achieved would have sent shockwaves through the football world. To the relief of the establishment, Leeds lost the Championship to Manchester United on goal average on the very last day of the League programme and were then beaten 2-1 by Liverpool after extra-time in the FA Cup Final. The *Daily Mirror* lamented the Wembley spectacle: 'Their football did not win them many friends. Possibly it lost the game quite a few, especially the sheer Leeds defensive tactics. If this is the football of the future then give me the football of not such a distant past.'

Revie defended his team's strategy later arguing that, 'it was essential to adopt a "tight" system of play in our first couple of years in the First Division while we consolidated our position.' Leeds' rise to prominence coincided with a natural movement away from the gung-ho approach of the 1950s and early 60s. European competition taught English sides that an iron strong defence was essential if success was to be had against skilful and often brutal sides from Italy, Spain and the Balkan states. The old 'WM' formation was no longer fit for purpose. 4-2-4 came into fashion which soon morphed into the more defensive 4-3-3 and 4-4-2 configurations, the latter being adopted by England's 'wingless wonders' in the 1966 World Cup Final. The lexicon of field positions changed too. Inside and centre forwards became strikers, outside forwards known as wingers and half backs were renamed midfielders. The upshot of this tactical overhaul was a considerable reduction in goals, not only in Europe but in the domestic game too.

The disappointment of letting the double slip through their hands would have crushed many outfits but the Leeds team was nothing if not resilient. 'Keep Fighting' was the message nailed to the dressing room wall and they did, in more ways than one. Under the strict regime of club coach Syd Owen and trainer Les Cocker, they were the best drilled team in the land. Revie's role was father figure, nurturing and motivating his faithful young charges and instilling in them enormous self-belief and a powerful 'all for one and one for all' team spirit.

To opposing players and supporters 'The Don' was less father, more godfather, a gangland boss who each weekend sent out eleven hired assassins to kill the game stone dead. Jimmy Greaves was left with the impression that the Leeds team was fed on a diet of raw meat and nails. Brian Clough, one of the club's most venomous and vociferous soap-box critics, repeatedly accused them of being a bunch of cheats and urged the Football League to kick them out of the First Division.

Despite the flak, Leeds - as the club anthem goes - went marching on together in a relentless, some might say ruthless, quest for a trophy. They did it, too, without their inspirational skipper. In October 1965, Collins shattered a thighbone in a horror challenge during a match against Torino. The tough little Scot never fully recovered and fourteen months later, after five years invaluable service, he moved to Bury on a free transfer.

Leeds were Division One runners-up again in 1966, this time to Liverpool. The following year they finished fourth, reached the FA Cup Semi-Final - an Elland Road attendance record of 57,892 was set against Sunderland in the fifth round - and lost 2-0 on aggregate to Dynamo Zagreb of Yugoslavia in the Final of the Inter-Cities Fairs Cup, the forerunner to the UEFA Cup. On a personal level, however, the period 1965-67 was one of great achievement for the veteran of the side, Jack Charlton. A gangly, big-mouthed, no-frills defender, he collected the first of 35 international caps for England in 1965 when almost 30 years old. The following year, he won a World Cup winners' medal[1] playing alongside his younger brother Bobby, and in 1967 he was voted Footballer of the Year. And still he soldiered on, finally retiring in 1973 at the grand old age of 37 and with a club record 772 appearances to his name.

As a replacement for Collins, Revie tried but failed to

prise another World Cup star, Alan Ball, from Blackpool. Instead he spent £30,000 on Huddersfield Town's right winger Mike O'Grady and moved Johnny Giles into the midfield engine room. It was a momentous decision. The Collins-Bremner combination was good but Giles and Bremner were exceptional. Small in stature but huge on talent, they brought verve and craft as well as steel and a competitive spirit to the midfield. Johnny was a composed player, cool and calculating, who used the ball intelligently and sprayed passes, long and short, with pinpoint accuracy. Billy was, by contrast, tigerish, impetuous, passionate, the pumped-up heart of the side who never gave less than total effort. A brilliant passer of the ball, he had a happy knack of scoring vital goals in important matches. Handed the captain's armband, Bremner toned down his fiery temper and waspish tongue to mature from a gifted but nasty piece of work into one of the finest all-round midfielders the game has ever seen.

Leeds United finally broke their cup hoodoo in 1968. In March, they beat Arsenal 1-0 in a dour League Cup Final at Wembley, the decisive goal being scored by speedy left-back Terry Cooper who, in trademark white boots, developed into one of the world's finest exponents of the overlapping full back. Then, in September, Leeds ground out a 1-0 aggregate win over favourites Ferencvaros of Hungary in the Fairs Cup Final, the crucial strike this time coming from Mick Jones, an ungainly but brave-hearted target man who arrived from Sheffield United for £100,000 the previous summer.

Leeds' confidence grew exponentially. During the 1968/69 season they cantered to the Division One title losing just two games, conceding only 26 goals and amassing a record-shattering 67 points. On the flip side, their output of 66 goals - Jones, with 14, was the only Leeds player to hit double figures - was fewer that any title-winning team since before the off-side law was changed in 1925.

The Championship was clinched at Anfield on 28th April, 1969 following a tense, nail-biting goalless draw against Liverpool, their closest challengers. At the insistence of his boss, Bremner took his team over to the Kop at the end of the match to salute the 27,000 home fans crammed inside, a brave act that could have resulted in the Leeds players being showered with coins, spit and vitriol. As it was, the vanquished supporters generously cheered and chanted 'champions'. Revie was clearly moved. 'The reception given to us by the sporting Liverpool crowd was truly magnificent,' said the Manager of the Year. His opposite number Bill Shankly sportingly hailed Leeds as, 'a great side'. Even the most sceptical of pressmen gave them grudging praise along the lines of 'we might not like you, but we admire you'.

Having proved themselves worthy winners, Revie decided the time was ripe to unleash his side's full potential. He gave his players license to thrill, to add adventure and imagination to hard graft and discipline. Wherever possible games were to be opened up, not ritually closed down. Bremner and Giles were the midfield maestros, conducting the tempo and style of the team's play. Gray brought guile and flair to the left wing in place of Johanneson. Lorimer - known as 'Lash' or 'Hot-Shot' for his cannonball shooting - pushed forward from the right side of midfield to give the attack an extra dimension. More firepower was added when Allan 'Sniffer' Clarke, a cocksure and dead-eye finisher, joined from Leicester City for £165,000 in a new British record deal. Over the next five seasons Clarke and the hardworking Jones, the rapier and the bludgeon, plundered almost 200 goals. The classic Leeds United team was complete: Sprake, Reaney, Cooper, Bremner, Charlton,

Hunter, Lorimer, Clarke, Jones, Giles, Gray - a mantra for their fans. Backing them up was Leeds-born Paul Madeley, an elegant and incredibly versatile footballer whose ability to play anywhere with the utmost ease - he appeared in every outfield position during his career - was rewarded with 24 England caps (1971-77).

Freed of their inhibitions, Leeds enjoyed many triumphal moments. Juventus were beaten in the 1971 Fairs Cup Final. Clarke put the ball in the Arsenal net to win the Centenary FA Cup Final the following year. A brilliant 29-match unbeaten run from the start of the season was the catalyst for a second League Championship in 1974. Hunter was named Player of the Year by fellow professionals. New stars like Joe Jordan, Gordon McQueen and Trevor Cherry lent extra lustre to an already sparkling squad. In 1970, Revie was made an OBE, Bremner voted Footballer of the Year and 22-year-old Scotsman Eddie Gray, who teased full backs before skipping past them with an explosive burst of speed, scored one of the finest solo goals ever seen at Elland Road, slaloming like Franz Klammer past several Burnley defenders in a tightly packed penalty area and throwing in a couple of drag-backs before burying the ball in the back of the net. A few weeks later, the Caledonian starlet gave Chelsea right back David Webb a torrid going over in the FA Cup Final, prompting some judges to predict that he would become as great a player as George Best. Such forecasts were, unfortunately, premature when, not long afterwards, he picked up a recurring thigh injury which for the next five years decimated his fledgling career.

Memorable matches abounded, the pick of a substantial bunch being a 7-0 hammering of Southampton in March 1972. Reaching near perfection, Bremner and Giles toyed with Saints like cats with mice, playing keepy-up and performing other training ground tricks towards the end of the match. At one stage the whole team strung together some 25 uninterrupted passes to cries of '*Ole*' from the home fans, prompting *Match of the Day* commentator Barry Davies to rhapsodise: 'To say that Leeds are playing with Southampton is the understatement of the season, poor old Southampton just don't know what day it is. Every man jack of this Leeds side is now turning it on, it's almost cruel.'

Not so much 'Dirty Leeds' anymore as 'Super Leeds', United were streets ahead of the competition in England and superior to all but a handful of European sides. Their champagne squad bubbled over with international players, Billy Bremner heading the list with 54 caps for Scotland.

And yet there was also a huge sense of under-achievement. Diabolical refereeing decisions, crooked match officials, miraculous saves, injuries and pure bad luck in cup finals, crucial matches and dramatic last-game climaxes conspired to rob Leeds of potentially two European Cups (1970, 1975), a hat-trick of League Championships (1970-72), two more FA Cups (1970, 1973) and a European Cup Winners' Cup (1973). In 1972, the double was theirs for the taking but they contrived to lose their last match 2-1 to Wolves at Molineux. The gut-wrenching finale was made worse by the fact that the title went instead to Brian Clough's Derby County.

Leeds were labelled 'Big Match Chokers' but the truth of the matter is they were too good for their own good. As the old riddle goes, 'What do Leeds and a darts champion have in common?' Answer: 'They are always chasing doubles and trebles'. By the time the business end of a season came around, Bremner and Co. were exhausted and facing an energy-sapping fixture backlog. Physical fatigue more than any kind of mental meltdown was behind their failure to win further silverware. 'Just our second places alone would have satisfied most clubs, but we also won a hell of a lot,' reflected Revie although his superstitious nature must have had him cursing the Fates.

By the 1974 close season, Don Revie had achieved all he had set out to do. He had built Leeds United up from nothing into one of the biggest teams in Europe. Average gates at Elland Road had ballooned to 39,000 and large swathes of the general public and the media were now of the opinion that this was a team not to be reviled but revered; championed, maybe even loved. Mission accomplished, Revie resigned and took over as England boss from sacked World Cup legend Sir Alf Ramsey.

The split was not a happy one for either party. In their infinite non-wisdom the Leeds board notoriously appointed as their new manager not Revie's recommendation of Giles but the club's nemesis, Brian Clough. It was like asking Arthur Scargill to take over as leader of the Conservative Party. 'Old Big 'Ead' was undoubtedly a brilliant and super-confident manager, but he was also egotistical, antagonistic, outspoken and an irrepressible braggart. He came to the club he despised above all others only because it offered him another crack at the European Cup - his Derby side were beaten by Juventus in the semi final in 1973. But telling the injury-jinxed Gray that, 'if you'd been a racehorse they'd have had you shot', or the team as a whole that, 'you can all throw every one of your medals in the bin [because] you never won any of them fairly', was not the way to go about it. Bremner, his fury boiling over, got himself sent off in the Charity Shield at Wembley for fighting with Liverpool's Kevin Keegan, who also saw red. The dressing room mutinied and after 44 stormy days the club directors caved in - 'Player Power', the newspapers called it - and sacked Clough.

He was replaced by the genial, pipe-smoking Jimmy Armfield, a far more diplomatic man who brought calm to troubled waters. The Leeds players responded by powering through to the 1975 European Cup Final against Bayern Munich. It was the perfect setting for Bremner, Giles and the rest of Revie's ageing stars to go out with an almighty bang but, once again, Lady Luck deserted them. Leeds dominated the match from start to finish but two shocking decisions by the referee - waving play on when Clarke was scythed down in the penalty box by Franz Beckenbauer and disallowing a Lorimer volley for an offside that never was - cost them dear. Against the run of play, the Germans scored twice in the last half-hour.

The aftermath was dismal. In a disturbing sign of things to come, Leeds fans rioted. The violence was so bad and given such international exposure on live TV that UEFA banned the club from playing in Europe for four years. Thereafter, Revie's brilliant team was dismantled, terrace hooliganism at Leeds matches became rife and on-pitch fortunes waned to such an extent that in 1982 the club was relegated.

Meanwhile, Revie as England manager came to the conclusion that there was a dearth of genuine talent in the country. He tinkered and fiddled with team selections in the hope of stumbling across a winning combination and all the while England's chances of qualifying for the 1978 World Cup were evaporating. Sensing that he was about to be sacked, Revie negotiated a secret four-year deal worth £340,000 to take over as national coach of the United Arab Emirates. In July 1977, he sensationally walked out on the England job without informing the Football Association, sold his story to the *Daily Mail* for another £20,000 and then boarded a plane bound for the Middle East.

Revie claimed he did what he did to secure his family's financial future but the knives were out and sharpened. Incensed, the FA slapped a 10-year ban on him for bringing the game into disrepute. The constraint was overturned by the High Court in 1979 - the same year, incidentally, in which Clough won the European Cup with Nottingham Forest - but it was a hollow victory. The judge scathingly described Revie's resignation as, 'a sensational, outrageous example of disloyalty, breach of duty, discourtesy and selfishness.' Revie was vilified by the press as a greedy, deceitful rat who deserted the good ship England as she sunk. The *Daily Mirror* even accused 'Don Readies', as they dubbed him, of corruption, dredging up old but unproven allegations that the former Leeds boss had tried to bribe Wolves players £1,000 per man to throw the 1972 title-decider.

Innocent or guilty, Don Revie's reputation was in tatters. He never worked in English football again. In 1987, the most successful manager in the history of Leeds United and, for that matter, Yorkshire football was diagnosed with Motor Neurone Disease. He died two years later on 26th May, 1989, aged 61. At his funeral service in Edinburgh his football 'family' turned out in force headed, as ever, by Bremner and Giles, his two favourite 'sons'. The FA and Football League had neither the wit nor the compassion to send a representative. Even in death Don Revie remained an unforgiven pariah.

FOOTNOTE

[1] In addition to Jack Charlton, the 1966 World Cup winning team included goalkeeping great Gordon Banks, a native of Catcliffe, Rotherham, and left back Ray Wilson, who played over 250 games for Huddersfield Town (1955-64). Two non-playing members of the squad were Charlton's defensive partner at Leeds, Norman Hunter and Sheffield Wednesday keeper Ron Springett.

18

'Black Magic'

WHEN Leeds United's Albert Johanneson ran out at Wembley on 1st May, 1965 for the FA Cup Final against Liverpool he did so as the first black player to feature in English football's blue ribbon event. In a decade when coloured footballers were few and far between, 'Black Flash' was a trailblazer who proved that race was no barrier to sporting success, that natural skill, blistering pace and a keen eye for goal were essential building blocks in creating a top class winger, not Caucasian DNA.

Born into poverty in the townships of Johannesburg, South Africa on 13th March, 1940 Johanneson was 'discovered' playing on the wing for a local colliery team by a schoolteacher who had links with Leeds United. Offered a three month trial in March 1961, the lithe, cropped-haired outside left followed in the footsteps of another black South African, Gerry Francis, a strong running but unreliable winger who played sporadically for Leeds between 1957 and 1961. Within days of landing in England, Albert was snapped up by an impressed Don Revie on a permanent deal, all for the price of a plane ticket.

Johanneson made an immediate impact on his debut, swinging in a perfect cross for Jack Charlton to head in one of the Leeds goals in a 2-2 draw against Swansea Town on 8th April, 1961. He quickly became a key - if atypical - member of the early 'Mean Machine', described by Rob Bagchi and Paul Rogerson in *The Unforgiven*, chronicling the Revie Era, as, 'the only element of glamour in a drab Leeds side'.

'Black Flash' made creating history something of a habit. On 20th March, 1965 in a 4-1 home win against Everton, he became the first black player to be shown scoring a goal on the BBC's new football highlights programme, *Match of the Day*. The following year he scored Leeds' first hat-trick in Europe, in a 5-1 win over DWS Amsterdam in the Inter-Cities Fairs Cup.

Leeds supporters adored the dazzling wing wizard who raced down the left flank each week, chanting 'Albert, Albert, Albert' as he tormented back-peddling full backs with his breakneck speed and close ball control. Bobby Collins, the Leeds captain, was one admirer: 'Albert could fly and I could put the ball on the spot for him. When he was in his stride there weren't many who could catch him.'

Not everyone, though, was so enamoured and Johanneson was subjected to racial taunts from ignorant, small-minded bigots, not all of whom stood on the terraces. In one bitter, foul-strewn confrontation between Leeds and Everton at Goodison Park during the 1964/65 season Johanneson complained at half time that an Everton defender was calling him a black bastard. Revie's advice was to fight fire with fire: 'Call him a white bastard back.'

The solution might have seemed simple to the manager

but for a gentle man who had escaped the evils of apartheid in his homeland and come to a supposedly civilised and tolerant country, such acts of prejudice must have been distressing. Johanneson had all the natural ability in the world but brittle self-confidence, born of his upbringing in a segregated world and reinforced by the racial abuse meted out to him on the pitches of his adopted land, prevented him from conquering the football world.

He was handicapped, too, by big match nerves. As Leeds scaled the football mountain and expectations began to soar, the intense pressure became too much to bear. The 1965 FA Cup Final was a watershed moment. Like so many of his team-mates he had a stinker of a game but, unlike the others, he never rediscovered his mojo. A sensitive nature, inconsistent performances, niggling injuries and the emergence of Eddie Gray combined to turn him from first-team regular into peripheral squad member.

In the summer of 1970, aged 30 and a shadow of the exciting young thing that had arrived in Yorkshire on a cold and snowy day nine years earlier, he left Leeds after scoring 68 goals in 200 appearances in the No. 11 shirt. He joined York City, of the Fourth Division, helping them to win promotion in his first season before hanging up what were once seemingly jet-propelled boots a year later.

Albert Johanneson was a trendsetter, by common consent the first black footballer to make an outstanding contribution to the English game. Or was he? Rumours persist to this day that his Leeds team-mate Paul Reaney, a swift and tough-tackling right-back who liked to gallop forward on the overlap, was of mixed race parentage. Although regarded at the time as white - much as Ryan Giggs is today even though he has a black father, former rugby league international Danny Wilson - Reaney's swarthy complexion, distinctive facial features and wiry hair suggest black roots. If that is the case then 'Speedy' should be recognised not only as the first player of black origin to play in an FA Cup Final, jointly with Johanneson, but also the first to be capped by England. His international debut, as a substitute against Bulgaria in December 1968, came a full decade before Nottingham Forest full back Viv Anderson claimed the honour to much fanfare. Although he played more games for Leeds (745) than anyone else bar Charlton and Billy Bremner and was able to mark George Best out of a game like no other, he collected just two more caps. Had he not broken a leg early in 1970, then he would probably have earned a call-up to the England World Cup squad.

Questions over Reaney's heritage will no doubt continue. Perhaps he was content to be regarded as white at a time of mounting racial tension. The end of the Second World War triggered mass immigration into Britain from the Commonwealth, chiefly from the West Indies, India and Pakistan. Settling in large numbers in deprived areas of cities such as Leeds, Bradford and Sheffield, their sudden appearance was treated with suspicion and not a little loathing and they were generally treated as third-class citizens. Programmes such as *The Black and White Minstrel Show* perpetuated negative racial stereotypes whilst caricature TV characters like Alf Garnett regurgitated a common belief that ethnic minorities were nicking white working-class people's jobs and houses. From this melting pot of intolerance and ignorance there bubbled up in 1967 the far-right, whites-only National Front. The following year Conservative MP Enoch Powell made his infamous 'Rivers of Blood' speech in which he warned of civil war should immigration continue unchecked. Little wonder Albert Johanneson cracked under the strain.

Racial discrimination in football was not new. Long

before Johanneson arrived in West Yorkshire, Arthur Wharton, English football's first black player and a lively goalkeeper who starred for Rotherham Town and Sheffield United in the 1890s, was barracked as a 'darkie' by sections of fans and had his intellect questioned by some newspaper reporters.

That people took a dim and narrow-minded view of Wharton is not wholly surprising. The British Empire was at its peak when he was carving out a career in football and the world order was that white men ruled and black men served. To their credit, however, the majority of observers regarded the athletic showman from the African continent - he was born in Accra, the capital of the Gold Coast (now Ghana), in 1865 - as an exotic curio who brought a dash of glamour and excitement to English football in much the same way as his contemporary, Indian Prince KS Ranjitsinhji, did to English cricket.

The son of a white Methodist missionary father and a native black mother, Arthur enjoyed a comfortable middle class upbringing. He was sent to London to be schooled and returned to England in 1882 to train as a minister at Cleveland College in Darlington. While there, he demonstrated a prowess for sport, excelling at cricket, cycling and athletics as well as soccer. Tall and slim with extravagant waxed moustaches, he turned his back on religion and became a semi-professional footballer in 1886, signing for Preston North End, then the mightiest team in the North of England. In the same year, he set a world record for the 100 yards sprint, clocking 10 seconds flat at the Amateur Athletics Association championships at Stamford Bridge.

How curious then that a man timed as the fastest human on earth should end up playing football in goal. Described by Rodney Hinds in *Black Lions* as, 'an unorthodox and entertaining performer' with, 'a phenomenal punch',

Wharton starred for the 'Invincibles' of Preston for three years during which time he played in an FA Cup semi final, before swapping the red rose for the white when joining Rotherham Town in 1889.

For five years, Wharton thrilled the Rotherham crowds during which time his new club won successive Midland League titles in 1892 and 1893. In the summer of 1894 he was lured away to Bramall Lane by the prospect of playing First Division football. However, he was past his prime and found his route into the Sheffield United first team blocked by the ample body and abundant talent of 20-year-old Bill 'Fatty' Foulke. After three senior appearances he returned to Rotherham and later played for Stalybridge Celtic, Ashton North End and Stockport County before retiring from the game in February 1902.

Wharton then hit on hard times. Eking out a living as a haulage hand at the Yorkshire Main Colliery in Edlington, he became an alcoholic and died, of cancer, in a Doncaster sanatorium in December 1930. He was buried in an unmarked pauper's grave, a sporting hero forgotten by the world. That dreadful wrong was put right in 1997 when 'Football Unites, Racism Divides' - an organisation set up in 1995 by a group of Sheffield United fans - unearthed and retold Arthur Wharton's pioneering story and erected a memorial headstone in tribute to his landmark achievements.

Sandwiched in between Wharton and Johanneson was Yorkshire's first 'home grown' black professional. Charles Adolphus Williams, better known as Charlie Williams, was born in the small mining village of Royston near Barnsley, the son of a white Yorkshire mother and a black Barbadian father who served with the Royal Engineers during World War One. He spent most of the Second World War working down the pits at Upton Colliery and played football for the same works team that produced Doncaster's Clarrie Jordan and Rotherham's Len White. A physical, no-nonsense centre-half - 'I was never a fancy player, but I could stop them buggers that were' - Williams signed for Doncaster Rovers in October 1948. He had to wait, though, until January 1955 before making the No.5 shirt his own and for the next three years played Second Division football in a capable side that also contained wonderkid Alick Jeffrey and Northern Ireland international goalkeeper Harry Gregg.

After 171 appearances and one solitary goal, Williams left Belle Vue in 1959. He kicked off a new career as an entertainer, touring the Northern variety club circuit first as a crooner with the Jeffrey Trio, alongside former team-mate Alick Jeffrey and Jeffrey's father, and then as a stand-up comic who became well known for his cheeky patter and big smile. In the early 70s he hit the big time, earning a regular spot on Granada Television's smash-hit show *The Comedians*. Nationwide exposure turned Charlie Williams into a household celebrity. He was the new King of Comedy with a Rolls-Royce and a posh house to show for it, a working-class lad made good.

Black rights activists thought otherwise. They condemned Williams for pandering to his mainly white audiences' prejudices with gags like, 'It was so sunny today I thought I'd been deported'. But as the first well known black comedian, Williams found himself in an unusual situation. He was, in many ways, just like the white people who came to see him perform. Born and bred in Yorkshire, he experienced the deprivation of the 1930s and lived through the war. His close family relations were white. He went to school with white schoolmates, worked alongside white miners and played football with white team-mates. As Lenny Henry observed, he was someone, 'who talked like them, who thought like them, but who just happened to be black.'

Williams' glittering showbiz career faded but supporters at Belle Vue never forgot the wholehearted displays he put in, voting him Doncaster Rovers' 'All-time Cult Hero' in a poll organised by the BBC's *Football Focus* programme in 2004. Two years later Charlie Williams MBE, footballer and funny man, died, aged 78, at home in Barnsley.

He once said that laughter is the finest medicine in the world but while he was able to laugh off Britain's endemic racism, other black footballers found life tough going in the Seventies. It seemed to be of no consequence that a brilliant Brazil side won the World Cup with a largely black XI in 1970 or that Pele, the best footballer on the planet, was dark skinned. Antipathy towards black players in England increased in line with an alarming growth in support for an ever more confrontational National Front. Britain was crippled by high inflation, rising unemployment, strikes, power cuts and fuel shortages and it was all too easy to blame immigrants for the desperate situation. The skinhead slogan of, 'There ain't no black in the Union Jack' struck a chord in young white males up and down the country and who spent Saturday afternoons at football grounds verbally abusing black blokes dressed in the away team's kit.

Nevertheless, those on the pitch survived the booing, monkey noises, banana throwing and vile songs and did so in ever growing numbers. In the decade of Glam Rock, they brought to the game, as Garth Crooks, the ex-footballer turned pundit, puts it in *Black Lions*, 'a certain flair and exuberance [and added] some real spice to what was rather a dull dish'. The most famous black players of the day were Viv Anderson (Nottingham Forest), Clyde Best (West Ham), Justin Fashanu (Norwich City) and West Brom's tastelessly so-called 'Three Degrees' of Brendon Batson, Laurie Cunningham and Cyril Regis. But in Yorkshire it was another Cyril who made the biggest impression - Cyril 'Ces' Podd, of Bradford City.

An intelligent, if at times cavalier, right back with a decent turn of speed and a distinctive haircut, Podd was a living legend in Bradford. In a career spent exclusively in the lower divisions, he pulled on the claret and amber shirt 574 times - more than any other player in the club's history - and scored four goals between 1970 and 1984. He, like Williams before him, disproved the utterly absurd but widespread belief that black players were 'fair weather' performers who enjoyed showboating in the sun but had no stomach for a fight in the middle of a freezing cold English winter.

Born on the Caribbean island of St Kitts in August 1952 but raised in Leeds after coming to the UK at the age of nine, Podd studied at the Bradford College of Art but found greater enjoyment and comfort as a pro footballer at Valley Parade. 'I got on so well with the Bradford fans. They were my security blanket,' he said.

Podd's testimonial in March 1981 pitted Bradford City against a Harlem Globetrotters-style representative team called 'The Black All-Stars' which included Regis, Batson, Fashanu, Vince Hilaire, Luther Blissett, Ricky Hill, George Berry and Remi Moses. Also in the squad was Leeds United striker Terry Connor and Podd's team mate and fellow West Indian Joe Cooke, a heavyweight defender-cum-striker who played over 300 games for City and scored the goal that clinched promotion from Division Four in May 1977.

The crowd of 3,381 for Ces's big night was, on the face of it, disappointing but it was none the less some 500 more than City's average attendance that season. Podd remains a big crowd favourite at Valley Parade. In July 2007, fans voted for him to be one of three ex-Bantams (the others were Stuart McCall and John Hendrie) to have a specially brewed ale named after them in aid of charity.

Race relations in England were at breaking point by New Year 1981 and in early summer they snapped with explosive effect. Riots broke out across the country - including in the Chapeltown district of Leeds - as disaffected black youths hurled petrol bombs, smashed windows and battled with police in violent protests against widespread discrimination and social depravation. Around the same time, racist chanting at football matches reached unprecedented levels. Among the worst culprits were a large minority of Leeds United fans who conveniently overlooked the contributions given to their club by Johanneson, Francis and Connor and made Elland Road a living hell for black players to visit. Outside the ground the National Front magazine *Bulldog* was openly on sale; inside it the atmosphere was thick with hatred and hostile songs and chants.

Something had to be done, not just at Leeds but throughout professional football. At first, individual clubs and various Football Supporters' Associations attempted to address the deplorable problem on a local and piecemeal basis. It took another decade for a coordinated national movement to swing into action. The 'Let's Kick Racism Out Of Football' campaign was launched in 1993 by the Professional Footballers' Association and the Commission for Racial Equality and backed by the FA A ten point action plan was implemented across the board and steadily attitudes among supporters, players, managers and directors changed for the better.

By the early 1990s, the trickle of black players had become an unstoppable torrent. Many were now English-born which meant the national side benefited too. Lanky Sheffield United striker Brian Deane became the first black player from a Yorkshire club to play for England when he came on as a second half substitute against New Zealand in June 1991. When Leeds were crowned the last champions of the old First Division in 1991/92 they had Chris Fairclough and Chris Whyte shoring up their defence and Rod Wallace creating havoc up front. The racist chants that had emanated from Elland Road less than a decade beforehand were nowhere to be heard. Sheffield Wednesday recruited the groundbreaking Viv Anderson and Des Walker, capped 59 times by England and a star of Italia '90. Elsewhere in the county the likes of Keith Walwyn (York City), Carlton Palmer (Sheffield Wed and Leeds United), Tony Agana (Sheffield United), Noel Blake (Leeds and Bradford City), Chris Kamara (Leeds, Bradford City and Sheffield United) and Shaun 'The Goat' Goater (Rotherham United) made massive impacts.

The launch, in May 1992, of the Premier League gave participating clubs the financial clout with which to buy foreign talent from all corners of the world. Leeds, having finally shed their unwanted right-wing image, made the most of the new pulling power, attracting black international players of the calibre of Jimmy Floyd Hasselbaink (Holland), Oliver Dacourt (France), the hugely popular Lucas Radebe (South Africa) and striker Tony Yeboah (Ghana) who broke the club's transfer record when he arrived from Eintracht Frankfurt for £3.4 million in 1995. More recently Hull City have used their elevation to the Premier League as leverage to broker a deal with the much travelled and vaunted Brazilian playmaker, Geovanni.

In the new millennium, black footballers are an accepted part and parcel of the English game, comprising a quarter of all Premier League players. The England national team has had up to six black players in its starting line-up. In 2002 Rio Ferdinand became the world's most expensive defender when he moved from Leeds to Manchester United for £29.1 million. Black players have started to break into club management too, Anderson (Barnsley, 1993-94) and Kamara (Bradford City, 1995-98) being two notable pioneers. As Hinds says: 'The black footballer has turned from freak show into a respected member of the football fraternity.'

That is not to say that racism in football has been totally conquered. In 2004, TV pundit Ron Atkinson shockingly abused Chelsea's Marcel Desailly when he thought he was off-air and, post 9/11, there have been reoccurrences of race riots, notably in Bradford, allied to a growth in popularity for the BNP and the English Defence League as sections of white Britons fight back, sometimes literally, against Islamic extremists.

Such prejudice is not helping British Asians to prosper in professional football. Yorkshire should be a hotbed for Asian talent but the county's Muslim, Sikh and Hindu communities remain largely untapped. Midfielder Adnan Ahmed has played for Huddersfield Town (2004-07); Harpal Singh, a left winger from Pudsey, was tipped for England honours while he was a youth player at Leeds United but failed to live up to expectations; Anwar Uddin was briefly on Sheffield Wednesday's books and defender Zesh Rehman is currently skipper of Bradford City. That, sadly, is about it. Maybe Rehman, one of only five Asian players in the top four divisions, can help reshape the football landscape. As an ambassador for the Asian Football Network he is leading the crusade, 'to tackle the numerous challenges facing the Asian football community'. Fingers crossed, his work will bear fruit in the coming years and pave the way for the next generation to come through in greater numbers as players and fans.

So what of trailblazer Albert Johanneson? Sadly his story does not end happily. Mirroring the fate that befell Wharton, in retirement he became dependent on alcohol and died, aged 55, alone, penniless and largely unremembered by the football world. His body lay undiscovered in a council flat in a Leeds tower block for several days, a pitiful end for a player who gave the Elland Road crowds much entertainment in the mid-Sixties. The late, great George Best, who lost his own battle against the demon drink, said of him: 'Albert was quite a brave man to actually go on the pitch in the first place, wasn't he? And he went out and did it. He had a lot of skill. A nice man as well ... which is, I suppose, the more important thing isn't it? More important than anything.'

19

Here Come The Girls

NOT SO very long ago, the commonly held belief - and one which persists in some quarters - was that any woman taking part in football matches were butch or lesbians, or more likely both. The very idea prompted sniggers and ridicule among many red-blooded males, after all, football was a man's game, wasn't it? Always has been. Women were neither physically nor psychologically built for football, they should, as the inimitable Ron Atkinson once said, 'be in the kitchen, the boutique, the disco but not in football.'

Into this male dominated and chauvinistic world was born, in 1969, the most famous of all ladies' football teams, Doncaster Belles. It was the year when America put a man on the moon but the Belles' first big step was rather more down to earth. Led by Sheila Edmunds, who is now the club's president, a group of young female Doncaster Rovers fans selling 'Golden Goal' tickets on the Belle Vue terraces on Saturday afternoons decided to form their own football side as a bit of fun. Initially going by the name of Belle Vue Belles, they were coached by a man (they did not appoint a female boss until the mid-90s) and played matches here and there against a few other local ladies teams.

The Belles were at the forefront of renewed interest in football among women after England won the World Cup in 1966. The game was first played by well-to-do ladies wearing baggy blouses and even baggier knickerbockers in London way back in 1895. By the end of World War One, women's football was thriving especially in the industrial North where the suffragette movement was strong and millions of women had shown their mettle by working in munitions factories while their men-folk went off to fight Kaiser Bill.

Ladies' teams appeared in Bradford, Huddersfield, Hull, Keighley and, fittingly, Doncaster. The most renowned side of the era, however, was the Dick Kerr Ladies, female employees of a large tramway and railway equipment factory in Preston. Attired by now in genuine football kits, except for hats resembling crocheted tea cosies, they played in numerous matches for charity, winning virtually all of them, drawing large crowds of up to 53,000 and raising around £50,000 for good causes, a sum equivalent to several million pounds today.

But such benevolence did not move the powerful men who sat in the offices of 42, Russell Square, London WC1, the home of the Football Association. On 5th December, 1921, FA chairman Charles Clegg and his fellow council members voted unanimously to ban women from playing football on League grounds. Furthermore, the Council felt, 'impelled to express their strong opinion that the game of football is quite unsuitable for females and ought not to be encouraged.'

In the face of such strong opposition, women's football

faded. Not until November 1969, when 44 women's clubs bandied together to form the Women's Football Association (WFA), did female football reassert itself.

In the early '70s, sexism was still prevalent in Britain. The butt of many a stand-up comic's jokes, women were portrayed in programmes such as *On the Buses, The Benny Hill Show* and the *Carry On* films as either buxom sex objects or haggard old nags. In reality, married women were still generally tied to the kitchen sink. Those who did go out to work found employment as secretaries, cleaners, office clerks and shop assistants notwithstanding the growing awareness of the women's liberation and feminist movements. It is, therefore, surprising that, at that time, the ultra conservative Football Association chose to lift their 50-year ban on women playing football on League grounds. In the same year, Belle Vue Belles took their own historic decision, changing their name to Doncaster Belles as they expanded their horizons beyond their home town. Steadily the Donny lasses climbed the rungs of an expanding ladies scene and, in 1976/77, won their first major trophy, the Notts League title, a regional competition which they dominated for the next dozen years, winning it ten more times before the end of the Eighties.

In the decade of Britain's first female Prime Minister, Margaret Thatcher, the Belles went cup crazy. Packed with England internationals, the team reached six successive WFA Cup Finals between 1983 and 1988, holding the trophy aloft three times (1983-87-88). The Belles were head and shoulders above all other ladies teams in the country. At their heart lay two extraordinary performers, Sheila Edmunds, who played for the club for 25 years, and Gillian Coultard, one of the greatest women players ever to kick a football.

A dynamic, competitive, box-to-box midfielder, in her

heyday Coultard was often described as, 'the Bryan Robson of women's football' and won more England caps (119) than any other player. Small, combative and technically adept, no one could touch her for all-round ability. 'She was a very talented player in every area of the game,' reflects Edmunds. 'She always gave 100 per cent, had a non-stop work rate and her skill and determination won many a game even at the highest level.' A teenage star, Coultard made her England debut just before her 18th birthday against Republic of Ireland in May 1981. She featured in the inaugural FIFA Women's World Cup in Sweden in 1995 and in four Women's European Championships and in a long career turned down several offers to move abroad and turn semi-pro. After playing more than 300 games for the Belles, Coultard, age 37, hung up her boots in 2000. Six years later she was inducted into the English Football Hall of Fame, the sixth female to be so honoured.

Into the Nineties and, while women's football expanded at a pace, one aspect remained constant, Doncaster Belles' near-total dominance. Coached by Paul Edmunds, husband of Sheila, they won the North East Regional League and the North East League Cup in 1989/90 and 1990/91. When the W.F.A launched a National League in 1991/92 they won that too, capping a memorable season by winning the Cup to complete the double, all without losing a single game. In 1993/94 the Belles repeated the feat and, astonishingly, their Cup triumph came in their eleventh final appearance in 12 years.

Success breeds interest and, around this time, the BBC pitched the idea of an end-of-season documentary. The girls agreed to it but in the subsequent programme they were shown to be beer-swilling ladettes who loved a night out, getting completely trashed in a nightclub 38 hours before a cup decider. This was the generation of 'Girl Power' when young women became more emancipated and the lines that once demarcated girls and boys became increasingly blurred.

Back on the pitch, Karen Walker, described as, 'a big, strong, old-fashioned centre-forward who knew where the goal was' quarried out a tonne of goals in the Belles' thick seam of success. A former county standard basketball player, Walker may have lacked finesse and a little pace but her fighting spirit and tremendous ability in the air rattled most defenders. In a glittering career spanning three decades, she plundered a trove of league and cup medals, scored a hat-trick in every round of the 1991/92 W.F.A Cup, including in the final against Red Star Southampton and, between 1987 and 2003, set an England scoring record of 40 goals in 83 international games. Moving to Leeds United Ladies in the 2004 close season, in her last match, the 2006 FA Women's Cup Final against Arsenal at The New Den, she left the pitch to a standing ovation. The following year she was inducted into the English Football Hall of Fame.

Riding high on the crest of a wave, the Belles could not have imagined that they were about to crash on the rocks and that the 1993/94 double would be their last major trophies. Times were changing rapidly and the balance of power was about to tilt towards London. Obeying a FIFA directive to have all football run by a single body, the FA took over the women's game lock, stock and barrel in the summer of 1994. The move was met with a good deal of scepticism, not least because it appeared as though they had been forced into it against their will. 'A lot of people felt very bitter,' reflected Linda Whitehead, secretary of the WFA. 'It wasn't what they wanted ... They [the FA] just ran roughshod over us.' Sheila Edmunds' view was that the FA wanted, 'to control us, to keep us in our place.'

The cynicism was understandable but, as things turned

out, also misplaced. Contrary to initial fears, the men from Lancaster Gate were not indifferent but committed, to the tune of £8 million, to developing the women's game, 'from grassroots to elite level'. Centres of excellence for girls were established nationwide. Sponsors were found for the FA Women's Challenge Cup, FA Women's Premier League and FA Women's League Cup, as the three major competitions were renamed. Sky, BBC, ITV and, from 2011, ESPN struck deals to televise big matches. And, in 1998, Hope Powell was appointed the first female coach of the England national squad, a post she holds to this day.

Women's and girls' football experienced phenomenal growth, the number of participants rocketing by 600 percent in less than a decade. By 2002 it had overhauled netball as the most popular female sport in England. The rapid progress exceeded even the FA's expectations, bringing, as the then chief executive Adam Crozier said, 'women's football onto a higher level'.

As it gained in popularity, so the top end became increasingly commercialised and competitive. Doncaster's tight grip on silverware was wrenched away by a London cartel of Croydon, Millwall, Fulham and Arsenal Ladies. The latter were formed in 1987 with the full backing and support of their parent club. They represented a departure away from older sides like the Belles who, at best, had loose ties with their local men's professional outfit. Nor did it take them long to get into their stride. In 1992/93, the girls from Islington performed the treble, including a 3-0 defeat of the Belles in the cup final and they have lifted at least one of the three top prizes on offer in every season, bar one, since 1996/97.

When Arsenal Ladies won the second of a record ten FA Women's Cups in 1995 they did so by beating Liverpool Ladies 3-2 in the decider. In the losers' line-up that day was a gifted all-round sportswoman from Huddersfield, Clare

'Romper' Taylor. If Coultard can be described as a female Bryan Robson then Taylor could be said to be the fairer sex's equivalent of Denis Compton, a double international who represented England at cricket and football. A nagging medium-paced seamer for Yorkshire Ladies and a solid central defender for first Bronte Ladies of Bradford and then Liverpool, Taylor uniquely appeared in the Women's World Cup in both sports, lifting aloft the trophy in the former at Lords in 1993 and reaching the quarter finals of the round ball equivalent in 1995. A veteran of five cricket World Cups and one of only five women bowlers to have taken 100 one day international wickets, 'Romper' was awarded the MBE in 2000 for services to women's sport.

Their aura of invincibility shattered, Doncaster Belles, who inspired the BBC drama *Playing the Field* (1998-2002) starring James Nesbitt and Ricky Tomlinson, struggled to keep pace. Arsenal Ladies were able to tap into a vast reservoir of resources, attracted bigger gates and sponsorship deals and, in 2002, became the second club after Fulham to turn professional, which enabled them to enlist many of the country's best players.

To their credit, Belles have gallantly fought back and since the turn of the century have come close several times to picking up more silverware. Under the management of first Julie Chipchase and then former Doncaster Rovers and Leeds winger John Buckley they reached the FA Women's Cup Final in 2000 and 2002 (losing to Croydon and Fulham respectively), finished runners up behind Arsenal in the Premier League in 2003/04, and reached the Premier League Cup Final in 2009, only for the ladies from Arsenal to wallop them 5-0.

Amid this flurry of activity, relegation was narrowly avoided in 2005 when club captain Vicky Exley, a woman with more than 50 England caps, scored a lifesaving goal on the last day of the season. Within weeks of their great escape, Doncaster Belles announced a partnership with Doncaster Rovers in a bid to remain competitive at the highest level. The alliance allowed them to play some home matches at Belle Vue, saw them adopt the red and white hoops of Rovers and triggered a name change to Doncaster Rovers Belles. In 2007 both clubs vacated Belle Vue and moved to the £32 million, 15,000-capacity Keepmoat Stadium on Lakeside to the south of Doncaster Racecourse.

Doncaster Rovers Belles undoubtedly went up in the world in terms of facilities and commercial potential but at the same time they lost their pre-eminence in Yorkshire. Leeds Carnegie Ladies, formerly Leeds United Ladies who were formed in 1989, won promotion to the Women's Premier League in 2001 and have since then established themselves as one of the best sides in the country. Boasting a host of international players, the team, which changed its name after striking a big money sponsorship deal with Leeds Metropolitan University in 2007, has reached four cup finals since 2006, finally lifting a first major trophy in February 2010, when they beat Everton Ladies 3-1 in the Premier League Cup Final.

The victory was bitter sweet, however. The future of the club is seriously in doubt after Leeds Met confirmed it could not bankroll them to the tune of £250,000 per year to compete in a new full-time professional Women's Super League. Due to be launched in March 2011 and designed to halt a recent drain of talent to the USA, the Super League will at least feature Doncaster Rovers Belles, one of eight clubs who have entered, even though they are among the current Premier League's poorer relations. That Leeds Carnegie might even cease to exist in an ultra-competitive form is desperately sad, especially as they have proved themselves more than capable of challenging for honours.

The women's game has evolved tremendously in the 40 years since those Yorkshire lasses selling lottery tickets on the Belle Vue terraces decided to have a kick-about. There are now some 7,000 teams, including Sheffield Wednesday Ladies, Huddersfield Town Ladies, Hull City Women, Leeds City Vixens and Barnsley Ladies, and more than 150,000 females of all ages competing at every level. The standard of women's football rivals that of the men's in terms of skill if not physicality. Attendances have grown to the extent that cup finals and international matches attract crowds of up to 20,000 and more. England players, including Carnegie's spiky-haired, effervescent winger Sue Smith (80 caps and counting), now receive central contracts worth £16,000 per year, small fry compared to what the men earn but a huge step forward from the days when the Belles paid for everything out of their own pockets and got changed in the backseat of their cars.

It is doubtful that the women's game will ever compete with that of the men's in terms of popularity, status and financial rewards but female footballers have come of age, they are no longer a laughing stock. Perceptions and attitudes have changed, respect has been earned and few have done it better than the trailblazing, famous Doncaster Belles.

20

The Glam And The Punk

THE 1970s was when glam rock collided with punk at football grounds. On the pitch, glamorous, long-haired Ziggy Stardusts with personalities as big as Elton John's platform boots and private lives as colourful as the bright and breezy kits they wore, entertained crowds with displays of outrageous individual skill. Off it, snarling youths, often fitting the stereotypical bovver boy image of skinhead, tight jeans and Doc Marten boots, got their teenage kicks from having a right old punch up on the terraces. The age of the football hooligan had arrived.

At first glance nothing appears to connect the creative and carefree spirits of George Best, Tony Currie, Frank Worthington, Stan Bowles, Rodney Marsh, Duncan McKenzie and their ilk with the brawling Alpha males who created 'Anarchy in the UK' on Saturday afternoons. One camp put the fun back into football; the other viciously snatched it away. But these two diametrically opposed groups were tied together by a common bond - a disdain for rules and authority.

Of all the so-called maverick entertainers who graced the game in the period, Tony Currie - a shaggy haired, skilful midfield schemer for the Uniteds of Sheffield and Leeds - was, after Best, probably the most naturally gifted. An effervescent magician around whom the England team should have been built, he had a box of tricks that Ali Bongo would have been proud of. Big and strong but as balanced as a trapeze artist, 'TC', as the fans nicknamed him, bamboozled the best of them, effortlessly switching play with a pinpoint diagonal pass or throwing in a subtle feint here or a snaky body-swerve there to glide past defenders. He scored plenty of goals too, over a hundred of them, ranging from delicate chips to screaming pile-drivers. One typically brilliant effort, in which he waltzed through a bewildered West Ham United defence, came on his 300th appearance for Sheffield United in March 1975 and had *Match of the Day* commentator John Motson purring: 'A quality goal from a quality player'.

That such a quality player won only 17 caps for England is scandalous. A knee injury in the early months of 1974 and loss of form during the 1975/76 season were contributory factors, but the biggest reason for his lack of international exposure was Don Revie. The former Leeds boss mistrusted improvisers like Currie who had flair and imagination in abundance but not so much inclination to track back or to race around the pitch like headless chickens. 'I believe I'm a naturally gifted player - if that doesn't sound immodest,' Currie said, looking back in 1978. 'But over the years I've been left out of the England side in favour of donkeys in terms of vision and football skill.'

His fabulous attributes were appreciated better at club level and nowhere was he idolised more than at Bramall Lane. 'TC' was worth the admission price alone. A Londoner by birth, he arrived in South Yorkshire as a precocious 18-

year-old from Watford for £26,500 in February 1968, a successor to Alan Birchenall, another colourful character beloved by Blades fans, who had joined Chelsea the previous November. Currie promptly scored on his debut against Tottenham. It was a case of 'the King is dead, long live the King'.

Currie's captivating performances had the Shoreham Street boys singing his praises while his clowning around had them roaring with laughter. He was known to blow kisses and wave at fans while dribbling with the ball and in a 5-0 thrashing of Arsenal at Bramall Lane, in September 1973, he sat on the ball, goading Alan Ball, who had taunted United in similar vein during their previous encounter at Highbury, to come and get it off him. Then there was that kiss with former favourite Birchenall in the final home match of the 1974/75 season. Ending up on their backsides following a tussle for the ball, Currie and Birchenall, now with Leicester City, exchanged a mock peck on the lips to 'kiss and make up'. It was pure showmanship but nevertheless it managed to raise the hackles of traditionalists - what was wrong with a firm handshake? Questions were even raised in Parliament.

Currie was the fulcrum of a Sheffield United side which won promotion from Division Two in 1970/71 and punched above their weight to finish sixth in Division One in 1974/75, missing out on a place in Europe by one point. It was during this period that Currie made an inauspicious start to his international career, substituted on his debut against Northern Ireland in May 1972. The following June he played in the infamous 1-1 draw against Poland at Wembley which cost England a World Cup place and legendary manager Alf Ramsey his job.

At Bramall Lane Currie developed an almost telepathic understanding with Alan Woodward, a powerful winger with a booming shot who effortlessly latched on to his raking passes. 'TC' and 'Woody', the holder of a post-war club record 175 goals in 595 games, went together like strawberries and cream. The rest of the team was just as sweet. Centre back Eddie Colquhoun played nine times for Scotland. Free-scoring left winger Gil Reece pulled on the Wales jersey 29 times. Alan Hodgkinson, a short but reliable goalkeeper who won five England caps in the late 50s, brought the curtain down on a long and fulfilling career. Striker Billy Dearden, a former plumber from Chester, scored 61 goals in 175 League appearances. Buccaneering right back Len Badger, from Darnall, hardly missed a game between 1964 and 1975 and gained 13 England Under-23s caps without ever being selected for the full national side. Mexborough-born Geoff Salmons made 199 appearances alongside Currie in midfield before being sold to Stoke City for £200,000 in 1974. And when not playing for United, left back Ted Hemsley turned out for Worcestershire CCC as a steady middle order batsman, scoring over 13,000 runs in 20 seasons.

Hemsley was one of the last men to combine top flight football with first-class cricket and is a reminder of the strong bonds that once held the two sports together, dating back to the formation of Sheffield FC in 1857. Another to play soccer and cricket professionally was Chris Balderstone, from Longwood, who entered sporting folklore when he turned out for Doncaster Rovers and Leicestershire on the same day in September 1975. In the afternoon the all-rounder scored 51 not out for the Foxes against Derbyshire at Chesterfield. Then he dashed off to Belle Vue to help Donny grind out a 1-1 draw with Brentford in the evening. The next day 'Baldy' returned to the crease and completed a well deserved, if rather exhausting, century.

Over the years there have been several Yorkshiremen

who have made the grade in both the summer and winter games, including 'Nudger' Needham, Brian Close and Ken Taylor. The best of the lot, though, is surely Willie Watson, a double international from Bolton-on-Dearne. The son of Billy Watson of the great Huddersfield teams of the 1920s, Willie was a cultured wing half for Huddersfield and Sunderland and a stylish left-handed batsman for Yorkshire and Leicestershire. In the early 1950s he won four international caps at football and played 23 Tests, including three when England, captained by Len Hutton, regained the Ashes in 1953.

The uncoupling of football and cricket gathered pace in the county when Yorkshire CCC played their last match at Bramall Lane in the summer of 1973. The old pavilion was left stranded as the £1 million South Stand went up on the cricket square to finally make the Lane a four-sided soccer stadium. The new grandstand was opened ahead of the 1975/76 season, a campaign in which Tony Currie's form deserted him - he was even substituted for the first time - and United, glued to the foot of the table after losing 18 of their opening 22 fixtures, suffered relegation.

With a record of 66 goals in 376 games, 'TC' left Sheffield in the summer of 1976. He travelled up the M1 and signed for Leeds for £250,000, inheriting the No. 10 shirt from Anderlecht-bound Duncan 'Magic' McKenzie, another fully paid-up member of football's 'Culture Club' who Brian Clough signed during his tempestuous 44-day reign as manager. Over the next three years, Currie played arguably the best football of his career and was voted 'Player of the Year' by Leeds fans in 1978. The post-Revie/Bremner Leeds side boasted some marvellous talent - Currie, Arthur Graham, Brian Flynn, Paul Hart, Trevor Cherry and a recuperated Eddie Gray - but they could not add any more silverware to the club's trophy cabinet. Three losing semi-finals (FA Cup 1977, League Cup 1978, 1979) and a fifth placed finish in Division One in 1978/79 was as good as it got.

Currie's flagging international career was rekindled by Ron Greenwood, the new boss of England, who threw him in against Brazil at Wembley in April 1978. 'TC' responded with a vintage display which moved Greenwood to say: 'Tony showed skill, composure and controlled the game ... He outdid the Brazilians in both strength and flair.' Picked nine more times in the next fourteen months, scoring twice, including a 30-yard corker against Wales, Currie's England career came to a permanent close in August 1979 when he joined Second Division QPR, who he captained in the 1982 FA Cup Final against Spurs. It is of interest to note that after his recall to the national team England did not lose a match when Currie played, a statistic which suggests that had Revie had more faith in his maverick spirit, then England may have qualified for the 1978 World Cup in Argentina.

Another victim of Revie's aversion to unconventional players was Frank Worthington, a swashbuckling striker from Shelf, near Halifax. Embarking on an extremely long football career with Huddersfield Town in November 1966, he had little respect for managers like Revie who, he said, 'seemed determined to squeeze out individual flair'. Tall and with a mane of dark hair and huge sideburns like Elvis, his great musical hero, Worthington won just eight England caps, six of them in 1974 when Joe Mercer was the caretaker manager.

'Worthy' was superficially a languid player but beneath the seemingly lazy style and off-the-cuff creativity there lay plenty of substance. His shooting was often spectacular, his ball control a marvel - a quality which enabled him to 'kill' the ball instantly and set up a team-mate with a subtle pass or flick - and he could create vital space in a packed penalty area to have a pop at goal. No one scores 234 league and cup goals without having something special about them.

A born entertainer - best illustrated by his strike for Bolton against Ipswich in April 1979 when he juggled with the ball with his back to goal, flicked it over a defender's head, swivelled and volleyed it into the net - Worthington was as renowned for his off-field antics. Whether quaffing champagne, smoking pot or entertaining pretty girls - a Swedish teenager and her mother were apparently one of his many sexual conquests - he lead an eventful and not so private life. In 1972 a dream move to Liverpool, then managed by ex-Terriers' boss Bill Shankly, fell through after he failed his medical because of high blood pressure, brought on, so said the doctors, by too much sex. Frank Worthington could not help himself. The draw of the playboy lifestyle was irresistible, his ardour untameable. As he once said: 'George Best wants every girl to love him. I just wanted them to go to bed with me.' Not for nothing was his best selling autobiography entitled *One Hump or Two?*

Worthington's jack-the-lad image and his magical ability to do whatever he wanted with a leather ball made him a big hit with the younger generation. He was an important member of the Huddersfield team that enjoyed a magnificent run to the League Cup semi final in 1967/68 only to see their dream Wembley date with neighbours Leeds United crushed by Arsenal, 6-3 on aggregate. In 1969/70 Worthington bagged 18 League goals for a dynamic and youthful side which, under captain Jimmy Nicholson, a former Busby Babe and Town's most-capped player with 31 international appearances for Northern Ireland, positively sprinted to the Second Division Championship and returned the club to the top division after 14 years in the wilderness.

Thereafter, Huddersfield took the adage 'build from the back' to extremes. In the 1970/71 season they conceded five less goals than Wolves who qualified for the UEFA Cup and yet finished eleven places below them because of their shot-shy attack. In the following year Town let in fewer goals than Manchester United but were relegated in bottom place after pilfering only 27 of their own, the worst scoring record of any demoted team since Woolwich Arsenal in 1912/13.

Such a defensive mindset was not exactly conducive to Worthington's *laissez-faire* style of play although, interestingly, his older brothers Bob and Dave both played professionally as stoppers. Having scored 48 goals in 193 games for The Terriers he joined Leicester City for £100,000 in August 1972. So began a nomadic life in which, playing on into his 40s, he clocked up 757 League appearances and turned out for umpteen teams home and abroad, League and non-league, including Leeds (15 goals in 35 games, 1982), Guiseley (1989-91) and his hometown Halifax Town (player-coach, 1991). As with Currie, he was treated somewhat shabbily by his country. Had the pair been born French or Dutch then the selectors would have fallen over backwards in their desire to pick them for the national XI.

Following Worthington out of Huddersfield in the summer of 1972 were Trevor Cherry and Roy Ellam, the Beauty and the Beast, one a polished defender, the other an ungainly yet effective enforcer. Their solid performances in the heart of the Town back four prompted Don Revie to shell out a combined fee of £100,000 to bring them to the FA Cup holders. Ellam - christened 'Kipper Feet' by Terriers' fans who loved his robust if awkward style - proved a misfit and soon returned to Leeds Road. Cherry, however, went from strength to strength. Converted into a left back to cover for the injured Terry Cooper, he won a League Championship medal with Leeds in 1974, became club captain in 1976 and collected 27 England caps in the late 70s.

Shorn of their three best players, Huddersfield Town

went downhill fast. Twelve months later they suffered a second relegation and two years after that they finished bottom of Division Three; First to Fourth Division in three seasons. Attendances crashed to below 3,000 in 1974/75 when, only a few short years before, the stadium had rocked to packed gates of more than 40,000 for the visits of Leeds and Manchester United.

Although they plummeted farther and faster than the rest Huddersfield were not the only Yorkshire club to hit upon hard times in the mid-70s. With the nation beset by miners' strikes, fuel shortages and power cuts, it was as if somebody had turned out the light on the county's football. In 1976, ten years after appearing in the FA Cup Final, Sheffield Wednesday escaped the ignominy of relegation to Division Four by the skin of their teeth, beating already doomed Southend United 2-1 at Hillsborough in the last match of the season. In the same campaign, Sheffield United were dumped out of the First Division; three years later they suffered demotion to the third tier of the Football League for the first time in their illustrious history.

Bucking the trend, for a while at least, were York City. Kitted out in an iconic maroon and white strip with a distinctive big 'Y' on the shirt fronts, they broke virgin territory by reaching the Second Division in 1974 for the first and only time in their history. But then they too slipped back into the familiar surroundings of the Fourth Division. Frequenting the basement with them at one time or another were Bradford City and Barnsley, their past glories but a hazy memory, Rotherham United, Halifax Town and Doncaster Rovers. Even Leeds, one of the dominant forces in Europe at the start of the decade, took an almighty tumble after Revie left the club. Three semi finals in as many years might have been viewed with green eyes by some of their county brethren, but for United it represented an uncomfortable fall from grace.

No Yorkshire club suffered more in the Seventies, though, than Bradford Park Avenue. Anchored at the bottom of Division Four for the third time in a row at the end of the 1969/70 season, their abysmal record during those years of woe included 87 defeats with 284 goals conceded. The writing was not so much on the wall as plastered all over it. Forced to seek re-election for a fourth successive time, they lost the vote 17-31 to Cambridge United. After swimming around the Football League for more than 60 years Avenue plunged into the humble backwaters of the Northern Premier League.

Bradford left behind some lasting achievements. They scored 100 or more goals in a season three times on the trot between 1925 and 1928. Locally-born Albert Geldard, a nippy outside right who later played for England and won the cup with Everton in 1933, became the youngest player to appear in League football when he made his debut, aged 15 years and 158 days against Millwall in September 1929. In December 1942 they spanked Bradford City 10-0 at Valley Parade in a never-to-be-forgotten Wool City derby. Six years later, almost 83,000 fans watched them hold Manchester United, the eventual winners, to a 1-1 draw in the FA Cup at Maine Road as Old Trafford was still out of action after being bombed during the war. On 25th April, 1964, Jim Fryatt scored the fastest League goal on record, after four seconds against Tranmere Rovers, and youthful striker Kevin Hector, who was destined to win the championship with Derby County and play for England, lead the Football League's scoring charts with 44 goals in 1965/66.

To keep the wolves from the door, Bradford Park Avenue sold their antiquated ground to a property company in April 1973. Matters were compounded for their dwindling fan base by a move to Valley Parade, home of their archrival Bradford City. The final home game of the 1973/74 season drew a miserable gate of 698 people, hardly enough to finance debts of £57,000. Shareholders were left with little option. On 3rd May, 1974 at a special meeting at Bradford's Midland Hotel, the club was liquidated. Proud old Bradford Park Avenue ceased to exist.

Happily, that was not the end of the story. A dedicated band of enthusiasts resurrected the name and for the next decade played under its banner as amateurs in Bradford's Sunday League scene. In 1988 they disbanded to allow the 'old club' to reform which then joined the West Riding County Amateur League. Several changes of address - they now play at Horsfall Athletics Stadium - and promotions later, Bradford PA currently compete in the Unibond League Premier Division. In 2009/10 they missed out on elevation to the Blue Square Conference North, finishing one point behind champions Guiseley and then losing to Boston United in the play-off final.

While Bradford lurched from one crisis to the next, Scarborough FC made big waves beside the seaside. Formed in 1879 by members of the town's cricket team, in the 1970s they underwent a remarkable transformation to become one of the big hitters of non-league football. They regularly finished in the top-five of the Northern Premier League but it was in cup competitions that they really excelled. Four times they reached the FA Trophy Final at Wembley (1973-75-76-77), triumphing on three occasions and twice reached the third round of the FA Cup. In January 1976, *Match of the Day* cameras and nearly 10,000 excited Seadogs were present at the Athletic Ground to watch 'Boro narrowly lose 2-1 to Crystal Palace and, in January 1978, a crowd of more than 22,000 at the Goldstone Ground saw them lose 3-0 to Brighton & Hove Albion who would themselves reach the final five years later.

The blue touch paper of success was lit by a local lad, Colin Appleton, the ex-Leicester City skipper who played in two Wembley cup finals in the Sixties. Appointed player-manager in August 1969, he went close to guiding Scarborough to the 1980/81 Alliance Premier League title and possible election to the Football League before being poached by Hull City in June 1982. Star striker was Jeff Barmby, father of England international Nick, who scored 156 goals during those years of plenty while Harry Dunn was their most loyal servant, twice voted 'Clubman of the Year' and who played in a colossal 901 matches for the club between 1965 and 1986.

The quaint Victorian resort conjured up images of fish and chips, buckets and spades, sun, sea and sand, but elsewhere football was growing ugly. Young men, full of bravado, beer and the tribal instinct, created 'aggro' throughout the country. 'They get too emotionally involved. They support from the heart and this sort of thing happens,' said Leeds boss Jimmy Armfield, with massive understatement, after a section of his club's fans trashed Parc des Princes, Paris during the 1975 European Cup Final. Football clubs responded to the terrace charges, pitch invasions and vandalism by segregating the 'animals' in iron fenced cages, an understandable but drastic measure which had tragic consequences at Hillsborough in 1989. In the Seventies, black players were ritually targeted and humiliated by the mob and chants were often aggressive and riddled with invective. 'You're going home in a Yorkshire ambulance' was a threat which, all too often, became real. Peaceable supporters, unsurprisingly, grew disillusioned. What was the point of risking life and limb every Saturday for the sake of a game of football? Hooliganism and declining success caused attendances in Yorkshire to fall sharply, a slide which was to deepen in the Eighties. The brief flourishing of charismatic footballers like Tony Currie and Frank Worthington was sadly at an end but that was the least of anybody's worries for the game was about to get a whole lot worse.

21

Foreign Invasion

25th JUNE, 1978 and amid snowstorms of tickertape and wild celebrations, Argentina beat favourites Holland 3-1 to win the World Cup on home soil. A fortnight later, Tottenham Hotspur pulled off a sensational double transfer, paying £750,000 to buy two key members of the Argentina squad, Osvaldo Ardiles and Ricardo Villa.

Ardiles, a small and gaunt looking master craftsman whose performances in midfield were pivotal in his nation's success on that wonderful night in Buenos Aires, was to become a hugely popular figure at White Hart Lane. The bearded Villa, a non-playing substitute in the final, was a tall and powerful midfield hustler who won renown for scoring a spectacular solo goal against Manchester City in the 1981 FA Cup Final replay at Wembley.

The groundbreaking transfers which lifted a long standing ban on overseas players caused great excitement and many hundreds of column inches to be written. 'It was as if the janitor had gone to buy a tin of paint and had come back with a Velasquez,' commented *The Guardian* in colourful tones. A little known fact about the deal, however, is that it was brokered by Harry Haslam, the 56-year-old manager of Sheffield United. Arriving at Bramall Lane from Luton Town in January 1978, the cheery Mancunian immediately set up a scouting system in Argentina, an unusual and forward thinking step at a time when English football was still very insular, an attitude reinforced by its clubs' successes in European competitions. There seemed to be no need to scour beyond the British Isles for talent, but home grown flair players like Tony Currie and Frank Worthington were becoming increasingly hard to find. And so some enlightened people within the game, like 'Happy Harry', decided the time had come to look further afield.

Ably assisted by Danny Bergara, a Uruguayan by birth, Haslam identified a group of young Latin footballers who he thought could bring back the razzmatazz to Bramall Lane which had been lacking since Currie's departure to Leeds in 1976. Top of his shopping list was a precocious 17-year-old on the books of Argentinos Juniors. So determined was he to get his hands on the barrel-chested boy wonder with the golden feet and dead eye for goal that he agreed a staggering fee of £400,000 with the club and the Argentine FA. His hopes were crushed, however, by a cash-strapped board which baulked at paying such a huge sum for an unknown teenager from some foreign land. After all, Yorkshire-born England star Kevin Keegan had moved from Liverpool to SV Hamburg in June 1977 for only £100,000 more. So it was that the little kid with the massive talent called Diego Armando Maradona slipped through the Sheffield dredging net.

Winning the World Cup sent the valuations on Ardiles' and Villa's heads shooting through the roof. Haslam could no longer afford to buy them either so he gave Spurs boss

Keith Burtenshaw the lead in and turned his own attentions and limited transfer kitty to another rising star, 23-year-old Alejandro 'Alex' Sabella.

Nicknamed *El Mago* ('The Magician') for his captivating ball skills and *Pachorra* ('Slowcoach') for his unhurried style, the uncapped Sabella was beginning to make a name for himself as a clever, if laidback, midfielder with River Plate of Buenos Aires, one of South America's top sides. The deal was rubberstamped on 19th July, 1978 at a far more reasonable cost to Sheffield United of £160,000. Sabella's unveiling was greeted with a mixture of surprise, enthusiasm and scepticism in South Yorkshire. A nice shiny adornment to the Sheffield United side, maybe, but could this short and slender Latino hack it on the heavy quagmire pitches of an English winter? Only time would tell.

In that cool summer of 1978, Sabella was part of a foreign raid which also included left back Alberto Tarantini, a bubble-haired bad boy of Argentine football who was snapped up by Birmingham City; Dutch Master Arnold Muhren, lured to Ipswich Town by Bobby Robson, and Poland captain Kazimierz Deyna, who joined Manchester City.

English football had not seen the like before. There had been the odd overseas player here and there in the past, usually from some far flung outpost of the Commonwealth, such as Arthur Wharton (Ghana) and Albert Johanneson (South Africa). Hull City gave Danish international Viggo Jensen, a versatile player who could do a decent job anywhere on the field, a regular run out in the 1950s. Then there were Chilean brothers Jorge ('George') and Eduardo ('Ted') Robledo who made their Football League bows with Barnsley in the 1940s and won the Cup with Newcastle United in 1951 and '52 - George scoring the winner against Arsenal in the latter final - before returning to their homeland to link up with Colo Colo of Santiago. The Robledos could, however, be described as adopted Tykes for their mother was a Yorkshire girl and they were brought up in the Dearne Valley after emigrating as small boys from Chile before the war. This latest wave was completely different, one which thirty years later has spawned football squads resembling meetings of the United Nations.

Wearing no shin pads and with his No.10 shirt habitually hanging out, Sabella made his debut for Sheffield United against Leyton Orient on 18th August, 1978. If the fans were expecting a miracle worker then they were sorely disappointed. What they got instead was the equivalent of a misfiring Ferrari. All the parts were in place for the Argentinian ace to excel but he just could not get going properly. A massive dose of culture shock, both on and off the pitch, was at the root of the problem but it did not help that he was a big fish in a small pond. The United squad he joined was a pale shadow of its former self and an ageing Alan Woodward would shortly join a mini exodus of British players to the up-and-coming North American Soccer League.

On occasions, Sabella showed what a class player he could be but he flattered to deceive, often going missing in games, his fragile skills swamped by the hustle and bustle of the English Second Division. United continued to slide and at the end of the 1978/79 season they were relegated to Division Three, their fate sealed by defeat against Leicester City in the final home game, a match marred by crowd trouble.

That Alex Sabella should end up competing against the likes of Chesterfield, Bury and Exeter was a depressing sight. For all his inconsistency, he was extremely gifted and his talents deserved a far bigger stage. All the same, he and his team-mates made a good stab of the situation and by

Christmas they were sitting proudly at the top of the table. An instant return to Division Two beckoned. But then they visited Hillsborough on Boxing Day and, in front of a heaving crowd of 49,309 - a Third Division record - were walloped 4-0. All of a sudden the wind went out of their sails. Cast into the doldrums once more, United ended the season in mid-table while Wednesday, who had been struggling up until that derby massacre, went into overdrive and won promotion.

Up to their necks in debt, Sheffield United cashed in on their biggest asset. The spluttering Sabella, scorer of eight goals in 76 League games, was sold to Leeds for £400,000 in the 1980 close season. The sum gave the club a tidy profit but it was, nevertheless, small change in what was by now a spiralling transfer market, in which Trevor Francis became British football's first £1 million player when he moved from Birmingham City to Nottingham Forest in February 1979.

Blades fans were left with the overriding feeling of frustration. Sabella was capable of producing sparkling moments of pure magic but they were fleeting and certainly insufficient to arrest the club's decline. At Elland Road the feeling was less frustration more utter disbelief as the little Argentinian flopped big style. 'Samba with Sabella!' proclaimed hastily printed T-shirts but failing once more to adequately fill the No.10 shirt vacated by the sublime Currie, he turned out for Leeds on just 23 occasions.

In December 1981, shortly before the outbreak of the Falklands War, Sabella returned to his homeland and joined Estudiantes de La Plata with the chant, 'what a waste of money' ringing in his ears. Comforted by familiar surroundings, he readily produced the red-hot form that had been so lacking in his three years in Yorkshire, helping his new club to win back-to-back National Championships (1982-83) and winning a call up to the national side.

Blades fans might care to ponder what might have happened to their club had chunky Maradona come to Bramall Lane rather than the slim-line Sabella. Would the greatest footballer since Pele have struggled to fit in to a new way of life and a whole different style of play as Alex had? Or would he have been a roaring success, like Ardiles and, to a lesser extent, Villa? Considering Maradona almost single-handedly propelled Argentina to further World Cup success in 1986 and transformed Napoli from football donkeys into thoroughbred Italian champions in the late-80s, one suspects the latter.

A few years later, ahead of the 1986/87 season, the rumour mill in West Yorkshire ground out an amazing story. Leeds United, then mired in the Second Division, were on the verge of making an audacious bid for the world's best player. A few weeks earlier a slyly punched goal and an amazing dribble from Maradona contentiously knocked England out of the World Cup in Mexico. In light of his 'Hand of God' con trick and on the back of jingoistic feelings aroused by war with Argentina over the Falkland Islands, Diego Maradona was, in many English supporters' eyes, Public Enemy Number One, a fat, big-headed, cheating bastard.

In Leeds, however, there was a palpable buzz about the place. Speculation and gossip, egged on by some carefully chosen words from club director, Bill Fotherby, was rife. But in the end nothing came of the wild proposal. Leeds were flat broke, they could hardly afford to finance domestic transfers let alone the megabucks it would have cost them to buy Maradona.

The indifferent performances of Sabella and Tarantini put English managers off South American players. Their gaze turned instead across the North Sea to Scandinavia and Holland where footballers were perceived to have more of the attributes considered necessary to succeed in the hurly burly of British football, not least dependability and a willingness to 'get stuck in'. There was still no huge influx but protagonists of the calibre of Frans Thijssen (Ipswich), Jan Molby (Liverpool), Jesper Olsen (Manchester United) and Johnny Metgod (Nottingham Forest) left indelible marks on the English game.

The first foreigners after Sabella to make any kind of impression in Yorkshire were two Vikings for Sheffield Wednesday. Siggi Jonsson, a midfielder from Iceland, arrived in February 1985 and played 67 games over four years. He was followed by Swedish international right back Roland Nilsson, a £375,000 buy from IFK Göteborg in December 1989. An instant hit, he played more than 150 matches and appeared in three FA and League Cup finals over the next four and a half years. Homesickness prompted his return to Sweden at the end of the 1993/94 season, much to the disappointment of Owls supporters who hail him the best in position ever to play for their club.

Joining Nilsson at Hillsborough were John Harkes, an American midfielder of Scottish descent who also played in those Wembley finals, and an arrogant and impetuous French striker with an unenviable reputation as an *enfant terrible* - Eric Cantona. The ill-disciplined but gifted 25-year-old France international came to Sheffield on a one week trial in January 1992 with a litany of fines, fall-outs and suspensions trailing in his wake. He wished to resurrect a career which, in a characteristic fit of pique, he had jacked in the previous month after the French Football Federation banned him for two months - one month as punishment for throwing the ball at a referee, the other for calling each of the committee members at his hearing an idiot. He was worth having a punt on but when Owls boss Trevor Francis told him that he wanted to extend the trial period by a further week the moody Frenchman walked out ... straight into the squad of Yorkshire rivals Leeds United.

His coupling with Howard Wilkinson, the Leeds manager, seemed a very odd marriage - the uncontrollable law unto himself and the single-minded disciplinarian who demanded nothing less than complete obedience. The honeymoon period was serene. Cantona, a French cavalier among roundheads, added a certain *je ne sais quoi* to the Leeds team at a critical stage of the season. He lifted everyone's spirits, not least those of the fans who took the Marseille maverick to their hearts. The Kop resonated to the tunes of, 'Ooh, Aah, Cantona!' and *La Marseillaise* at every home game. Three goals in 15 appearances, one an outstanding volley against Chelsea from an acute angle after twice juggling the ball over the head of a bemused Paul Elliott, went a long way in helping the Whites to snatch the First Division championship from pacesetters Manchester United on the penultimate weekend of the season.

The love affair did not last long, though. Cantona's last memorable act was scoring a hat-trick in a 4-3 victory over Liverpool in the Charity Shield at Wembley in August 1992. Wilkinson soon concluded that the Frenchman was a disruptive influence in the dressing room while Eric claimed his boss could not handle a strong personality like himself and was jealous of the way the fans worshipped him. In a hastily arranged divorce settlement worth a paltry £1.2 million, Wilkinson bade his troublesome striker *au revoir* in November 1992, throwing him into the grateful arms of Sir Alex Ferguson at Manchester United. Leeds fans were outraged by Cantona's willingness to hop into bed with their hated enemy and many have never forgiven their old idol's treachery.

With his shirt collar ritually turned up, 'King Eric' ruled imperiously at Old Trafford. His showmanship, inventiveness, technical brilliance and uncanny ability at finding the net from seemingly impossible positions laid a foundation stone for the Red Devils to dominate English football. In 1996 he became the fourth foreigner to be voted 'Footballer of the Year'; since then only four Englishmen have won the award, a clear sign of the changing times.

Controversy dogged Cantona. No stranger to the red card, in 1993 he was fined £1,000 by the FA for spitting at a Leeds fan during an electrically-charged return to Elland Road. In 1995 he received a record eight-month worldwide ban and 120 hours community service for infamously kung-fu kicking a jeering Crystal Palace fan. The wild but entertaining Frenchman brought the curtain down on an eventful career in 1997, turning his talents instead to acting. It was a well chosen profession for a man who on the football pitch had played the role of pantomime villain to perfection.

By the time he left the stage the sporadic foreign incursions had become a full scale invasion. Players touched down from all corners of the globe. They came in the name of money and lots of it. The formation of the FA Premier League in 1992 and the multi-million pound TV and sponsorship deals it entailed, at a stroke, made member clubs richer than ever before. For the first time they could compete in the global transfer market with the glitterati of European football, a situation made still easier by the Bosman ruling of 1995 which gave players greater freedom to move between EU states. Gorging themselves fat on some of the world's best players, Premier League clubs reversed the trend that had previously seen great British products like Gary Lineker, Chris Waddle, Glenn Hoddle and Paul Gascoigne exported to continental Europe. Instead, Italians, Frenchmen and Spaniards chose to slum it in England, tempted across the Channel by the pots of gold on offer in football's new *El Dorado*.

In Yorkshire, Leeds and Sheffield Wednesday used the extraordinary pulling power of the Premier League to scoop up a veritable pick 'n' mix of international stars, none more popular than Lucas 'Chief' Radebe, a black South African who reigned supreme in the heart of the Leeds defence and wore the captain's armband with distinction for more than a decade. Many easy on the eye performers turned up in Yorkshire, such as Brazilian striker Marcelo who scored 32 goals in 61 games for Sheffield United (1997-99); Benito Carbone, from Italy, who lent a touch of silky class to the Wednesday and Bradford City attacks either side of the millennium; Aussie pin-up Harry Kewell, an exceptionally quick and strong running winger for Leeds who had a penchant for scoring spectacular goals and Sheffield United's Paul Peschisolido, an instinctive striker from Scarborough, Canada.

Even the traditional role of the big 'barge 'em over and bang 'em in' centre-forward was taken on by non-Brits. Norwegians Jan-Aage Fjortoft and Jostein Flo starred for Sheffield United and Barnsley; Ghanaian Tony Yeboah wowed the Leeds crowds with his thunderbolt shooting, picking up the 'Goal of the Season' award in 1995/96 for a wonder strike against Wimbledon and Mark Viduka, a hulk of a Croat-Australian, hammered in 59 goals in 130 League games for Leeds following a £6 million move from Celtic in 2000. In recent years, Sheffield United has gone one step further than merely recruiting foreign mercenaries by establishing global links with Ferencvaros (Hungary), Chengdu Blades (China), Royal White Star (Belgium) and Central Coast Mariners (Australia) to nurture young talent across the world.

The sheer number of foreigners in the English game has had, say the critics, an adverse affect on the England national team. What cannot be denied, though, is how foreign players as a whole have improved the quality of English domestic football immeasurably, fashioning what was once a rather drab lump of coal into a sparkling diamond, at least in the Premier League. They have been aided and abetted in their endeavours by foreign managers whose continental outlook on tactics, team formations, fitness regimes and diets has had a profound effect upon the game which is now quicker, slicker and more skilful than at any time in living memory.

Not every foreign player has been a resounding success. One man who can challenge 'King Eric' in the bad boy stakes is Paulo Di Canio, a self-proclaimed fascist who Nazi saluted right-wing fans when he played for Lazio. The Italian hot-head was, like Cantona, a fabulously talented schemer but, in September 1998, he was punished with an 11-match ban for pushing referee Paul Alcock to the ground after he was sent off playing for Sheffield Wednesday against Arsenal at Hillsborough.

The performances of another Wednesday striker, Darko Kovacevic, and those of tubby Swede Tomas Brolin for Leeds exasperated the crowds at Hillsborough and Elland Road respectively. Others made the fans' blood boil. Step forward Belgian forward Gilles De Bilde, another one on Wednesday's books, whose sneering, 'could not care less' attitude incensed Owls supporters and was deemed a primary factor in the club's relegation to Division One in 2000. For a decade, foreign mercenaries had helped Wednesday remain seated at the top table of English football; now they cost them their prized place in the Premier League.

Yet more, like Holland striker Jimmy Floyd Hasselbaink, were seen as greedy. Initially a big hit with Leeds fans, bagging 42 goals in two seasons, the 'Flying Dutchman' lost their goodwill when he threatened to go on strike in a row over a new contract. Leeds offered him a five-year deal worth a massive £6.5 million but it was not enough for Hasselbaink who wanted £7.5 million and not a penny less. When the board rebuffed his demands he put in a transfer request and refused to play again for the Whites, making a mockery of his agent's claims that, 'Jimmy loves the fans … He would have loved to have stayed at the club'. In the end Hasselbaink got his way. He was sold to Atletico Madrid for £12 million in August 1999. It was player power gone mad. A year later he was back in England with Chelsea and the reception he received whenever he revisited Elland Road was colder than an Arctic blizzard.

Then there was Macedonian striker Georgi Hristov, signed by Barnsley in 1997 for a club record £1.5 million, who told a Belgrade sports magazine that, 'The local girls are far uglier than the ones back in Skopje. Our women are much prettier. Besides, they don't drink as much beer as Barnsley girls.' Not the best way to win friends and influence people.

For good or bad, there is no sign of the foreign influx letting up. The days when Yorkshire clubs fielded sides jam packed with names and characters like Wilf Copping, Ernie Blenkinsop and Sam Wadsworth are long gone. Hull City's rainbow squad for 2009/10 was representative of the Premier League: Geovanni (Brazil), Boateng (Ghana/Holland), Zayatte (Guinea), Vennegoor of Hesselink (Holland), Altidore (USA), Mouyokolo and Mendy (France), Garcia (Australia), Ghilas (Algeria), Olofinjana (Nigeria), Sonko (Senegal), Halmosi (Hungary) and Zaki (Egypt).

Overseas players have percolated down into the lower echelons of the football pyramid too. Last season Barnsley, in the Championship, and Leeds, in League One, between them fielded multi-national teams that contained natives of Brazil, Malta, Iceland, Nigeria, Ivory Coast, Poland,

Portugal, Denmark, Australia, Slovakia and Zaire. Both clubs also had an Argentine on their books, midfielder Hugo Colace turning out for the Tykes and forward Luciano Becchio for United, modern heirs to their pioneering compatriot Alex Sabella.

We will never know how bright Sabella's star would have burned had he been in the main body rather than the vanguard of the foreign takeover. But one thing is certain, when he traded South America for South Yorkshire back in the summer of 1978, Sheffield and English football were as foreign to him as he was to us.

Tragedy

BRADFORD - 11th May, 1985; Sheffield - 15th April, 1989; two indelible dates for cities with football tragedy at their heart. Yorkshire football will forever be haunted by the hellfire that consumed Valley Parade and the overwhelming crush at Hillsborough which together claimed the lives of 152 supporters and left many more terribly scarred for life. Time, they say, is a great healer. But no one present at either stadium on those ill-fated days or who watched the traumatic scenes unfolding before their eyes on TV or heard them on radio will ever forget the utter sense of despair and helplessness they felt as scores of people died in the name of football.

Some 11,000 Bradford City fans and civic dignitaries were blissfully unaware of the nightmare that was about to extinguish their dreamland when they arrived at Valley Parade in carnival mood for the last game of the 1984/85 season against mid-table Lincoln City. The Bantams were about to be crowned champions of Division Three. The ground was awash with beaming faces, chests were puffed out with pride, claret and amber scarves waved in the air and everybody sang their hearts out for the lads. And why not - three years before, the team was playing Fourth Division football. The previous year the average gate at Valley Parade had slumped to below 3,000 and, worst of all, in the summer of 1983, the team, beleaguered and bankrupt, very nearly went out of existence.

With barely four hours left before the axe fell, former chairman Stafford Heginbotham and ex-board member Jack Tordoff rode to the rescue, buying the tottering club for a pittance and transferring its assets into a new company, thereby saving it from following old neighbours Park Avenue into Football League oblivion. That City were now standing on the threshold of Division Two for the first time since before World War II was an extraordinary turnaround and a damn good excuse to have a party.

The Champions had a team to relish. In spite of financial restrictions, player-manager Trevor Cherry and assistant Terry Yorath, two old Leeds United team-mates who linked up again at Valley Parade in December 1982, had worked wonders, blending home grown products with transfer market bargains. The quality of the side can be gauged by the fact that three of its members - locally-born skipper Peter Jackson, Scottish winger John Hendrie and 20-year-old midfield terrier and City legend in the making Stuart McCall - were later sold to Everton and Newcastle United for a combined transfer fee of £1.6 million, a very healthy sum in the 1980s. Then there was Bobby Campbell, a big, brave but temperamental centre forward from Belfast who Halifax Town once sacked for 'persistent misconduct'. Beloved by City fans, the twice-capped Northern Ireland international banged in 26 goals in 1984/85 and obliterated Frank O'Rourke's club scoring record, which had stood since 1914, by netting 143 goals in 320 games between December 1979 and October 1986.

The Bradford eleven that took to the field on that sunny Saturday afternoon in May 1985 did so to rapturous applause. The game was tense - the score remained 0-0 as half-time approached - but the Kop remained in full voice. Then, at 3.40pm, a Mr Brownlie sitting in Block G of the Main Stand, a ramshackle wooden structure erected in 1908 and running the whole length of the pitch, felt his right leg getting warm. Wisps of smoke rose from beneath the floorboards. At first the danger seemed small and fans sitting close by were reluctant to move. But, fanned by a strong breeze, the flickering flames rapidly turned into a wall of fire. Plumes of dense black smoke belched into the sky. Pandemonium broke out among the 3,000 fans in the stand. Many clambered on to the pitch, mercifully unimpeded by the anti-hooligan perimeter fences that were in place elsewhere around the ground. One can only imagine how high the death toll would have reached otherwise.

Many more panic stricken supporters tried escaping the fireball via entrances at the back of the stand but to their horror they found them padlocked shut. As burning roof timbers and tarpaulin rained down on them they found themselves caught in a terrifying death trap. Here in the cramped and bottlenecked corridors at the back of the stand was where the fire claimed most of its victims.

Yorkshire Television and BBC, whose cameras were present to record the promotion celebrations for *The Big Match* and *Grandstand*, broadcast the awful drama live to the nation. By the time the fire brigade arrived it was already too late to save the Edwardian grandstand. It took less than five minutes for it to be engulfed by the inferno. When the flames were finally brought under control all that remained was a skeleton of metal stanchions and a mass of charred and smoking wood.

Fifty-six men, women and children, ranging in age from 11 to 86, some still sat bolt upright in their seats, perished in the pyre. Of those, 54 were Bradford City fans, including a former chairman, Sam Firth, and two from Lincoln. The grim total would have been higher had it not been for the courage of fellow supporters and police officers - six of whom were awarded the Queen's Gallantry Medal for their actions - heroically dragging comrades from the blaze.

At least 265 people were treated in hospital with burns that evening. One was McCall's father who was hospitalised for several weeks and needed skin grafts on his hands and head. The city of Bradford went into mourning, coach Yorath speaking for many when he lamented: 'It is the worst day in my life.'

Poignantly, City officials had earmarked £400,000 to be spent on replacing wooden flooring and seating and installing steel in the roof of the Main Stand. Work was due to begin on the Monday following the match. The Bradford Disaster Appeal Fund was immediately launched and in the space of a few months raised almost £4 million, much of which was distributed to families of the bereaved and the injured. The rest of the money was donated to a specialist burns research unit at Bradford University that was established following the fire.

The Valley Parade Fire was the worst stadium disaster to hit British football since 66 supporters were killed when a stairway collapsed at Ibrox in January 1971 at the end of a Rangers-Celtic derby. Alas, it was a tragedy waiting to happen. Wooden grandstands at Elland Road, Leeds and Leeds Road, Huddersfield burned to the ground in the 1950s and in the ensuing Valley Parade inquiry, Mr Justice Oliver Popplewell noted that between 1977 and 1983 some 86 fires broke out in various grandstands, thankfully all without loss of life.

He published his full findings on 16th January, 1986. 'I am quite satisfied,' he reported, 'that the cause of the fire was the dropping of a lighted match, or a cigarette or tobacco, on to debris beneath the floorboards.' He went on to say that the club had been warned of the fire risk posed by the rubbish, adding: 'Had the Green Guide [first published in the aftermath of the Ibrox disaster] been complied with, this tragedy would not have occurred.' As is often the case, a catalogue of small errors combined to cause a catastrophe.

In a long list of recommendations, Popplewell called for wooden stands to become things of the past, better evacuation procedures, trained stewards, suitable and adequate exits and tighter restrictions by the fire authorities. In short, the wellbeing of spectators was to become paramount. Many of his suggestions were subsequently embodied into the Safety of Sports Grounds Act, 1987.

Up and down the country dilapidated and antiquated structures, most of them belonging to poorer clubs who could not afford to replace them, were closed down. The whole of Valley Parade was condemned as unfit for purpose. Bradford City were obliged to play their 'home' fixtures in the 1985/86 season at Leeds, Huddersfield and Bradford Northern's Odsal Stadium. That City managed to finish the season well above the relegation zone was a highly commendable achievement[1].

Barely-healed wounds were ruthlessly reopened, however, on 20th September, 1986 when during a Bradford-Leeds derby at Odsal a bunch of moronic Leeds yobs, chanting sickening songs about the fire, torched a burger van situated at the back of the terracing. Hundreds of frightened fans took refuge on the pitch, delaying the match for 20 minutes. 'To do that so soon after the [Valley Parade] fire was beyond belief,' said McCall, the City captain. 'Smoke was billowing into the sky. People were panicking, kids crying.'

Valley Parade lay derelict for over a year. Rumours circulated that City would never go back, that they would remain co-tenants at Odsal, a stadium owned by Bradford Council. But City officials, fans and local MPs refused to let the club lose its ancestral home. Through various loans, grants and insurance payouts they raised the £2.6 million needed to redevelop the venue. Work began in June 1986 and within six months Valley Parade was reborn. Pride of place went to a brand new 5,000-seater Main Stand made of steel and concrete and fitted out with plastic seating in the club colours. The Kop was extensively rebuilt and covered for the first time too, new turnstiles and a sophisticated CCTV system were installed, and exit gates were added to perimeter fences in case of emergency.

The new-look, safety-conscious Valley Parade was officially opened on 14th December, 1986 by Mr Justice Popplewell. The Bishop of Bradford, the Right Reverend Robert Williamson, unveiled a commemorative bas-relief sculpture on the outer wall of the Main Stand. Then a full-house of 15,000 generated an emotionally charged atmosphere in which City took on and beat an England International XI containing stars like Kevin Keegan and Peter Shilton. But the night was not about who won or lost. It was about coming home, about the rebirth of a spiritual home and, most of all, about remembering the 56 people who died that terrible afternoon. On 11th May, 2010 Bradford city centre fell silent at 11am as some 2,000 people bedecked in claret and amber observed a minute's silence at a 25th anniversary remembrance service in Centenary Square. The Bradford public will never forget.

On the same day as the Bradford Fire, a young Leeds United fan died at St. Andrews, Birmingham when a wall collapsed on top of him following pitched battles between Leeds and Birmingham City hooligans. A fortnight later, on the evening of 29th May, 1985, 39 people (31 of them Italian) were trampled to death in a riot inside the Heysel Stadium, Belgium, shortly before the European Cup Final between Liverpool and Juventus.

Popplewell took these two further calamitous events into account when formulating his recommendations for crowd safety. In the resulting report he championed, among many other proposals, a national membership scheme for football fans. Margaret Thatcher and her Conservative government seized upon the idea as a way of tackling soccer hooliganism once and for all. In the early months of 1989, the Football Spectators Bill was unveiled with a target date for it becoming law of spring 1990. The cost of bringing in ID cards was estimated to be more than £30 million and football clubs were told in no uncertain terms that it would be they who would be footing the bill, not the taxpayer. Should they refuse to comply then a levy would instead be imposed on transfer fees. The FA and the Football League were dumbstruck but before the Bill was able to reach the statute books there came the Hillsborough disaster.

Spring sunshine greeted fans of Liverpool and Nottingham Forest as they flowed into Sheffield for a repeat of the previous season's FA Cup semi final. Hillsborough was capable of holding more than 50,000 spectators and well used to staging big matches. For the third successive year and for the 28th time since the Second World War, the ground was chosen to host one of English football's gala events. There was no reason to suppose that operations would run other than smoothly.

However, while Liverpool fans had been allocated the

cavernous Kop end in 1988, this year they were given the smaller Leppings Lane end. It was a ludicrous decision to allocate the reigning League champions 6,000 tickets less than Forest despite them having a far greater fan base. The two-tiered area behind the goal comprised a seated stand above a terraced paddock split into pens which swept up into a large bank behind one of the corner flags. Half an hour before kick-off, the pens behind the goal were already heaving with Liverpool supporters but the bank to their left was half empty.

As the clock ticked down, thousands of them, some without tickets, were still outside the ground and increasingly desperate to get in. The pressure in the walled courtyards in which the turnstiles were situated intensified, the force becoming so great that a police horse was lifted bodily from the ground. People screamed. The police lost control of the crowd. One officer called for the kick-off to be delayed - a request that was denied. At 2.52pm, as the congestion reached dangerous levels, Chief Superintendent David Duckenfield, who had minimal experience of policing a football match, gave the order to open a set of exit gates known as Gate C. In doing so he made a bad situation far, far worse.

Supporters flooded down a dark, 30-yard long tunnel which led directly into the two central pens behind the goal, pens that were already overcrowded. Some 6,000 people, nearly twice the capacity, tried to cram into space that simply was not there. The pressure became unbearable. Anti-crush barriers twisted and warped as if they were made of plasticine. Men, women and children literally had the life squeezed out of them. Those who slipped unconscious to the floor were trampled underfoot. Distressed supporters yelled and pleaded for help. Some managed to wriggle free of the fearsome crush, clambering over bodies and fencing to safety. Others at the back of the pens were yanked from the masses into the upper tier by fellow fans. And yet, amid all this chaos, the game kicked off as intended, as if nothing was happening.

Inside the ground, the police assumed Liverpool fans were rioting, just as some of them had at Heysel four years before. Duckenfield - who later denied giving the command to open Gate C, telling senior FA officials that Liverpool fans had forced it open themselves - sent in reinforcements, including dog handlers, to quell the 'pitch invasion'. But this was not an act of hooliganism; it was a desperate situation in which people were dying. At 3.06pm the referee abandoned the game, to howls of derision from frustrated Forest fans in the Kop who were unaware of the gravity of the situation.

Grandstand relayed the harrowing sights into the homes of millions of people. Numb with shock, we witnessed weeping men in Liverpool shirts and hats ripping advertising hoardings from their moorings and frenziedly ferrying them back as makeshift stretchers to help friends and family. Police officers now joined in the frantic efforts to save people's lives but all the while the rescue attempts were frustrated by those damned anti-hooligan fences. Dozens of bodies were strewn across the pitch. The volunteers of the St John Ambulance Brigade tried their best to assist but they were ill-equipped for a disaster of such magnitude. Bungled communication meant that the first paramedic crew did not arrive for ten minutes. Even at 3.30pm there was still only one ambulance at the Leppings Lane end.

That evening Sheffield's *Green 'Un* reported that there had been more than 30 deaths from compressive asphyxia and several hundred injured. Four days later the death toll rose to 95. The 96th and final victim, Tony Bland, aged 22, passed away on 3rd March, 1993 when his life support machine was switched off. He had never regained consciousness. In addition, a number of suicides can be attributed directly to the psychological trauma of that day.

On Merseyside, Anfield became a shrine, the pitch in front of the Kop a sea of flowers as the city paid homage to its fallen. While they tried to come to terms with their sorrow Liverpool fans had to put up with a smear campaign by some of the red-tops. 'Dead Fans Robbed By Drunk Thugs', screamed the *Daily Star*. 'THE TRUTH: Some fans urinated on the brave cops. Some fans beat up PC giving kiss of life,' stormed *The Sun*, a tabloid which was subsequently boycotted in Liverpool and is still reviled by a significant number of Scousers to this day.

Liverpool manager Kenny Dalglish, the anguish showing in his face, said simply: 'Football is irrelevant'. Players attended funerals across the area. 'You'll Never Walk Alone', the club anthem, never seemed more apt. A fortnight later the decision was made to replay the semi final, this time at Old Trafford. Liverpool won the tie 3-1 and in the 'Requiem Cup Final' at Wembley beat city rivals Everton 3-2 to lift the FA Cup for the fourth time, a tribute of sorts, some said, to those who had been killed.

Lord Justice Peter Taylor was appointed to investigate this latest disaster. In his 104-page report, published on 29th January, 1990 few escaped his wrath. Sheffield Wednesday, Sheffield City Council and the FA were all criticised, as were 'a drunken minority of fans' for aggravating the problems. But the main reason for the disaster, he concluded, was the failure of police control. 'It is astounding' he said, that '95 people could die from overcrowding before the very eyes of those controlling the event.'

Survivors and families of the deceased blamed South Yorkshire Police for the disaster and Chief Superintendent Duckenfield in particular, pointing to alleged alterations of self-written statements as evidence of a cover up. They were appalled when an inquest returned a verdict of accidental death against all the victims. A judicial review in 1993 reached the decision that, 'it would not be right to quash the verdicts' and, in 1997, a scrutiny by Lord Justice Stuart-Smith came, 'to the clear conclusion that there is no basis upon which there should be a further Judicial Inquiry'. To this day, the bereaved families believe they have not received a fair hearing, never mind justice for their loved ones.

In his report, Lord Justice Taylor submitted 76 recommendations to improve crowd safety and behaviour. He challenged clubs to face up to their responsibilities, to improve the squalid conditions prevalent at their crumbling grounds and to stop caging fans in like, 'prisoners of war'. The most far-reaching consequence of his report was all-seater stadiums. He recommended that they should be introduced into the upper two divisions of the Football League by 1994 and into the lower two by 1999. In the meantime the capacity of terraces, he declared, should be cut by 15 per cent. Finally, the proposed and controversial national membership scheme should be dispensed with on the grounds that it would not be effective and could compromise fans' safety at turnstiles. Taylor's proposals were unequivocally accepted by the government.

Despite the horror of Hillsborough, there was much quibbling over making terraces a thing of the past. Impoverished clubs claimed that the huge cost to convert their grounds, estimated to be £300 million, would put many of them out of business and hordes of supporters argued that the unique atmospheres generated in packed standing areas would be lost forever.

The game, however, found an unlikely ally in John Major, the Chancellor of the Exchequer and soon to be Prime Minister. In his Budget on 20th March, 1990 he announced that the Football Pools tax would be cut by 2.5 per cent and that £100 million would be made available over five years via the Football Trust to help clubs transform outdated grounds into modern all-seater stadiums. And so began the most extensive rebuilding programme since the Edwardian heyday of Archibald Leitch.

Twenty years on and Lord Justice Taylor's vision has become reality. Football grounds are now sleek and contemporary testaments to architectural design. Fortunes have been ploughed into renovating Hillsborough, Elland Road, Bramall Lane, Valley Parade, Oakwell, The Shay and Bootham Crescent, refurbishments which have gone well beyond just putting in a few extra seats and removing fences. Existing stands have been extended and covered, whole new grandstands have been built, none more impressive than Leeds' 17,000-capacity East Stand on Lowfields Road which, when it opened in 1993, was considered to be the largest cantilever structure in the world.

Meanwhile, fans of Hull City, Doncaster Rovers and Huddersfield Town may more readily admit that although it may have been gut-wrenching to leave their historic but decaying homes of Boothferry Park, Belle Vue and Leeds Road, the comfort and views afforded by the state of the art KC Stadium, Keepmoat Stadium and award-winning Alfred McAlpine Stadium (now the Galpharm Stadium) in many ways makes up for the initial sense of loss. Indeed, the McAlpine with its striking design of four domed stands was a trendsetter, a blueprint for other cutting-edge sporting arenas that followed such as the Riverside (Middlesbrough), Reebok (Bolton), Stadium of Light (Sunderland), City of Manchester (Manchester City), Emirates (Arsenal) and the new Wembley.

It took two devastating disasters for football to come to its senses and realise that those who patronised it deserved a modicum of luxury and respect rather than piss-poor facilities and contempt. The legacy of the Valley Parade Fire and the Hillsborough Disaster are grounds that are far removed from what they were two decades ago. Our rose tinted memories tell us that the atmospheres inside today's stadiums are not as passionate or as loud as they were when most of us stood crowded together on the terraces. But is it mere coincidence that attendances have grown year on year since the introduction of comfortable, all-seated and non-combustible stadiums? We might like to remember the terraces as the golden age of following football but go to Valley Parade and Hillsborough and read the 152 names engraved on memorial plaques. They were fans, like us, who were fatally let down by men in suits who thought that we would put up with anything so long as we could watch our team play.

FOOTNOTE

[1] Trevor Cherry's 'reward' was to be sacked on 7th January, 1987, less than a month after Bradford City made their triumphant return to Valley Parade. Although the Bantams had slipped into the relegation zone, his removal nonetheless shocked fans who admired how he had driven the team forward when the club was homeless and penniless and, more importantly, shown compassion in attending many funerals in the city.

23

The Worst Of Times

WHITE ROSE football hit rock bottom in the 1980s. Even without the great loss of life at Valley Parade and Hillsborough it was the worst of times; an age in which attendances crashed, clubs went bust, the aesthetically displeasing long-ball game arrived and yobbish behaviour all the while blighted the sport.

In the decade of IRA bombs, CND marches, race riots, yuppies and Margaret Thatcher - a woman who, in Yorkshire especially, was like Marmite - some loved her while most despised her doctrine and condescension - supporters drifted away from the game in their droves. The reasons are many fold but the two most potent were an escalation in hooliganism and a deep recession at the start of the decade exacerbated in places like Barnsley, Rotherham and Doncaster by the year-long and bitter miners' strike of 1984-85.

Followers of Sheffield Wednesday set the tone for the period when thousands of them poured over the Pennines for a match against Oldham Athletic on 6th September, 1980. When Wednesday's fiery striker Terry Curran was sent off for punching an Oldham player it was like a ton of Semtex had gone off in the away end. The fans exploded, scaling the fences to invade the pitch and hurling bricks, concrete, coins - anything they could get their hands on. Owls boss Jack Charlton, who had taken charge of the club in the autumn of 1977 and masterminded their promotion from Division Three in the season just gone, was reduced to tears. He beseeched the fans to stop but all he got for his troubles was to be hit by a missile. The match was held up for more than half-an-hour as police attempted to restore order; incredibly, only nine people were arrested amid the disturbances.

Violent, tooled up, dressed in designer gear - the era of the football casual had arrived - and sometimes several hundred strong, the louts ganged together in organised firms that have become infamous within the football world: Headhunters, Bushwackers, ICF, Zulus. Sheffield Wednesday's mob was called the Owls Crime Squad. Their city rivals christened themselves Blades Business Crew. Rotherham's fringe was the Tivoli Crew, Hull had City Psychos. Every club in Yorkshire, however large or small, had their 'top boys' who were prepared to stand up and fight for their team.

No firm, though, was more notorious or active than the Leeds Service Crew. Formed in 1974, they were named after the ordinary scheduled trains on which they travelled to away matches. They came to prominence with that high profile riot during the 1975 European Cup Final but it was in the Eighties, either side of Leeds United's relegation from Division One in 1982 - which left Yorkshire without top flight representation for the first time since the reign of Queen Victoria - that they cemented their place in hooligan folklore. Everywhere the Service Crew went, from West

Brom to Chelsea, Huddersfield to Derby, Grimsby to Birmingham, they trashed grounds and city pubs and caused innocent bystanders to cower in terror. The ramification of their mayhem was to put the future of the club at stake. To the horror of non-violent Leeds fans there was genuine talk of closing Leeds United down and having done with the thugs.

Football's administrators were determined to purge the yobs from the game. They implemented a variety of Draconian measures: more police and improved surveillance, perimeter fencing and CCTV, banning orders, all-ticket matches, prohibiting the sale of alcohol inside grounds, switching the kick-off of high risk games to Sunday lunchtimes. But the hooligans just kept coming back.

The so-called 'English disease' and the economic downturn combined to slash total attendances at matches by a third in the six years between 1980 and 1986, down to a post-war low of 16.5 million. Nowhere was the slump more keenly felt than in Yorkshire. Leeds' average attendance in 1985/86 was 13,200, half the figure it had been in 1979. Sheffield United's was 10,800, Huddersfield Town's 6,800, Barnsley's 6,000. Bradford City, Rotherham United, York City, Doncaster Rovers and Halifax Town all recorded League gates in the single thousand. Even Sheffield Wednesday, who finished fifth in Division One and reached an FA Cup semi final for the second time in three years in 1985/86, experienced a sharp drop, down by 15 per cent on the previous season to an average 23,100.

The collapse had a severe and wide ranging effect. In February 1982 Hull City went into receivership, followed by Bradford City in June 1983 for failing to settle tax bills. York, Doncaster and Halifax, a club which spent the best part of the decade languishing near the bottom of the League, had their heads permanently in the financial guillotine. Huddersfield leaked money and cash-strapped Leeds had a transfer embargo imposed upon them and in the summer of 1985 sold their Elland Road stadium to the city council for £2.5 million. They unveiled exciting plans to transform the site into a multi-purpose complex which, in addition to football, would have a shopping centre, ice rink, cinema, nightclub, café, restaurant and leisure centre. Nothing ever came of them. Three years earlier, Sheffield United chairman Reg Brealey proposed a similar idea to exploit spare land around Bramall Lane. The redevelopment, he argued, would drag the Blades, who were more than £1 million in debt, back into solvency. But Sheffield City Council rejected the 'Bramall Centre' scheme, leaving Brealey bitterly disappointed. 'A golden opportunity to re-establish Sheffield United among the country's top clubs has been lost,' he lamented.

Rotherham fans, meanwhile, must have wished they never clapped eyes on a flashy, cigar smoking self-publicist from Essex by the name of Anton Johnson. Paying £62,000 for what was a modestly profitable club in December 1979, careful husbandry of tight resources was never going to be the new owner's style. He splashed out £400,000 - money United simply did not have - on bringing in ex-Liverpool and England captain Emlyn Hughes as player-manager, star striker Ronnie Moore from Cardiff City, veteran ex-Manchester City midfielder Gerry Gow, Halifax's 18-year-old keeper Bobby Mimms and wingers Tony Towner from Millwall and Everton's Joe McBride.

This 'speculate to accumulate' approach initially produced the desired results. Fans' favourite Moore scored 45 goals as United won promotion to Division Two in 1981 and then went to within four points of reaching Division One the following year. But the team was unable to sustain the forward momentum and at the end of the 1982/83 season were relegated back from whence they came. Johnson immediately bailed out, leaving behind him a mountain of debt and tales of dodgy dealings. Rotherham were saved from the scrap yard by local metal dealer Ken Booth who, in May 1987, stepped in with a rescue package which at a stroke wiped off the club's burgeoning liabilities of almost £800,000. By then Johnson had quit football altogether, scared off by the threat of a Football League investigation into alleged financial malpractice while at Rotherham and for breaching its rules on being involved with more than one club at any one time - he also had ties with Bournemouth and Southend United.

That should have been the last anyone heard of one of the game's colourful yet also shadiest characters. But the 'King of Clubs' bounced back in 1997 as the public face of a consortium seeking to wrest control of struggling Doncaster Rovers from Ken Richardson for £2 million. After negotiations broke down, Johnson wormed his way into Scarborough FC, becoming their majority shareholder in August 1998. Continuing his reverse Midas touch, at the end of the season Boro were relegated to the Nationwide Conference, thereby bringing to an end an historic 12 year period in the ranks of the Football League.

Just as war is the mother of invention so, perhaps, depression is the father of necessity. In the face of ever diminishing returns at the turnstiles, clubs, individually and collectively, scrambled to find new revenue streams in order to survive. Out of this desperation was born the embryonic era of sponsorship. The Football League struck sponsorship deals with the Milk Marketing Board for the League Cup in 1981 and Japanese camera giants Canon for the League itself in 1983, not insignificant achievements given the game's tarnished image. Shirt sponsors appeared for the first time too. To begin with they were low key and low earning - RF Winder (Leeds), Conveyer Improvements Ltd (Doncaster) and MacDee sanitary systems (Halifax), for example - but as the decade wore on household names like Greenalls (Huddersfield), Finlux (Sheffield Wednesday), Burton (Leeds) and Lyons Cakes (Barnsley) signed money-spinning contracts. Over time, some sponsors became synonymous with the teams they partnered, such as Hansa Beer (York), Parkgate retail outlet (Rotherham) and thriving timber merchant Arnold Laver (Sheffield United). With their HQ next door to the football ground on Bramall Lane, Laver was the most local of sponsors and one of the most supportive too. Not only did they advertise their product on the Blades' shirts for ten years (1985-95) but they also sponsored for a long time the South Stand which to this day some fans still refer to as the 'Laver Stand' and Andrew Laver, grandson of the company's founder, has become vice-president of the club.

First Division matches were televised live for the first time in November 1983, and on a Sunday to boot, another new departure. Being at the beck and call of TV executives is an accepted part of the modern game but back then supporters were incensed at being forced to watch matches at any other time than 3pm on a Saturday.

Fans found innovate ways to try and reclaim the sport as theirs. Often crude and tub-thumping, football chants can also be passionate, rousing and, at times, amusing. Take the classic *Greasy Chip Butty* song, for instance, sung to the tune of *Annie's Song* by John Denver and adopted by Sheffield United fans in the mid-80s:

You fill up my senses
Like a gallon of Magnet
Like a packet of Woodbine
Like a good pinch of snuff

Like a night out in Sheffield
Like a greasy chip butty
Oh Sheffield United
Come thrill me again...
Na Na Na Naa Naa Naaaaa, Oooh!

Such humour trickled off the terraces and into the pages of an Eighties phenomenon - the football fanzine. Put together by devoted fans on early home computers and peddled outside grounds on match days, they were a cheaper, wittier and more irreverent alternative to the stuffy match programme, like buying a copy of *Viz* instead of *The Times*. One of the earliest to come rolling off the black-and-white dot matrix printer was York City's now defunct *Terrace Talk*, whilst the oldest surviving one, predating the nationally acclaimed *When Saturday Comes* by more than a year, is Bradford City's *The City Gent*. Named after a cartoon character in a bowler hat that was introduced by the club in the 1960s, *The City Gent* was first published in November 1984 under the tagline: '16 pages of the best drivel available for the princely sum of 20p!' It has since sold more than 300,000 copies, not bad going for an amateur production.

Fanzines, droll songs, chubby cheerleaders shaking pompoms in club colours and police dogs chasing down 'crooks' making not so very quick getaways on rickety bicycles, they all brought some light relief to matches which were, with astounding regularity, mind numbingly boring in the 80s. The ugly long-ball game, with its big hoofs up field and emphasis on physicality rather than artistry, gained widespread popularity. Two leading exponents of this unrefined style were ex-Wimbledon and Watford boss Dave Bassett and former Notts County manager Howard Wilkinson who both used it to great effect in guiding Sheffield United (1989/90), Sheffield Wednesday (1983/84) and Leeds United (1989/90) to promotion to Division One, although, to be fair to both men, they occasionally tried to play 'proper' football.

Different in character as chalk and cheese - Bassett was an effervescent Londoner with the gift of the gab, Wilkinson a taciturn Yorkshireman - both men shared a belief that nothing could be achieved without sheer hard work. They created industrious teams packed with gritty defenders like Paul Stancliffe, Lawrie Madden and Mel Sterland; direct wing men such as Brian Marwood - who started out at Hull and won the League title with Arsenal in 1989 - and Scottish international star Gordon Strachan; midfield runners including ex-hod carrier Vinnie Jones and Gary Megson - the son of Don Megson, captain of the Owls' 1966 FA Cup Final side - and lanky front men such as Lee Chapman and the surprisingly deft Brian Deane. On the rare occasions that either manager dabbled with out and out flair - as 'Wilko' did at Leeds with brooding French forward Eric Cantona - the experiment was usually counterproductive.

So successful was Wilkinson at turning Wednesday from a competent Division Two outfit under Jack Charlton, whom he succeeded in 1983, to a top five Division One side that the club was invited during the 1985/86 season to join the biggest party in town - a proposed breakaway Super League. Instead of lucrative TV and sponsorship deals being divvied up between the 92 Football League clubs, the participants would keep every last penny for themselves. Capitalism over socialism you might call it, but a rich/poor schism was avoided, for the time being at least, by panicky League officials appeasing the rebels with the offer of a much bigger slice of the cash cake.

Wednesday regularly and unusually posted profits in the 80s, thanks largely to their chairman Bert McGee keeping a firm grip on the financial tiller. His extreme prudence, however, alienated Wilkinson who came to the conclusion that he could not take the club any further if he continued to be hamstrung in the transfer market. Blaming, 'those bastards in the boardroom' for his decision, Wilko reluctantly walked out on his boyhood heroes in October 1988 and joined Leeds who were prepared to back him to the hilt to get back to the very top, an aim which in due course was handsomely achieved.

Elsewhere in the county there was a short-lived managerial craze for former Leeds players, the train of thought being that top footballers would have learned a lot from a manager like Don Revie and would therefore make great bosses themselves. The results were mixed. Jack Charlton (Sheffield Wednesday), Allan Clarke (Barnsley & Leeds), Eddie Gray (Leeds), Billy Bremner (Doncaster & Leeds), Norman Hunter (Barnsley & Rotherham), Bobby Collins (Barnsley, again) and Trevor Cherry and Terry Yorath (both Bradford City) all gave it a bash without ever accomplishing much more than the odd promotion here and there. In 1986/87, Bremner led Leeds to an FA Cup semi final and within ten minutes of promotion to Division One via the newly introduced play-offs, glory being denied by Coventry City and Charlton Athletic respectively. The nearest any of the ex-pros came to matching their old mentor's achievements was 'Big Jack' who saved his best days for the international arena, leading a Republic of Ireland side cast in his image - straightforward and durable - to Italia 90 and USA 94.

Huddersfield Town illustrated the fickle nature of football, scoring 101 goals to win the Fourth Division championship in 1979/80 but conceding 100 in finishing bottom of Division Two in 1987/88, a tally which included a club record 10-1 defeat by Manchester City at Maine Road in November 1987. 'My most humiliating day within football,' was how Town manager and ex-Newcastle, Arsenal and England striker Malcolm MacDonald described the annihilation, 'Supermac' resigning his post before the end of the season.

Meanwhile, Bradford City, after enduring that horrendous stadium fire and playing home matches away from Valley Parade for more than a year, came to within an ace of reaching the First Division in 1988. Front runners for much of the first half of the season, with two matches to go they were still very much in the mix. One more victory and they would have been promoted; two wins and the championship title would have been theirs. But with six clubs all vying to go up they crumbled. Both games ended in defeat and they finished the season in fourth place just one point behind runners-ups Aston Villa and then in the play-off semi final they were beaten 3-2 by Middlesbrough. City quickly went from looking forward to competing against Liverpool, Manchester United and Arsenal to having to sell their crown jewels Stuart McCall and John Hendrie and suffering relegation back to Division Three in 1990.

Halifax remained in the doldrums throughout. Four times they sought re-election and a famous 1-0 victory over Manchester City in the FA Cup third round in January 1980 was compensation for humbling defeats in the same competition by non-leaguers Whitby Town, South Shields and Kettering. Better news for Hull City, who put their financial woes behind them and regained some of their past form after ex-Scarborough supremo Don Robinson took over as club chairman in 1982. He installed Colin Appleton in the managerial hot-seat and the former Boro boss immediately instilled the same kind of winning mentality in his new team as he had in his old one. Over the next three years the Tigers rose from the Fourth to the Second Division and came closer than any other Yorkshire team in the 80s to winning one of the knockout competitions, losing 2-1 to Bournemouth in the final of the much maligned Associate Members' Cup at Boothferry Park on 24th May, 1984.

Meanwhile, the fortunes of York City, who in 1981 held up the rest of the Football League, were revitalised by former Stoke City team-mates Denis Smith and Viv Busby. In 1983/84 the Minstermen scored 96 goals and racked up a mammoth 101 points under the new three-points-for-a-win system to romp to the Fourth Division championship, the club's only major trophy to date. They also gloriously reprised their giant killing role of yesteryear, knocking Arsenal out of the FA Cup in January 1985 thanks to a dramatic last minute penalty by Keith Houchen - a future Cup winner with Coventry - and twice holding mighty Liverpool to draws in front of full houses at Bootham Crescent. Such jubilance was tempered, however, by a 7-0 thrashing in one of the replays at Anfield, York's biggest ever cup defeat.

The main man at the Crescent in those days was Keith Walwyn, a tall, brave and bustling centre-forward from St. Kitts & Nevis in the Caribbean. A genuine cult hero beloved as much for his cheery nature as for his attacking prowess, he plundered 140 goals in 269 games between 1981 and 1987, a club total that has only ever been surpassed by Norman Wilkinson, a star inside forward of the 50s, who needed 110 more matches in which to score three more times. Walwyn hit the 20 goal mark in all but one of his six seasons and was twice voted 'Clubman of the Year' (1982, 1987) before being sold, rather surprisingly, to Blackpool for £35,000. Many tears were shed when 'Big Keith' died, aged just 47, in April 2003 while undergoing heart surgery. But the legend lives on at York City, his place in the fans' affections assured for the major part he played in arguably the club's most triumphant period of its history.

Walwyn's strike rate, as impressive as it was, was eclipsed by Keith Edwards. A short and clever centre forward from Stockton-on-Tees with astonishing pace, he scored 256 League goals between 1975 and 1991, the great bulk of which came in the colours of Hull City and Sheffield United. One of the most prolific strikers ever to patrol the lower divisions, there have been few, if any, footballers to rival him for the sheer number of goals scored for Yorkshire clubs. He was at the height of his powers with the Blades in the early 80s, rattling in 35 goals during their Fourth Division championship season in 1981/82 and 33 as they won promotion to Division Two in 1983/84. That he only made a handful of appearances in the First Division - in 1975/76 for relegation-doomed Sheffield United - is a huge shame and undeserving of his wonderful gift in front of goal.

Walwyn and Edwards were not the only fans' favourites to strut their stuff for Yorkshire teams in the 1980s: John Sheridan (Leeds), Ronnie Glavin and Mick McCarthy (Barnsley), Ronnie Moore (Rotherham), Terry Curran (Sheffield Wed), Stuart McCall and Bobby Campbell (Bradford City), Gareth Roberts (Hull), Paul Stancliffe (Rotherham & Sheffield United), Mark Lillis (Huddersfield) - all claimed a cherished, enduring status at their workplaces.

That the little men can have their day in the sun was again illustrated by Scarborough who, in 1987, 108 years after they were formed and marshalled by an outspoken 37-year-old Sheffielder called Neil Warnock, won the GM Vauxhall Conference title to become the first team to gain automatic promotion to the Football League. And what an opening fixture they were handed, Wolverhampton Wanderers, once the best team in the country, at home. But was it a good idea to allow Wolves fans, who had a tasty reputation for violence, to come to a seaside resort in August? In retrospect the answer has to be no. The Seasiders' dream start to life in Division Four was shattered by those in the visiting colours' lamentable behaviour which involved smashing up the away end at the Athletic Ground and clambering on to the terrace shed roofs. Boro earned a creditable 2-2 draw in front of a crowd of more than 7,000 but their big day was overshadowed by the crowd trouble, a state of affairs that all too often replicated itself at football matches up and down the country.

The 1980s truly was the decade from hell for football. It is a minor miracle that every one of Yorkshire's professional football clubs survived its trials and tribulations, coming out the other end battered and bruised but alive. Having hit rock bottom, there was only one way for football to go, and that was up.

24

Boom...

AFTER THE dark and barren years of the 1980s, Yorkshire football entered a period of prosperity. Football stadiums underwent expensive makeovers that would have made Trinny and Susannah proud, money poured into the game, attendances went up, hooliganism down and success returned to the county's clubs on a scale not seen for many a year.

The cavalry charge for silverware was lead by Sheffield Wednesday - somewhat of an irony given Howard Wilkinson's assertion that he had taken the club as far as it could go - who on Sunday 21st April, 1991 beat Manchester United 1-0 at Wembley to win the Rumbelows (League) Cup for the club's first major trophy since 1935. Wednesday went into the final as underdogs, a Second Division team, they slipped out of the top tier the year before, versus the FA Cup holders. But they were heading for an instant return to Division One and were very much in form. With skipper Nigel Pearson putting in a Man of the Match performance in the heart of defence, they nullified the threat posed by Paul Ince, Bryan Robson, Mark Hughes *et al*. A ragged game was settled in the 38th minute by a moment of pure genius from Republic of Ireland international John Sheridan, an exquisite midfielder of guile and vision, who stunningly volleyed the ball into the net from outside the box. The blue and white half of the 77,612 crowd went crazy and so did thousands of fans watching the game live on television back in Sheffield. Yorkshire TV incurred the latter's wrath, however, by cutting short the post-match celebrations in order to show *War of the Monster Trucks*, a deplorable decision which brought about accusations of anti-Sheffield bias against the Leeds-based broadcaster.

Leading Wednesday to victory over one of his old clubs was Ron Atkinson, a charismatic and colourful manager who led Manchester United to Wembley glory in 1983 and 1985. Bejewelled in gold bling and with a quip or two never far from his lips, 'Big Ron' championed champagne football, insisting that the ball be played on the deck, not among the pigeons and the planes. Although his teams all had an iron core, he packed around it stylish playmakers who had the craft and the imagination to unlock the tightest of games.

Atkinson joined Wednesday in February 1989 after a short and turbulent spell at Spanish side Atletico Madrid ended in the sack. Given a war chest of £5 million to spend, mainly by Bert McGee's successor as chairman, Dave Richards, he used the money wisely, buying quality players like Sheridan, former England stars Viv Anderson and Trevor Francis, foreign internationals Roland Nilsson and John Harkes, beanpole midfielder Carlton Palmer, Northern Ireland wide man Danny Wilson and Dalian Atkinson, a skilful forward.

Atkinson improved the quality of the football on show - some of the best seen at Hillsborough since the days of Vic

Buckingham in the early 60s - but Wednesday, nevertheless, were relegated in 1990 on goal difference after losing five of their last six games. 'Big Ron' tendered his resignation but Richards, a future head of the soon to be launched Premier League, refused to accept it, convinced that he was still the best man for the job and what a vote of confidence that turned out to be.

After popping the League Cup in their trophy cabinet, Wednesday sealed promotion back to Division One with a 3-1 home win against Bristol City in the penultimate game of the 1990/91 season. Scoring two of the goals that day was David Hirst, an electrifying striker who was simply hero-worshipped by Wednesdayites. Signed from Barnsley in August 1986 during the McGee-Wilkinson era, his career took off under Atkinson. Possessing all the attributes needed to make it at the top - power, pace, dribbling ability, a thundering shot and a God given talent for putting the ball in the back of the net - 'Hirsty' scored 149 goals in 358 appearances in 11 years at the club and was the object of six unsuccessful bids by Manchester United boss Alex Ferguson. But for a series of injuries hampering an embryonic international career (3 caps, 1 goal, 1991-92) then he, rather than Alan Shearer, might well have inherited Gary Lineker's mantle as England's premier goal poacher.

Wednesday fans' jubilant celebrations suddenly went flat when rumours swept the city that Atkinson was about to leave for Aston Villa. After a hastily arranged meeting with his chairman, however, 'Big Ron' announced: 'I must be barmy to think of leaving this club ... I couldn't turn my back on people who have been so good to me.' A week later he did just that and went to Villa, his boyhood team. It was a sour end to a very sweet season.

On a much sadder note, York City's 25-year-old striker David Longhurst collapsed and died of a heart attack during a Fourth Division match at home to Lincoln City on 8th September, 1990. He was the first player to pass away in a Football League match for 69 years. The Shipton Street End at Bootham Crescent was renamed the David Longhurst Stand in his memory.

The pendulum of success now swung the way of Leeds United. In less than three years, Wilkinson had transformed the Whites from a floundering club heading towards Division Three into a well drilled, competitive outfit able to win the Second Division championship in 1990 and finish fourth in Division One and reach the Rumbelows Cup semi final the following year.

Dubbed 'Sergeant Wilko' - a play on Phil Silvers's American TV character *Sergeant Bilko* and alluding to his regimental style of management - Wilkinson stamped his authority from the outset, telling captain Mark Aizlewood that he would never wear the white shirt again after he flicked the V-sign at the Kop and selling crowd favourite John Sheridan to Nottingham Forest for £650,000 in August 1989 following a bust up. Bizarrely, Brian Clough then stuck Sheridan in the Forest reserves for three months before offloading him to Wednesday at a £150,000 discount.

The Sheridan sale could have backfired stupendously but the Elland Road crowd was mollified by the £300,000 arrival from Manchester United in March 1989 of winger-cum-midfielder Gordon Strachan who, like Clem Stephenson, Jimmy Seed and Bobby Collins before him, belied his age and the critics to become the inspiration behind his team's march to the top. Even at 32, the wee ginger-haired Scotsman with the caustic tongue had more energy than Ferrybridge power station. A natural born leader and a skilful yet tenacious player who scored plenty of goals pushing forward from midfield, he bore more than a passing resemblance to the ultimate Leeds hero, Billy

Bremner. Handed the captain's armband, he responded with a string of superlative performances which not only silenced the doubters but earned him a recall to the Scotland team (he went on to collect 50 caps) and the 1991 'Footballer of the Year' award.

Given £10 million to spend, a sum he could only have dreamt about when he was at Sheffield Wednesday, Wilkinson had, by the start of the 1991/92 season, assembled a team capable of challenging for the title. The defence was strong and reliable, Rod Wallace and Lee Chapman, a classic small man/big man partnership, was highly productive up front and the midfield of Strachan, Gary McAllister, David Batty and Gary Speed was widely considered to be the best in the country, local boy Batty giving the side a distinctly steely edge.

Putting aside their manager's favoured long-ball game, Leeds produced some of the most fluent and compelling displays of the campaign, a slick 4-1 win at Aston Villa in November taking them to the top of the table and a 6-1 drubbing of Sheffield Wednesday at Hillsborough in mid-January confirming their championship credentials. By the end of February they had lost only four matches. But the challenge then began to falter and by early April it appeared dead in the water after Manchester City meted out a 4-0 hammering at Maine Road. With the finishing line in sight, though, the red side of Manchester also stumbled, dropping ten points from the next fifteen to gift the initiative back to Leeds. On a nerve jangling second-to-last weekend of an enthralling season, Strachan and company seized their chance, beating Sheffield United 3-2 in a red-hot atmosphere at Bramall Lane. Hours later Manchester United lost 2-0 away at Liverpool and the League championship trophy was heading across the Pennines for the first time in 18 years.

While Leeds basked in the afterglow of their triumph, English football underwent a revolution. On 27th May, 1992, seven years after a super league was first mooted, the First Division clubs resigned *en masse* from the Football League and formed their own Premier League under the auspices of the Football Association. Sky and BBC agreed to pay a whopping £304 million between them over five years for the exclusive privilege to broadcast Premier League games. The following campaign, Carling negotiated a four-year sponsorship deal worth £12 million. So began the process that has transformed the competition into the richest football league in the world and its leading players into global superstars.

Attendances at games were also starting to rise again, up from a record low of 16.5m in 1985/86 to 19.5m in 1991/92, partly as a result of hooligan gangs at matches finally being brought under control by far more effective methods of policing and stewarding. The fear factor of the 1980s was replaced by a fun one. Grown men in furry suits calling themselves Ozzie the Owl, Billy Bantam, Captain Blade and the like entertained the kids during pre-match warm-ups. At Hillsborough, the Kop Band, a ten-piece brass ensemble who found a wider audience at Euro 96, brought musical humour to proceedings. Kit designers joined in the frivolity too, coming up with some weird and wacky strips involving diamonds (Bradford City), harlequins (Sheffield United), fuzzy hoops (Doncaster) and even kitsch tiger print (Hull City - naturally).

The dazzling riches on offer in the new Premier League sparked a gold rush among those clubs left behind in the Football League. Two of the victors in this frenzied scramble for fame and fortune were Barnsley and Bradford City. Playing a stylish brand of football which was, as their fans joyously sang, 'just like watching Brazil', Barnsley gloriously reached the top flight of English football for the first time in their history in 1997, finally accomplishing the goal that the Rev Preedy had set them after their Cup triumph way back in 1912. Promotion was clinched in the last home game of the season, against (as fate would have it) Bradford City; diminutive West Indian striker Clint Marcelle scoring Barnsley's second goal two minutes from time to send a nervously excited Oakwell delirious. Manager Danny Wilson and his men spent just the one season playing alongside the Premier League big boys, suffering some terrible beatings along the way, but it was still a whirlwind trip which Tykes fans would not have missed for the world.

One man looking on in envy the day Barnsley won promotion was Bradford City chairman Geoffrey Richmond. A successful businessman born and raised in Leeds, Richmond bought City, then in Division Two, in January 1994 following a successful spell as chairman of Scarborough FC. Incredibly ambitious, he predicted his new team would be playing Premier League football within five years. He invested millions of pounds in buying new players (the club record fee was smashed several times) and £7.5 million more on transforming Valley Parade into a 25,000 capacity all-seater stadium worthy of the top division.

The dream became reality on the last day of the 1998/99 campaign when City beat Wolves 3-2 at Molineux to snatch the runners-up spot behind Sunderland. It was the first time in 77 years that Bradford City had reached such rarefied heights. Few pundits gave them any chance of staying there, however. But roared on by 18,000 Bradfordians, a 'Dads Army' of veterans featuring old favourite Stuart McCall - who re-joined the club as captain from Rangers in June 1998; midfielder Neil Redfearn, lately the inspirational skipper of Barnsley and the two Deans, Saunders and Windass, defied the odds and stayed up. A 1-0 home victory over Liverpool on the last day of the season guaranteed their safety, albeit with a record low of 36 points.

Turning the clock back to 15th August, 1992 it was Sheffield United striker Brian Deane who had the distinction of scoring the Premier League's first goal, netting after five minutes in a 2-1 win over Manchester United at Bramall Lane. Ten days later Eric Cantona became the first player to score a hat-trick, for Leeds United in a 5-0 defeat of Tottenham at Elland Road. Thereafter Leeds staggered through the season as if nursing a massive hangover. They limply surrendered their championship crown to a Cantona-inspired Man United, failed to win an away game all season, avoided relegation by a mere two points and proved a major disappointment in the UEFA Champions League, going out in the second round to Glasgow Rangers in what the tabloids predictably dubbed 'The Battle of Britain'.

Wilkinson tried desperately to recreate the magical winning formula but although he continued to spend heavily - £2.9 million on Brian Deane, £2.6 million snaring Carlton Palmer, £4.5 million wasted purchasing Swedish flop Tomas Brolin and £3.4 million to secure Ghanaian hit Tony Yeboah - the best Leeds could achieve was reaching the Coca-Cola Cup Final in 1996. They put on a dreadful performance, losing the game 3-0 to Aston Villa. Disenchanted fans called for Wilkinson's head and they got it too, in September 1996, after a 4-0 thumping by bitter rivals Manchester United. That Wilkinson had saved the club from relegation to Division Three less than a decade before was largely forgotten by those who had once sung 'Sergeant Wilko's Barmy Army' with such gusto.

For Sheffield Wednesday, the 1992/93 season was a dramatic but ultimately heartbreaking one which featured an unprecedented four trips to Wembley and a momentous

Steel City derby in the FA Cup semi final. The team was now managed by Trevor Francis, who brought to the post a single-minded approach that many people misinterpreted as obstinacy and aloofness. In his first season in charge Wednesday finished third in Division One and qualified for the UEFA Cup for the first time since 1964. That 'Tricky Trev' then guided them to not one but two cup finals in his second season is even more remarkable given that, at one time or another, he had to make do without four key players for lengthy periods: Hirst (broken ankle and thigh injury), Sheridan (knee operation), John Pearson (broken leg) and Peter Shirtliff (broken arm).

Sheridan was fully recovered and Hirst sufficiently so to start on the subs bench for the knockout clash with Sheffield United on Saturday 3rd April, 1993. The All-Sheffield tie was scheduled to take place at Elland Road but following an outcry by club officials, supporters, civic leaders and local MPs the FA acquiesced to demands for the match be switched to the grander surroundings of Wembley, a far more suitable arena for such a historic contest to take place.

Sheffield United boss Dave Bassett had performed minor miracles on a shoestring budget at Bramall Lane, guiding the Blades from the Third Division to the First in successive seasons (1988-90) and then to the brink of their first cup decider since 1936. A consummate wheeler and dealer in the transfer market, he created a utilitarian but highly effective side for which Deane scored more than 100 goals in five season after he was picked up for a pittance from Doncaster Rovers in July 1988.

A Wembley crowd of 75,364 made for a cracking atmosphere that was both intense in rivalry and carnival of mood for what everybody in Sheffield agreed was the real final. The game got off to a blistering start, England winger Chris Waddle, a £1.25 million summer capture from

Marseille and soon to be crowned 'Footballer of the Year', blasting in a 30-yard free-kick after just 62 seconds to give Wednesday the lead. Against the run of play, United equalized a minute before half time when veteran forward Alan Cork, who refused to shave during the cup run and so now looked like a member of ZZ Top, scored from just inside the box. Irish international keeper Alan Kelly then produced a string of outstanding saves to keep United in the game before Wednesday pressed home their advantage in extra-time, ex-Crystal Palace forward Mark Bright heading his 17th goal of the season to give the Owls a 2-1 victory. United suffered further FA Cup semi final agony in both 1998 and 2003 when they were knocked out 1-0 on both occasions by Newcastle and Arsenal respectively.

Uniquely, Wednesday drew Arsenal in the finals of both the FA Cup and the Coca-Cola Cup. Confident of landing at least one trophy, the Owls ended up empty handed after their creativeness was throttled by a dour, grinding, boring Arsenal side managed by George Graham.

The Coca-Cola Cup Final was notable for being the first European club football match to feature squad numbers on the players' shirts. Number 15 John Harkes gave the Owls an early breakthrough but Paul Merson inspired a fight back by Arsenal, scoring the equalizer and setting up the winner in a 2-1 victory. A month later and Hirst salvaged a draw in the FA Cup decider by drilling in a second-half equalizer. In the replay five days later the score was locked at 1-1 and heading for penalties until 50 seconds from the end of extra-time when goalkeeper Chris Woods fumbled a header by ex-Leeds defender Andy Linighan to gift the Gunners another 2-1 victory. A season which had promised Wednesday so much, in the end yielded them nowt.

It is of interest to note that in achieving their successes Sheffield Wednesday and Leeds United fielded only three players born outside the British Isles: Roland Nilsson (Sweden), John Harkes (USA) and Eric Cantona (France). The foreign invasion was coming though and by 2010 their numbers had swollen to such a degree that of the four 18-man squads named for the two Wembley finals, 38 players were from overseas.

Elsewhere, Huddersfield Town enjoyed a purple patch in the mid-90s, reaching the Autoglass Trophy Final in 1994, losing 3-1 to Swansea City in a penalty shootout, gaining promotion to Division One via the play-offs in 1995 and making a strong bid for Premier League football in 1995/96 until a poor run of form in the second half of the season sent them tumbling out of the play-off zone. Underpinning all of this were 100 goals from strikers Andy Booth and 'Rocket Ronnie' Jepson, the former an outstanding youth team graduate whose brilliance, especially in the air, earned him a club record-breaking £2.7 million move to Sheffield Wednesday in the summer of 1996. A flourishing career - he won three England U21 caps, scoring two goals, in 1995 - went stale during his five year stay at Hillsborough, however, and the man they call 'The Legend' in Huddersfield returned to his hometown club for a cut price £200,000 in March 2001. Rediscovering his touch and form, over the next eight seasons Booth upped his goals tally to 150, putting him third on the Terriers' all-time list behind Jimmy Glazzard and George 'Bomber' Brown.

In 1996, Rotherham United went one better than Town by winning the Auto Windscreens Shield, loan signing Nigel Jemson scoring both goals in a 2-1 victory over Shrewsbury Town at Wembley in front of 20,000 jubilant Millers fans. The following year United were relegated to Division Three but the club then pulled off a masterstroke by bringing back old hero Ronnie Moore as manager. Considered by many Rotherham supporters to be the club's greatest ever player, a man idolised as much for his banter and his antics - he once celebrated a goal by nicking a policeman's helmet and putting it on his head - as for his deadly marksmanship, 'Mooro', if anything, was worshipped even more as a boss. He had the golden touch, taking little Rotherham from the Third Division to what became known as the Championship in successive seasons (1999-2001) and then keeping them there for the next four years. Gates at Millmoor doubled to 7,500 as the likes of Mark Robins, Paul Hurst and Alan Lee turned on the style. The magnitude of Moore's achievements cannot be overstated. In their own way they were every bit as impressive as Leeds winning the League title and Sheffield Wednesday the League Cup. Alas, all good things eventually come to an end. In January 2005, with Rotherham already doomed to relegation after an atrocious start to the season, Moore departed for Oldham Athletic. It was a sad footnote, but the first 'Ronnie Moore' years will live long in the memory of Rotherham fans as an exhilarating period in the club's history.

Success came the way of the county's non-league sides too. Halifax Town won promotion back to the Football League in 1998 as champions of the GM Vauxhall Conference. Guiseley (1991), Bridlington Town (1993) and Whitby Town (1998) all won the FA Vase, Whitby beating North Ferriby United in the competition's only all-Yorkshire final to date. And the humble village of Emley, best known for its TV transmitter, went FA Cup ballistic. In 1991, Emley AFC qualified for the first round proper, losing 3-0 to Bolton in front of a bumper 9,000 crowd at Leeds Road, Huddersfield. Then, in 1997/98, they reached the third round, their deserved reward for which was to be handed an away tie at Premier League big guns West Ham United in front of the *Match of the Day* cameras. Against a Hammers team containing the youthful talents of Rio Ferdinand and

Frank Lampard, Emley put on a spirited performance, narrowly losing 2-1 but winning over many new friends. Sadly, the football team outgrew the village that gave birth to it way back in 1903. In 2000, they moved to Wakefield to satisfy new ground regulation rules, changed their name to Wakefield & Emley a couple of years later and became simply Wakefield FC in 2006 after a new club, AFC Emley, was formed by a group of disaffected officials and supporters and which brought senior football back to the moorland village's historic Welfare Ground.

In the late Nineties, the economy began to boom. Grubby old industrial cities like Leeds, Hull and Sheffield were transformed into modern metropolises of chic design and culture. This was the age of unlimited credit. There was unbridled optimism and an unquenchable eagerness to spend, spend, spend and in such a climate football sky rocketed. TV and sponsorship deals, ticket prices, players' wages and transfer fees all went through the roof. The Premier League became a multi-billion pound global brand to rival Coca-Cola and Microsoft. Merchant bankers and venture capitalists were football's new best friends, and there was nobody they liked more than Leeds United. When Peter Ridsdale - who gleeful agents nicknamed 'Father Christmas' - took over as club chairman in 1997, Leeds splashed the cash like Northern yuppies. Ridsdale was, as he freely admitted, 'a fan of Leeds United who happened to become a director [in 1986, as the representative of sponsors Burton], then chairman.' The bond between Mr Chairman and the supporters was strengthened by his display of genuine compassion and concern following the fatal stabbings of two Leeds fans, Christopher Loftus and Kevin Speight, on the eve of Leeds' UEFA Cup semi final match with Galatasaray in Istanbul in April 2000. Supporters loved him - he was one of their own - and he in turn adored the adulation. He resolved to turn his boyhood heroes into the best club side in Europe but in doing so drove them deeper and deeper into debt. In came a galaxy of international stars like Mark Viduka (£6 million), Olivier Dacourt (£7 million), Robbie Keane (£12 million) and Rio Ferdinand, who joined from West Ham in November 2000 for a new record fee of £18 million.

Manager David O'Leary, who stepped up from assistant manager on the resignation of George Graham who had replaced Wilkinson in 1998, blended the big money signings with a group of talented graduates from the club's youth academy, his so-called 'babies', whose number included Harry Kewell, Jonathan Woodgate, Ian Harte, Gary Kelly, Paul Robinson and Alan Smith. The end product was an exciting and attacking team which won over many neutral supporters and established itself as a major force in the Premier League and Europe, sweeping past AC Milan and Lazio to reach the Champions League semi final in 2001. There they were vanquished 3-0 by Valencia but most observers agreed that it was only a matter of time before Leeds cashed in on their heavy expenditure and won a trophy. But those games with the Spaniards marked the end of the boom times. A calamitous chain of events was about to bring Leeds United to its knees.

...And Bust

'LOOKING back, we made errors,' admitted Peter Ridsdale in his cathartic autobiography *United We Fall*. 'We messed up. We gambled. We won. Then we lost. Big time.' Too bloody right they did. 'Publicity Pete' and his fellow board members played Leeds United like the Monte Carlo Casino, staking everything they had - and more - on 'living the dream' of becoming the best club side in Europe. They very nearly pulled it off too but within six years of manager David O'Leary leading his exciting young guns to the Champions League semi final in May 2001, the club went bust and dropped into the third tier of league football for the first time in their history.

'Goldfish Gate' symbolised the rampant excesses of Ridsdale's reign. Once everything went belly up, what appalled the public more than anything, it seemed, was not the £100 million spent on big-name players or the galactic wage bill or the £600,000 annual cost for running a fleet of company cars or the £70,000 lavished on private jets for the directors to flit around Europe in luxury but the £280 frittered away each year on a tropical fish tank in the chairman's office.

Not that Leeds fans cared much about fish or profit and loss accounts while the going was good. They lauded the gregarious Ridsdale as a homespun hero who turned the club they all loved into a footballing powerhouse capable of holding its own against such European powers as AC Milan, Barcelona, Roma, Lazio and Anderlecht. Nobody worried about the crazy sums being shelled out so long as Leeds was winning but, in hindsight, perhaps they should have. Ridsdale and his corporate backers exposed the club to irresponsible financial risk, he hedged his bets, borrowing a staggering £60 million against potential future gate receipts and television revenue from the money-spinning Champions League, which made qualifying for the competition not just a desire but an imperative and increased the pressure on the manager and his team.

A fortune was spent on assembling a squad that teemed over with international players. Yet after that wonderful European adventure at the turn of the new century, O'Leary was unable to deliver Champions League football again and Ridsdale held his manager wholly responsible for the failure. O'Leary in turn pointed the finger of blame at two of his players, Lee Bowyer and Jonathan Woodgate, whose court case midway through the 2001/02 campaign for attacking an Asian student on a boozy night out, he claimed, adversely affected team morale and form. From topping the Premier League table on New Year's Day they ended up in fifth place and out of the Champions League.

The European dream turned into a living nightmare. Massive loans and operating losses of £28.2 million forced Ridsdale into taking the painful but necessary action of selling captain Rio Ferdinand to arch rivals Manchester

United for £29.1 million. The sale provoked a very public spat between manager and chairman which resulted in O'Leary, the nearly man who, in Ridsdale's words, 'gave us one hell of a ride but won us nothing', being sacked shortly before the record breaking deal was finalised.

A savage cost cutting exercise followed. Fans watched in disbelief as highly paid stars were sold off for next to nothing. £25 million-rated Aussie winger Harry Kewell epitomised the wretched situation when he joined Liverpool for £5 million, £2 million of which reportedly went straight into his agent's back pocket. One gallows humoured fan unfurled a banner at Elland Road which read: 'Players 4 Sale: Buy 1 Get 1 Free. Hurry While Stocks Last'. How unerringly near the truth that was.

Plunging from Superman to reveilled in a matter of months, Ridsdale succumbed to the fans' venomous demonstrations and even death threats and resigned as chairman in March 2003. He left behind £103 million of toxic debt. The following year Leeds tumbled out of the Premier League. Ownership of the club passed from Ridsdale to Gerald Krasner, an insolvency expert who reduced the crippling burden to £24 million, in part by flogging off Elland Road in a lease-back deal, and then on to ex-Chelsea owner Ken Bates in 2005. Belying his grandfatherly image of white beard, big glasses and gummy grin, 'Cuddly Ken' is a sharp-tongued, opinionated and belligerent character who does not care a fig what supporters think of him. A good job too, for two days before the final game of the 2006/07 season he earned Leeds fans' antipathy by entering the club into administration. The move incurred an automatic 10-point penalty which sent Leeds down to League One in bottom place with immediate effect.

Bates shrewdly figured it was better to lose points when all was doomed - to stay up Leeds would have had to have beaten Derby County 9-0 and hoped that Hull City lost - rather than having them docked at the start of the next season. Two months later a new concern, Leeds United 2007 Ltd, chaired by Bates, beat off several rival bids to buy the club from the administrators, KPMG. Bates' offer to creditors of 1p in the pound to settle the club's debts was readily accepted by three offshore companies, Astor Investment Holdings (Guernsey), Krato Trust Ltd (Nevis Island, West Indies) and, significantly, Forward Sports Fund (Cayman Islands) who, it transpires, is the owner of Leeds United 2007 Ltd. Mystery surrounds the company. The names and faces behind the corporate brand are anonymous so no one knows who is really behind Leeds United. Such secrecy breeds distrust, creates conspiracy theories and raises more questions than are answered.

Bates thought he had secured the valid Company Voluntary Arrangement (CVA) that would enable Leeds to have their 'golden share' membership of the Football League returned to them. But then Her Majesty's Revenue & Customs challenged and thereby nullified the CVA and suddenly Leeds' whole future was in doubt. Bates was fuming, not least because he had to rely upon the benevolence of other club chairmen to agree, somewhat reluctantly, to exercise an 'exceptional circumstances' clause to allow Leeds to compete in the coming season. Their charity came at a cost though - Leeds would start life in League One on minus 15 points. Blaster Bates huffed and puffed - 'We were damned if we did and damned if we didn't,' he stormed - but for once there was nothing he could do about it.

As the saying goes the bigger they are the harder they fall and Leeds United undoubtedly landed in League One with a resounding thud. Their misery was the result of Ridsdale's financial butterfingers, but he was no crook. The same cannot be said of Doncaster Rovers' former 'consultant' Ken Richardson who was sent to jail for four years for conspiring to torch the club's Main Stand in a bungled insurance scam.

Richardson, a millionaire businessman from East Yorkshire, was the public face of Dinard Trading Ltd, an Isle of Man-based company which gained a controlling interest of Doncaster Rovers in May 1993. He had a shady past. He was accused (but acquitted on a technicality) of stealing shares in a Liechtenstein company and, in June 1984, was found guilty of being involved in a horse racing betting swindle for which he was fined £20,000 and given a nine-month suspended prison sentence. Nevertheless, Richardson was welcomed with open arms at Belle Vue. At the time he was president of Bridlington Town, a club which he had bankrolled to two promotions and to victory in the FA Vase in the past three seasons. He seemed just the man to drive Rovers forward. 'This is the start of a new era for the club,' James Burke, the outgoing chairman, told the *Doncaster Star*, whilst one shareholder declared: 'We don't care if Attila the Hun is in charge as long as Rovers are successful.'

Richardson was more like Attila the Hedgehog, a prickly character who along with his sidekick Mark Weaver, Rovers' general manager, got under the skin of just about everyone, notably the fans. Richardson was reviled for his blunt avowal that without him there would be no Doncaster Rovers and that unless attendances improved significantly, twice they fell below the 1,000 mark in the league during his tenure, he would withdraw the club from the Football League and enter it into the Doncaster Senior League.

Supporters might have put up with the jibes, rants and the raves had Richardson turned the struggling Division Three club around. But after a brief honeymoon period in which funds were made available to buy a new team, it quickly became apparent that Rovers were going nowhere fast. Players went unpaid, a ban was imposed on further purchases, the whole squad was put up for sale and winding-up orders were issued against them thick and fast. All the while Richardson blocked a proposed move from Belle Vue - so dilapidated that Weaver likened it to bomb-torn Beirut - to a brand new community stadium to be built at Doncaster Council's expense. The sticking point was the 70-year lease on the existing venue. The council, who owned the ground, offered Dinard £50,000 for the lease, a sum labelled as 'derisory' by Richardson who came up with a staggeringly different value of £2.1 million.

With negotiations deadlocked, Richardson announced in May 1995 that Belle Vue would be redeveloped and that he would stump up the majority of the cash. Then, on the night of 28-29th June a fire mysteriously broke out in the Main Stand. An investigation established the cause of the blaze was arson. A police investigation lead them all the way to Richardson who, it was discovered, paid ex-SAS solider Alan Kristiansen £10,000 to carry out the dirty deed in what many observers believed to be an insurance fraud.

Richardson was arrested on 23rd March, 1996 but the court case was adjourned for three years. In the meantime everything went speedily downhill for Rovers. With the fans baying for his blood, Richardson put Doncaster Rovers up for sale, but whenever he came close to agreeing a deal - such as with a group headed by Anton Johnson (who had deserted Rotherham's sinking ship in 1983) - he just increased his asking price. With debts of £3.9 million the club dived into administration in June 1997. Down and very nearly out, Doncaster were relegated to the Football Conference the following year with a woeful record: Played 46, Won 4, Drew 8, Lost 34; goals for 30, against 113, Points 20. Resigned to their fate, fans went on a funeral march through the town, carrying a coffin and releasing hundreds of black balloons as symbols of the club's impending death. At Belle Vue a minute's silence was observed, wreaths were laid and a bugler sounded the *Last Post*.

But Rovers did not die, they limped on, aided and abetted by Richardson finally relinquishing control of the club to Aidan Phelan of Dublin-based Westferry Ltd in July 1998. They were still in business on 6th March, 1999 when Richardson, his mental state said to be in shreds, was found guilty at Sheffield Crown Court of conspiracy to commit arson and jailed for four years. The following year the FA banned him from all involvement in football for life. There was precious little sympathy to be found in Doncaster. Richard Hayley, chairman of the Save the Rovers action group, summed up the fans' feelings: 'He destroyed the club and destroyed our lives for a long time. I think a lot of people will be in a mood to celebrate.'

With the exceptions of Sheffield United and Sheffield Wednesday, whose mountains of debt accrued from living the Premier League high life could yet tip them over the edge, every one of Yorkshire's professional football clubs went into administration around the turn of the century.

Barnsley called in the administrators after suffering relegation to Division Two in 2002. It was the latest and most serious episode in a series of setbacks for the club. The euphoria of winning promotion to the Premier League in 1997 was followed the following year by the despair of going back down playing football that was more like watching Bognor than Brazil. Shortly afterwards, forward Ashley Ward was sold to Blackburn for a club record £4.5 million. Chronic overspending on transfer fees and players' wages and the building of a new all-seater North Stand was compounded by the £315 million collapse of ITV Digital in March 2002. Matters got a whole lot worse, though, when the administrators issued an ultimatum that if a new owner could not be found by the end of November 2002 then Barnsley would be shut down. Ten days before the dreaded deadline the town's mayor, Peter Doyle, made a surprise rescue bid which secured Barnsley's immediate future. But within a year he had sold out to another investor - Peter Ridsdale.

How sickened Barnsley fans must have felt when Ridsdale pitched up in town in September 2003. The former Leeds chairman's tattered reputation and Barnsley's precarious financial position made for a Molotov cocktail - and it proceeded to explode. Evidently learning little from his past mistakes, Ridsdale wanted his new interest to be the next big thing but in doing so he ran it, 'into a financial position that was less than comfortable' as his successor as chairman Gordon Shepherd tactfully put it. In other words Barnsley FC was more bust than ever. Ridsdale resigned on Christmas Eve 2004 following a boardroom power struggle from which Shepherd and the club's major benefactor, local millionaire and lifelong fan Patrick Cryne, who, together with Barnsley Council, owned Oakwell stadium, emerged the victors. Ridsdale sneaked off to South Wales where he has since destabilised the finances of Cardiff City too.

Huddersfield Town's slide into administration came in 2003 at the end of a depressing campaign in which they were relegated to the basement division for only the second time in their history. It was hard for Town supporters to believe that only four years before their team had been on the threshold of following Barnsley and Bradford City into the Premier League. In January 1999, technological entrepreneur Barry Rubery bought the club for £8 million. That summer he fired popular manager Peter Jackson and replaced him with ex-Manchester United defender Steve Bruce. Under Bruce, Huddersfield played some exhilarating football and by Christmas 1999 they were riding high at the top of the First Division table. Terriers' fans lapped up the most exciting times the town had seen since Worthington, Nicholson, Cherry and Ellam lorded it over Leeds Road. But they did not last long. In February, top-scorer Marcus Stewart was astonishingly sold to promotion rivals Ipswich Town for £2.75 million and without his glut of goals Huddersfield's form fell away alarmingly, so much so that they missed out on the play-offs altogether. As for Stewart, he did win promotion, scoring for Ipswich in the play-off final at Wembley and thus helping to stop Barnsley from making a swift return to the Premier League.

Bruce was sacked after an awful start to the 2000/01 season in which Town picked up eight points from their opening 19 league games. Rubery accused his 'egotistical' ex-manager of 'wasting' £3 million on substandard players and blamed him for triggering the desperate tailspin that not even the repatriation of Andy Booth from Sheffield Wednesday could arrest.

The problems of West Yorkshire neighbours Bradford City stemmed from what their chairman, Geoffrey Richmond, later ruefully referred to as his, 'six weeks of madness'. Following City's breathtaking last-match Premier League survival in May 2000, Richmond chucked money around like it was confetti. Millions of pounds were spent on snapping up moderately talented players at vastly inflated prices, weekly wages of £40,000 were paid to Italian playmaker Benito Carbone and the Main Stand at Valley Parade was rebuilt. The massive outlay was to no avail. Although they did reasonably well in the Intertoto Cup, before Russian side FC Zenit St Petersburg thrashed them 4-0 in the semis, in the Premier League City endured a torrid second season, going down in bottom spot. Also losing out in the ITV Digital crisis, they then suffered two more relegations in the next six years which dumped them in the basement division for the first time since 1982.

City's subsequent financial implosion was so acute that the fixtures and fittings at Valley Parade, and even captain Dave Wetherall, were sold to leasing companies. Lumbered with £13 million of debt, the club entered administration on 16th May, 2002 after which the squad was not so much trimmed back as butchered, leaving just five professionals on the books. With his grand dreams for Bradford City having gone up in smoke, Richmond fell on his sword and resigned. Joint control of the ailing Bantams passed to Bradford-born club director Julian Rhodes and to 26-year-old Scotsman Gordon Gibb, whose family own the Flamingo Land theme park near Malton. Gibb was no knight in shining armour though. He was an asset stripper who secured the freehold of Valley Parade and the surrounding 20 acres of land for the benefit of his family pension fund before unexpectedly quitting at the start of January 2004. City were involved in a doomed Division One relegation dogfight at the time and less than two months later they plunged into administration for a second time, their debts having mushroomed to £34 million. The club was in such dire straits that the administrators pleaded with Valley Parade's landlord to allow City rent-free use of the stadium for the next year. Gibb heartlessly refused to do so, a decision which could so easily have signed the club's death warrant, for at one stage they came to within 10 minutes of being closed down for good.

Gibb's tactic of splitting a club from its most tangible and valuable property - the stadium and surrounding land - was employed at York City by another Scotsman, Douglas Craig. A far from popular chairman, he caused alarm among supporters in 1999 when, to 'safeguard assets', he transferred the Bootham Crescent ground into a new company, Bootham Crescent Holdings plc. The fans' concerns over Craig's motives were confirmed three years later when Persimmon Homes bought a 10 per cent share in BCH and then lodged a planning application to build houses on Bootham Crescent, a prime piece of real estate in the centre of the historic city. A suggestion was mooted to pack the football club off to Huntington Stadium, home of York City Knights rugby league club but before the contentious move could come to anything York City FC went into administration in December 2002.

If there is one piece of advice that club owners and chairmen should heed it is this: screw the fans at your peril. Supporters are a passionate and loyal lot and City's 4,000 outraged followers quickly mobilised themselves into organised and vociferous action groups. Their team might be kicking around in the nether regions of the Football League and their ground might be cramped and tatty but it was still *their* team and *their* ground and they were prepared to fight to the death for them both. By early 2003, a record number of objections to the planning application had been lodged with the City Council and in March control of York City FC passed from the administrators to a newly formed Supporters Trust after the latter agreed to settle an outstanding tax bill of £100,000.

A new age had dawned but for all the supporters' erstwhile endeavours the team's on-field performances suffered during the turmoil. At the end of the 2003/04 season the Minstermen were relegated to the Nationwide Conference, bad news which was counterbalanced in the summer by the stunningly good news that the Supporters Trust had obtained a controlling interest in BCH and thus effectively reunited club and ground. After five long and hard years the battle was finally won but at the expense of York City losing their place in the Football League and the despised Craig making £2 million out of their predicament.

If he was regarded as a villain in North Yorkshire then in the South of the county Ken Booth and his sons were seen as some kind of bandits holding Rotherham United to ransom. For 17 years the scrap metal merchants had propped up the Millers, allowing everyone in the town to enjoy the Ronnie Moore years, but when everything turned sour - United were relegated from the Championship in 2005 on just 29 points - it was they who got it in the neck from the fans. Ken Booth Senior, now aged 83, decided he had had enough. In December 2004 he wrote off a £3 million overdraft and gave the club away for £1 to a group styling themselves Millers 05. All very laudable, you might think, but he and his family were canny enough to retain ownership, but not responsibility for the upkeep of, Millmoor. The club's new owners were thus obliged to pay them annual rent of £200,000 for the privilege of playing in the crumbling monolith.

In May 2006, with Rotherham haemorrhaging £140,000 per month and owing the Inland Revenue £500,000, Millers 05 sold their interest to Denis Coleman, a local builder and property developer. His first action was to put the club into administration to protect it against winding-up orders. His lobbying of creditors to agree a CVA was successful but there were certain conditions attached, including the payment of an additional £600,000 to the Booth family in respect to the Millmoor lease. On the pitch, United's fortunes continued to flag. Further relegation to League Two in 2007 was followed by a second spell in administration for which Coleman became the first person to be disqualified from running a football club for failing the Football League's 'fit and proper person' test. Of greater concern to the fans was a dispute between the club and the Booth family which ended acrimoniously with Rotherham United's eviction from their home of 101 years during the 2008 close season.

Cap in hand, United asked the Football League to let them play the 2008/09 season at the Don Valley Stadium in Sheffield, a request which was granted in return for a £750,000 bond. They were also handed a 17-point deduction for still being in administration, a penalty which cost them a play-off spot. The team showed they were capable of stringing good results together in unfamiliar surroundings but the six billion dollar question on every Millers fan's lips was would they ever again see their team play in Rotherham?

At least Rotherham United were still going. The malaise infecting Yorkshire football proved to be deadly for Halifax Town and Scarborough. Town, the poor relations of West Yorkshire football, had from their formation in 1911 fought a relentless battle to keep going. Somehow they managed to endure one financial crisis after another, even in the dark days of the 1980s, but come the 2007/08 season the death knells could no longer be silenced. Having been relegated to the Nationwide Conference for a second time in 2002, the Shaymen's plight became so desperate that in September 2007 they approached MyFootballClub as a potential saviour. Launched the previous April, MyFootballClub was a unique concept in Britain, a cooperative of thousands of soccer fans wanting to buy an equal share in a football club. Leeds United initially led the list of favoured targets but in February 2008 the members voted to take over a much more modest club from the Football Conference - not Halifax Town, however, but Kent-based Ebbsfleet United.

With that avenue blocked off and an interested party dragging its feet over a buyout, Halifax went into administration in March 2008. The knockout blow came on 8th May when HMRC, the club's major creditor, refused to accept an offer of 2.5p in the pound to settle an outstanding tax liability of £814,000. With the failure of a CVA to be passed, the proud old club collapsed. Within a week they were expelled from the Football Conference and formally wound up bringing to an inglorious end almost 100 years of history. The Shaymen had rarely lit up the back pages but their passing was nonetheless mourned by a small but devoted band of followers in the textile town.

Meanwhile, Scarborough FC, their glory years of trips to Wembley and promotion to the Football League far behind them, were allowed to perish by the Borough Council. The chips were well and truly down when, in March 2006, Boro unveiled potentially lifesaving plans which, if approved, would have seen their crumbling McCain Stadium on Seamer Road sold to Persimmon Homes for £4 million and a replacement 4,000-capacity stadium built on the outskirts of town. The council, however, pointed out that there was a covenant restricting the 108-year-old ground's use to sporting activities and that they would therefore not approve plans to redevelop it as a housing estate. A possible bright future suddenly became bleak again and looked bleaker still when Scarborough were relegated to the Blue Square Conference North at the end of the season.

With gates dwindling all the time the club went into administration. Boro began the 2006/07 season on minus 10 points, ended it with a further demotion to the Northern Premier League and throughout it all nervously awaited the fall of the axe that swung menacingly over their heads. Scarborough Borough Council purportedly had a last minute change of heart over the planning proposals but it was a case of too little too late. The final blow was delivered in the High Court on 20th June, 2007 when with debts of £2.5 million, Scarborough Football Club was liquidated.

Further down the East coast in Hull, David Lloyd, a professional tennis player in the 1970s who had amassed a fortune from building up and then selling a nationwide chain of fitness centres, breezed into the city in August 1997 as the new dual owner of Third Division Hull City AFC and rugby league side Hull FC. Lloyd immediately served an ace: he would build a swish new super stadium, boasting restaurants, bowling alley, fitness club and cinema, to be shared by both clubs. His vision was for the two clubs to realise their potential and become sporting powerhouses capable of competing against the very best teams in the country. 'The potential here is enormous,' he declared. 'I am excited by the prospect of building something special ... We are going to put Hull on the sporting map.'

But after initially getting Hull City fans on side Lloyd double faulted. Firstly, the former GB Davis Cup captain appointed an ex-Hull rugby league player, Tim Wilby, as City's chairman. Lloyd admitted he knew little about football, still less about rugby and was completely unaware of any demarcation between the two codes in the city. On the whole, you were either a football or rugby fan. As events panned out, Wilby, a gregarious but elusive character, did not last long. Secondly, Lloyd announced that he would sell clapped out Boothferry Park for upwards of £10 million and reinvest the funds in the construction of the new stadium. That in itself was not the problem. The bitter pill Tigers fans found hard to swallow was that in the meantime they would have to share The Boulevard, home of the rugby club. To many, the very idea was abhorrent. They objected strongly to any such move, no matter how temporary it might be.

Lloyd could have run roughshod over the supporters, of course, but his grand plan was trashed by Hull City Council, who rejected his planning application to redevelop Boothferry Park, and by the Kwik Save supermarket owners, which occupied one corner of the ground and refused to relinquish a 125-year lease unless they received a massive pay-off and a guaranteed alternative site.

Concurrently, affairs on the pitch went from bad to worse. City plummeted out of Division Two in 1996 and finished as low as 17th in Division Three in 1997. The recruitment of Mark Hateley, the ex-AC Milan, Rangers and England forward, as a 'big name' manager did not stop the rot. City plumbed new depths in the 1997/98 season, finishing in 22nd place, the club's lowest ever position. The fans revolted. They wanted Hateley and Lloyd out and protested by volleying hundreds of tennis balls onto the pitch before matches. Lloyd in turn lost his patience with the fans and the City Council for perceived intransigence over his scheme. 'The people of Hull are crap,' he fumed. 'They are living in the dark ages and they always will.' His comments were a PR disaster. There was no way back for him and in October 1998 he announced that, 'unless someone comes forward with £2m to buy the club by the end of the week I will be walking away [and] it will be the end of professional football in the city.' Lloyd had dug deep into his personal wealth, investing some £5 million on trying and failing to turn Hull City and Hull FC into major teams. He was, perhaps, the right man in the wrong place at the wrong time.

A consortium of businessmen bought the club for £200,000 although, crucially, the arrangement did not include Boothferry Park which Lloyd later sold to Mel Griffin, a 'property consultant', for £1 million. One of the new owners' first acts was to sack the manager and replace him with midfield player Warren Joyce. City were rooted at the bottom of the table and heading out of the Football League when Hateley was given the boot. But they survived after Joyce masterminded a reversal of fortunes of such epic proportions that it has gone down in City folklore as 'The Great Escape'. Finances remained a severe problem though. Lloyd twice locked City out of Boothferry Park in a dispute over unpaid rent of £100,000 and, in February 2001, the club was put into administration to protect them against creditors chasing them for unpaid debts totalling £1.8 million. Then there was Stephen Hinchliffe, the largest individual shareholder, who within days of the takeover being completed was disqualified from acting as a company director for seven years and later jailed for four years for bribery and corruption relating to his retail group, Facia.

A string of club chairmen and owners through financial mismanagement, greed, asset stripping, overstretched ambitions, corruption and plain old incompetency, loused up pretty much every one of the county's top football clubs. But Hull's destiny, at least, changed course in March 2001 when 36-year-old Adam Pearson, the commercial director of big-spending Leeds United during the Ridsdale era, became the '100 per cent shareholder' and chairman of Hull City. Speaking in plc terms - 'Hull City is one of the biggest franchises left in British football which is untapped in terms of potential and the size of its fan base' - Pearson was incredibly ambitious: 'I'm not saying we are going to be a Premier League club in five or six years, but we're going to give it a good try.' The Hull public dared to believe that he might be the man who Lloyd had promised to be, that it really was, 'a very exciting time', but few realised quite how far and fast Hull City's fortunes would be transformed.

26

Bouncing Back

IF YOU had told Hull City fans at the start of the millennium that before the decade was out they would see their team playing Premier League football, in a new state of the art stadium and would have a Brazilian star orchestrating attacks then they would have thought you had gone stark raving bonkers.

Adam Pearson's vision gave Hull fans hope but nobody seriously believed the new chairman's wild aspirations would ever be achieved, especially after initial attempts failed to go according to plan. By the summer of 2003, Pearson had already gone through two managers, Brian Little and Jan Molby, was on a third, Peter Taylor, the England Under-21 boss who was nicknamed 'tinker Taylor' by fans for his irritating chop and change selection policy, and had invested some £2 million on a merry-go-round of players, all to no avail. City remained an inconsistent Third Division side, one which had not won a single promotion since 1985, never mind the three it would take for them to go all the way to the top of the football tree. With each passing day the crazy talk of the Premier League seemed more and more like pie in the sky.

But Pearson was not about to let the dream die. Driven by an overwhelming desire to succeed, he knew that Hull City was a sleeping giant just waiting to be shaken from its soporific slumbers, a belief that was strengthened in December 2002 by the club's move to the KC Stadium at The Circle off Anlaby Road. Owned by Hull City Council, sponsored by Kingston Communications and built at a cost of around £44 million, the modern 25,000-capacity asymmetrical bowl consigned City's much loved but rusting old Boothferry Park to the annals of history. In its post-war heyday, Boothferry Park had been one of the biggest and best grounds in the country; it even had its own railway station. On 18th December 22,407 supporters joined the welcome party at the KC, a friendly game against Sunderland and, on Boxing Day, another 20,000-plus crowd turned out for the inaugural League match against pacesetters Hartlepool. Behind the euphoria of the move, however, there lay the sobering reality that Hull City were still tenants and about to incur an inflation-busting hike in their annual rent, making the need for consistently larger crowds imperative.

A new stadium is one thing but the best way to entice more people through the turnstiles is to have a winning team gunning for promotion. So it finally was for Hull, who in 2003/04 won their first promotion in almost two decades, as runners-up behind Yorkshire neighbours Doncaster Rovers, and averaged healthy gates approaching 17,000. That summer Pearson negotiated one of the biggest transfer coups in the club's history, signing 30-year-old former England star Nick Barmby on a free from Leeds United. Cynics accused the veteran of Euro 96 of being over the hill and wanting one final pay day before hanging up his boots but Barmby was adamant the reason he dropped down to League One to join his home city club was because of the tremendous ambition shown by the chairman. In short, Pearson used all his PR experience to sell Hull City to the pint sized midfielder-cum-striker and Barmby liked what he heard and saw. The club was going places.

Installed as favourites to go up again, Hull cantered into the 2004/05 season and by January they led the rest of the field. Despite a couple of subsequent setbacks, a second promotion was sealed with three matches left to play. The dream was coming true. Taylor, not so long ago a target of fans' frustrations, was now hailed as a messiah by ecstatic supporters. He did not always produce the most aesthetically pleasing of teams but he instilled in his players three qualities vital in any winning side: a strong work ethic, a solid defence and an indomitable spirit. No one exemplified those virtues better than skipper Ian Ashbee, a gritty, no-nonsense midfielder who drove his team mates on relentlessly in Hull's quest for success. Northern Ireland international winger Stuart Elliott scored 27 goals to earn a share of the Golden Boot award with Bradford City's Dean Windass and Barmby, who silenced the doubters with some sparkling displays, declared, 'This promotion really does mean as much as anything in my career.'

Pearson understood that the Championship would not be such easy meat for the Tigers to devour and so it proved, a dramatic late run of good results dragging Hull away from the jaws of relegation. The strain of working so hard to avoid the drop, however, opened up irreparable cracks in the relationship between chairman and manager which ended with Taylor resigning to take over at Crystal Palace.

Who would succeed Taylor? Mick McCarthy? Gary Megson? Joe Royle? All had the experience and profile but

Pearson bowled a googly, plumping instead for Phil Parkinson, the relatively unknown manager of Colchester United. After a shambolic start to the new season, though, he was fired and with Hull well and truly bogged down in the relegation quagmire Pearson went for the easiest and cheapest option, promoting Phil Brown from his position as first team coach, a post which he had held only for a month. Hull fans were dismayed. Who was this Brown guy? His CV wasn't exactly awe inspiring. A qualified electrician, in his playing days he had been a jobbing full back who trawled the lower divisions. On retirement he became Sam Allardyce's assistant at Blackpool and Bolton. In his only managerial post he lasted seven months at Derby County in 2005 and was unemployed from then until Hull threw him a lifeline.

Yet Brown quickly showed himself to be a great motivator, lifting team morale and improving results. To his inherited squad he added loan signings Ray Parlour, from Arsenal, and, significantly, 37-year-old Dean Windass from hard-up Bradford City. Born and bred in Hull, and returning to the club he began his professional career with in the early 90s, Windass bagged eight goals in the latter half of the season, none more decisive than the one he scored for a 1-0 away win at Cardiff City in late April which guaranteed his team's safety and sent Leeds United down. He is, perhaps, the most popular forward to have played for the club since Ken Wagstaff banged in the goals with astonishing regularity in the late 60s and early 70s, a hero among heroes to Tigers fans.

Hull City lived to fight another day in the Championship but they would have to do it without the man who had saved them from going bust. Unhappy at sluggish season ticket sales and amid rumours that his financial partner Peter Wilkinson, a Harrogate-based millionaire, was pulling the plug on further investment, Pearson suddenly quit at the end of July 2007. The club was sold for a reported £10 million to property tycoons Russell Bartlett and Martin Walker and media man Paul Duffen.

While the boardroom played musical chairs, Brown pepped up his attack, making Windass's loan deal permanent, shelling out a club record £1 million for Wigan's Caleb Folan, persuading Manchester United to loan him their young and exciting Frazier Campbell and luring 34-year-old former Bolton and Nigeria star Jay-Jay Okocha out of semi-retirement. Hull's early form and results were patchy and by Christmas there was little sign of the fireworks that was to come. But as the Windass and Campbell double act clicked, so City steadily climbed up the table. In late March they reached third place but their bid for automatic promotion was dealt a massive blow the following month by Sheffield United who, in the fiery cauldron of a Yorkshire derby, defeated them 2-0 at Bramall Lane.

City had to endure the nerve shredding experience of the play-offs instead. Their reward for swatting aside Watford in the semi final 6-1 on aggregate was the biggest game in the club's history, a titanic clash with Bristol City at Wembley worth £60 million to the victors. A keenly fought contest in front of 86,000 fans was settled just before half-time by Windass, his crew cut dyed platinum blond *á la* Gazza, who lashed in a thunderous volley from the edge of the penalty area. As the minutes ticked down and the tension cranked up, the West Countrymen surged forward in search of an equalizer. In stoppage time it looked certain they would score but Darren Byfield blazed over from six yards. At the final whistle the amber and black half of the ground erupted in an explosion of noise. After 104 years of trying and failing, Hull City were in the top flight. Ashbee, who experienced the whole bottom-to-top trip, proudly held the play-off trophy aloft. Barmby beamed like a Cheshire Cat from ear to ear, the champagne flowed and as the team went on its celebratory lap of honour exultant City fans chanted 'Deano' in homage to their goal king.

In five short years the Tigers had come from plugging away at spit-and-sawdust grounds of Rochdale, Macclesfield and Cheltenham to the brink of performing in the iconic amphitheatres of Old Trafford, Anfield and the Emirates Stadium. This really was Roy of the Rovers stuff. And it got better, starting with the stunning capture of attacking midfielder Geovanni, once of Barcelona and Benfica, from Manchester City. The brilliant boy from Brazil was soon followed by a host of other foreign recruits. Supporters responded by snapping up almost 20,000 season tickets as excitement levels in the city reached fever pitch.

Hull were made odds-on favourites to go straight back down, but this was one underdog that was not about to roll over. They took the Premier League by storm and, incredibly, by late October were joint leaders with Chelsea and Liverpool. The run included a memorable 2-1 victory away at Arsenal - 'Geo' scored a sensational equalizer from a fizzing, dipping, swerving 30-yard shot - which prompted Duffen to deliver one of the quotes of the season: 'Winning at Arsenal was not beyond my wildest dreams, because they involve Elle McPherson!'

The Gunners were not the only member of the Premier League glitterati to be given a kick up the backside. Manchester United won by the odd goal in seven at Old Trafford and Liverpool and Chelsea were both held in their own back yards. Geovanni, Barmby, Windass and George Boateng tended to receive the lion's share of the plaudits, but the man who got the fans' vote was 6ft 4in defender Michael Turner who was voted 'Player of the Year' for the second term running.

Against lesser opposition Hull's musketeers struggled to replicate their 'all for one, one for all' approach and, on Boxing Day, they went into the half-time interval 4-0 down against Manchester City. Brown was so angered by the performance that he gave his players a very public, on-the-pitch rollicking. The manager was pilloried in the media for his 'unprofessional' action, and came increasingly under fire too from frustrated fans as City's season quickly unravelled. Geovanni's thirst for goals dried up, Windass, to the chagrin of supporters, was loaned out to Oldham and Jimmy Bullard, a record £5 million signing from Fulham in mid-season, suffered a career-threatening knee injury on debut. From table toppers City descended into a relegation dogfight, one from which they emerged victorious but bloodied, finishing one point ahead of demoted Newcastle United. But the impossible dream of Premier League football was still very much alive.

Doncaster Rovers' fortunes, meanwhile, have been reconstructed to a remarkable degree by local born cosmetic surgery pioneer John Ryan. A former shareholder in the club who mistrusted Ken Richardson's motives, the multimillionaire popularly acquired control of the club on 3rd May, 1999 the same day Rovers beat Farnborough at a packed Belle Vue to win the Conference League Trophy. Possessing the same kind of drive and high ambitions as Adam Pearson and the financial clout to make things happen - he pumped some £4 million of his own wealth into the club - Ryan's avowed dream was to turn his boyhood team into a force to be reckoned with. A key component in that was moving to a brand new stadium. Doncaster Council, however, was reluctant to commit to the project. A frustrated Ryan went on the offensive in late 2001, storming that there, 'could be a bloody riot' and, 'blood on the streets' if the stadium was not built, an outburst for which he was fined £10,000 for bringing the game into disrepute. Ryan subsequently resigned as Rovers' chairman but not as its owner leaving his successor, Trevor Milton, to sweet-talk the council round to the club's way of thinking.

A quite extraordinary thing happened in the last league game of the 2002/03 season. Five days short of his 53rd birthday, Ryan fulfilled a lifelong desire when he donned the red and white hoops and trotted out for a three minute cameo appearance against Hereford, thereby becoming the oldest player to turn out for a professional football club. A couple of weeks later and manager Dave Penney's side thrillingly won promotion to the Football League after a gap of five years by beating Dagenham & Redbridge 3-2 in the Conference play-off final at the Britannia Stadium, Stoke.

That summer, exciting Scottish midfielder Michael McIndoe, one of Rovers' most popular players of modern times, was signed from Yeovil Town for £50,000. His pace and skill tormented opposition sides to such a degree that he was voted 'Third Division Player of the Year' in 2003/04. It was a great season all round. Doncaster won back-to-back promotions as champions ahead of Hull City, attendances reached their highest levels in nearly 20 years, Ryan returned as chairman with Milton moving upstairs as president and, to cap it all, Doncaster Council finally announced it would fund a £20 million, 15,000-capacity multi-activity complex at Lakeside for the benefit of the town's football teams, rugby league side and athletics club.

The Keepmoat Stadium - named after the construction firm which built it - was opened to great fanfare on New Year's Day 2007, a near sell-out crowd cheering Donny on in a 3-0 hammering of Huddersfield Town. With Penney surprisingly leaving the club at the start of the season, it was his replacement, former Bournemouth boss Sean O'Driscoll, who lead the club to their first major cup success in their

131-year history, the Johnstone's Paint Trophy. In a rip-roaring final at the Millennium Stadium, Cardiff, Doncaster beat Bristol Rovers 3-2 after extra-time to send the 20,000 supporters from South Yorkshire delirious. The triumph came a year after Rovers reached the Carling Cup quarter final, stunning Premier League sides Manchester City and Aston Villa and giving Arsenal an almighty scare, taking them to a penalty shootout, in three of Belle Vue's biggest nights out in living memory.

Things got better still the following season. Significantly, as events turned out, striker James Hayter arrived from Bournemouth for a new club record fee of £200,000. He was the latest addition to a vibrant team - captained by Wales international midfielder Brian Stock, another ex-Cherries player - which hustled and bustled its way into the play-offs. In the semi final, at the Keepmoat, Rovers crushed Southend United 5-1 to set up a grandstand finale with Leeds United at the new Wembley.

Sunday 25th May, 2008 is a date now etched in the DNA of every Donny fan. Seven years beforehand Leeds were Champions League semi finalists while Doncaster were making up the numbers in the Nationwide Conference. Now, at the national stadium, the two Yorkshire clubs, one very much on the up, the other on the slide, were both battling for a place in the Championship. Before a crowd of 75,132, Rovers attacked from the start, carving the Leeds rearguard open time and time again. Two minutes into the second half a bullet header from Hayter gave them a deserved lead and thereafter O'Driscoll's team thwarted the expected Leeds onslaught with a terrific display of steadfast defence. The shrill of the final whistle was met by a cacophony from the Doncaster end as overjoyed supporters celebrated going up for the third time in five glorious years and to the second tier of English football for the first time in half a century.

Doncaster Rovers have since established themselves as a Championship side capable of giving supposedly bigger teams a bloody nose. During the 2009/10 campaign, almost 270,000 spectators watched them play at the Keepmoat, a figure more than five times that at Belle Vue in the dark days of Ken Richardson's reign of the late 90s. The fairy-tale renaissance is every bit as impressive as that of Hull City and the fairy godfather to thank for it is John Ryan. When almost everyone else had given up on the club he put his money where his mouth was and dragged the team he loves out of the gutter and on to a road paved with gold.

Aside from Doncaster's triumph in the Johnstone's Paint Trophy, Yorkshire football has experienced several near misses in Cup competitions in recent years. In 2002/03 Sheffield United were one step away from reaching both the FA and Worthington (League) Cup finals. Their progress was checked by Arsenal and Liverpool, the latter overturning a 2-1 first leg victory by United at a pumped up Bramall Lane for a 3-2 aggregate win. Five years later it was Barnsley's turn to take centre stage in the FA Cup. Revitalised in the post-Ridsdale era, they KO'd the holders Chelsea and Liverpool, two heavyweights of football, *en route* to the last four only to have their challenge stopped in the penultimate round by fellow Championship middleweights Cardiff City who edged an entertaining encounter 1-0. Barnsley won promotion from League One via the play-offs in 2006 and since then they have clung on to their Championship status while also adding some 4,000 more spectators to the average Oakwell gate, no mean feat.

On their way up from League One Barnsley beat Huddersfield Town in the play-offs and the Terriers again missed out on promotion at the same stage the following season, this time losing 2-0 to Millwall. A steady improvement in the club's fortunes began in 2003 when Ken

Davy, the chairman of Huddersfield Giants, purchased the ailing club from the administrators. One of his first acts was to reappoint Peter Jackson as manager who on a threadbare budget took Town up from Division Three and to the cusp of the Championship. His 'reward' for a poor start to the next season was to be fired for a second time. Town celebrated their centenary in 2008 - a commemorative pre-season contest between Huddersfield and Arsenal for the Herbert Chapman Trophy was won by the Gunners - and the average home attendance is currently 14,381, the highest it has been since 1972, a clear sign that the club is going in the right direction again.

York City have twice suffered Wembley woe in the last two years, losing 2-0 to Stevenage Borough in the 2009 FA Trophy Final and then going down 3-1 against Oxford United in the Blue Square Conference play-off final. Both results were hugely disappointing but the future looks bright for the Minstermen. With gates having stabilised at around 2,500 - among the biggest outside the Football League - and after expending so much blood, sweat and tears on reuniting York City and Bootham Crescent, the club is looking forward to moving to a new multi-sports stadium to be built elsewhere in the city by 2015.

The tom-toms have beaten out the rumour that Bradford City might likewise vacate Valley Parade. The most likely option is a move to a proposed £75 million 'sports village' at Odsal which they would share with Bradford Bulls in the same kind of football-rugby league affiliation that exists in Hull, Huddersfield, Doncaster and Halifax. The current economic climate has forced Bradford Council to put the expensive scheme on the backburner but if it sees the light of day again, then it might just be the shot in the arm the club needs. Turning their backs on their historic 124-year-old home would not be popular among supporters but something radical needs to be done to drag the League Two club out of the doldrums. Not even the return of old hero Stuart McCall as manager could spark a promotion charge and in February 2010 he was replaced by ex-Hull boss Peter Taylor. At least a drive to get more fans through the turnstiles by slashing season ticket prices to some of the lowest in the Football League has worked. City are by far and away the best supported team in League Two. The potential is there, it just needs reigniting.

Sheffield United bounced back from their Cup disappointments to win promotion back to the Premier League in 2006. The clamour for tickets among supporters was so feverish that the average gate at Bramall Lane broke through the 30,000 barrier for the first time since the long haired, laconically-skilled days of Tony Currie and Alan Woodward in the early Seventies. But as with so many promoted teams, United found the gulf in standard between Championship and Premier League football almost too wide to bridge. Haunted by relegation all year long, Neil Warnock's men lost a last day, winner-takes-all encounter with Wigan Athletic at the Lane which saw the Latics leapfrog above them on goal difference and send United down.

The Blades were fuming. Not with Wigan but with West Ham United and the Premier League over 'The Tevez Affair'. From being dead and buried at the start of March, the Hammers staged a Lazarus like recovery, winning seven of their last nine games, including away fixtures at Arsenal and Manchester United, to hoist themselves off the bottom of the table and clear of the relegation places. Central to this late discovery of championship winning form was a glut of goals from Argentine striker Carlos Tevez. That he was playing at all infuriated Sheffield United for West Ham broke Premier League rules on third party ownership of players' registrations when they signed him (and his compatriot Javier Mascherano) from Brazilian side Corinthians. The Premier League fined the Londoners a record £5.5 million but did not ban Tevez from playing or impose a points' penalty, decisions which ultimately cost United their Premier League status. The absolute fortunes sloshing around in the gold pan of the Premier League has made competing in the uppermost echelon of English football a cut throat business and United took one almighty slash at West Ham's jugular, suing them for £45 million. The bitter dispute dragged on until March 2009 when the two parties finally agreed an out-of-court settlement understood to be £4 million per year for the next five years, a welcome payout but hardly enough to service mushrooming debt which in February 2010 was revealed to be in the region of £48 million. A gut-wrenching Championship play-off defeat by Burnley in 2009 may yet come back to haunt the Blades.

From ashes is born new life. Halifax Town and Scarborough FC might have died in body but in spirit they endured and shortly after their demises fans and officials of the old clubs filled the vacuum by forming two new teams, FC Halifax Town and Scarborough Athletic. Obliged to enter the Unibond (Northern Premier) League Division One North, FC Halifax, like their dissolved predecessor, took up residence at The Shay, a ground which in recent years has gone from blot on the landscape to comfortable 10,000-capacity stadium after a multi-million pound investment by Calderdale Council. From there they plotted promotion and achieved it in style, going up as champions after scoring 108 goals and accumulating 100 points. Meanwhile, Scarborough, who are run on a not-for-profit basis by supporters' organisation The Seadog Trust, were entered into the Northern Counties East League in 2007. With the McCain Stadium remaining empty and derelict and in the hands of the liquidators, Boro ground-share Queensgate Stadium with their East coast rivals Bridlington Town. Incidentally, Bridlington are a re-branding of a local pub team called The Greyhound which took on the mantle of an older Bridlington Town club that folded at the end of the 1993/94 season, following its president Ken Richardson's decision to seize control of Doncaster Rovers.

There were bucket loads of tears shed in Leeds and Sheffield at the end of the nail-biting, final round of matches in 2009/10 but for very different reasons.

At a rocking Elland Road they were of joy as 10-man Leeds United roared back from a goal down against Bristol Rovers to win 2-1 and with it promotion to the Championship. Writing himself into local folklore by scoring the clinching goal was striker Jermaine Beckford who for the second successive season racked up 30 goals, a club statistic which not even past 'greats' like John Charles, Allan Clarke and Peter Lorimer managed to achieve. The former Wealdstone player enjoyed a sometimes tempestuous relationship with the fans - some labelled him sulky and lazy - but he did the job he was paid to do and his reward for such proficiency in front of goal was a transfer to Premier League outfit Everton.

At an electrically charged Hillsborough there was overriding despair as the Owls suffered relegation to League One for the second time since the turn of the millennium, after failing to get the three points they needed in a must-win showdown with fellow strugglers Crystal Palace. Both results prompted pitch invasions at the final whistle but while thousands of happy and mightily relieved Leeds followers - a late collapse in form had almost pushed them into the play-offs for the third year running - turned Elland Road into a celebratory sea of white, yellow and blue, in Sheffield trouble flared between the two sets of rival fans as passions boiled over. Violence marred play-off matches too between York City and Luton Town at Kenilworth Road and Huddersfield and Millwall at the Galpharm Stadium, ugly scenes reminiscent of the bad old days of the 1980s.

Resentment for Wednesday's wretched decline is reserved largely for former chairman Dave Richards who resigned his post shortly before the club was relegated from the top tier in 2000 to take up a similar role with the Premier League. Wednesday Independent Supporters' Association accused him of leaving others to, 'sort out the mess of his stewardship', one which, sadly, remains. More than £20 million in debt, the club rejected as 'wholly unacceptable' an offer in May of £2 million for a 40 per cent stake from Chicago-based investment company Club 9 Sports. How long will it be, though, before another investment shark smells blood and comes in for the kill?

Agonisingly, Rotherham United missed out on promotion to League One in 2010 after losing a scintillating play-off final 3-2 against Dagenham & Redbridge at Wembley. It was a crushing blow for Millers fans present in the 32,000 crowd and also for a very familiar face sitting on the bench - Ronnie Moore.

The legendary player and boss returned as manager earlier in the season after Mark Robins was poached by Barnsley. He immediately rediscovered the golden touch of old and, by March, United occupied the third automatic promotion spot until four defeats on the bounce sent them into the play-offs lottery. The decision to bring 'Mooro' back was made by Rotherham United's new owner Tony Stewart, a local businessman with 'desire and ambition' who bought the cash-strapped club from the administrators in 2008. One tangible result has been the purchase of the former Guest and Chrimes Foundry site in the town centre which, in conjunction with Rotherham Council, will be redeveloped over the next two years as a 12,000-capacity sports stadium. Football is coming home to Rotherham.

The Tigers of Hull City lost their roar in an anti-climatic 2009/10 season. There was no fire-cracking start to the campaign, just a raft of negative results which embroiled the club in a relegation scrap from which, this time, there was no escape. The fans booed the team and jeered the manager who, it seemed, was losing the unity and respect of the dressing room. Worse still, the club was facing a financial meltdown of such magnitude that owner, Russell Bartlett, turned to the one man he thought could solve all their problems - Adam Pearson. Riding back into town like some kind of Wild West sheriff determined to clean up the detritus, Pearson was appointed Head of Football Operations. What he uncovered at the club was a runaway wage bill which was eating up 80 per cent of the club's £50 million annual turnover and nearly £6 million paid out in agents' fees in two years. He launched a scathing attack on outgoing chairman Paul Duffen, ridiculing his business sense and accusing him of spending non-existent money. Duffen, 'the whipping boy' as he himself observed, defended himself, blaming the club's financial ills on the credit crunch and saying that all he ever did was execute the board's consensus plan.

Meanwhile, out on the pitch things were going from bad to worse. In March, after a run of five straight defeats, Pearson took decisive action and placed Brown on 'gardening leave', a nice way of saying he was fired. He brought in the experienced, 'down-to-earth' Ian Dowie, an unpopular choice among the City faithful for the simple fact that he was the man who was at the helm when Newcastle United crashed out of the Premier League the year before. And he did it again with Hull, a 2-2 draw away at Wigan in the second to last match condemning the Tigers to relegation. The fantastical Premier League dream was over.

Having ridden the wave of good fortune for almost a decade Hull City are now perilously close to smashing against the jagged rocks of escalating debt. If administration is to be avoided then a gaping £21 million shortfall in the club's finances needs to be plugged and quickly. Pearson's plan of action is to offload expensively paid stars, thereby slashing the wage bill and, ominously, to borrow money against potential future revenue from ticket sales and TV rights. It is a risky strategy, one which bears an uncanny resemblance to the failed model implemented by Peter Ridsdale at Leeds United. Supporters can but hope that Pearson's business acumen will hold up to greater scrutiny. If it does then Hull City should emerge from their hellish predicament as a solvent Championship side. If it does not then the stunning bounce back of the last seven years might end in their dreadful demise.

What Next?

SO THERE you have it, the history of Yorkshire club football. With more ups and downs than the Dales, the story of the last 153 years has swung to and fro from exhilarating highs of triumph to depressing lows of failure and heart-rending disaster.

The county's sides have both dominated the game - winning 11 championship titles, 11 FA Cups, 2 League Cups, 2 Inter-City Fairs Cups and an assortment of minor trophies - and been at its mercy. Some clubs have come and gone, so too a veritable cast of star performers and colourful characters. Attendances have fluctuated from the incredibly huge to the worryingly small and everything in between. Yorkshire derby days have and still do elicit fans' fervour like no other tie. The county's clubs have championed innovations and rule changes, instigated floodlights, cup competitions, professionalism, women's football and the recruitment of black and foreign players. Tragedy has stalked the game. Hooligans have blighted it and betting scandals, player auctions, illegal payments and chairmen who have been all too willing to resort to skulduggery and underhand tricks have brought shame upon it too. But there have also been cult heroes and war heroes, not to mention some of the greatest players, managers and sides the sport of football has ever seen.

Through all this flux there has been one constant: Sheffield FC. Nathaniel Creswick and William Prest could not have imagined in their wildest dreams what the future had in store for 'Foot-Ball' when, on that walk in mid-summer 1857, they discussed forming a football club. Astonishingly, a century and a half later the oldest football outfit in the world is still going at full throttle. 'The Club' currently operates in the UniBond First Division South, seven levels below the Premier League, from the Coach and Horses Ground in Dronfield ... across the county border in Derbyshire! But their fame outshines that of many supposedly greater luminaries. Their 150th anniversary birthday bash on November 8th, 2007 was a star-spangled event attended by legends like Pele and 1966 World Cup hero Sir Geoff Hurst. Sheffield lost 5-2 to Inter Milan in a celebration match at Bramall Lane, watched by a crowd of 18,471. To emphasise the exalted company in which they now move, Sheffield FC and nine-times European Cup champions Real Madrid were the only two clubs recognised by FIFA with a Centennial Order of Merit in 2004 for significant contributions to football.

Exactly 100 years before, in 1904, their Edwardian counterparts gave the club its finest hour on the pitch, lifting the FA Amateur Cup when beating Ealing 3-1, in front of 6,000 supporters in the final at Bradford. Presenting them with the trophy was Charles Alcock, Vice-President of the Football Association and the mastermind behind the Cup and the annual England-Scotland international. 'It is a personal pleasure to hand the Cup to the Sheffield Club,' he declared to the gathered throng, 'especially when I recall its long and unique record in association football.'

Surprisingly, it took 'The Club' until 1961/62 to reach the Final of the Sheffield & Hallamshire Senior Challenge Cup, the modern name for the Sheffield Challenge Cup. There they were beaten 1-0 in a replay by their great rivals, Hallam FC. Amazingly, Hallam are also still plugging away, playing alongside the likes of Scarborough Athletic, Bridlington Town and Selby Town in the Northern Counties East League Premier Division, one rung below Sheffield. Celebrating their own 150th anniversary in 2010, what is equally astonishing about Hallam is they continue to play home matches at their original ground on Sandygate Road.

More than three million fans clicked through the turnstiles to watch the county's Premier League and Football League teams in 2009/10, a sure sign of the great appetite that exists for football in Yorkshire despite strong competition from rugby league. Hull City's KC Stadium was 96 per cent full to its 25,400 capacity. Leeds United (24,800) and Bradford City (11,400) were the best supported sides in League One and League Two. And Sheffield United and Sheffield Wednesday attracted a combined average attendance of over 48,000, 5,000 more than the Championship champions Newcastle United could muster in a one club city.

But what does the future hold? If the past is anything to go by, expect the unexpected. Have Hull City gone into administration? Have Sheffield Wednesday been taken over by foreign investors? Have the rumours circulating about Leeds United paying players' wages from offshore accounts been proven unfounded or true?

Given such unpredictability, perhaps we are as well to fall back on hopes and desires. Yorkshire derby days will always stir the blood and keep the passions flowing. The rivalry has been there from the start and it always will be. But would it not be fantastic to scan the Premier League table and see it dominated not by north west outfits or those from the capital but by Yorkshire clubs? Or to watch an all-Sheffield cup final, or to see Leeds or Hull or even Doncaster, Huddersfield, Bradford City and Barnsley qualifying for European competition, or for Rotherham to win the League Cup that they came so close to doing in 1961, or to welcome York City, Halifax, Scarborough and Bradford Park Avenue back into the Football League fold? Maybe it is all pie in the sky. Going back only a few years, no one then would have predicted Leeds plunging from a Champions League semi final to League One, or Hull City zooming from absolutely nowhere to the Premier League. Miracles do happen, and the possibility of them happening to our own club helps sustain us fans through all the bad times.

Enough about professional football, what of the honest and enthusiastic efforts of the tens of thousands of men, women and children who play the game week in, week out for no financial reward, and the armies of volunteers at the County FAs and at hundreds of local clubs who ensure the governance and smooth running of a myriad of district and regional teams and leagues. Why do they do it? Because they love the game, pure and simple. 'Foot-Ball' has come a long way since Creswick, Prest and their associates first got together. The game has grown exponentially into a multi-billion pound global concern. After the Olympics, the World Cup is the most prestigious sporting event on Earth. Star players have become mega-rich A-list celebrities. Interest and investment in the sport has never been higher. But scrape back the veneer of celebrity and commercialism and what you discover is the jumpers for goalposts spirit of those early pioneers at Sheffield FC alive and well, where the game is played not for fame and fortune but for fun and, if one is lucky, a slice of local glory.

The history of Yorkshire football came full circle on Tuesday 4th May, 2010 when at Hillsborough, Sheffield FC beat Hallam FC 4-2 to win the Senior Challenge Cup for the fourth time in six years. There is something rather fitting and romantic about the world's two oldest association football clubs locking horns in the final of one of the world's oldest Cup competitions.

To Boro Or Not To Boro?

MIDDLESBROUGH FC have not featured in this book so far but the question is: should they have done? On the one hand, the town was for many centuries a far flung outpost of the old North Riding of Yorkshire; on the other, it was absorbed into the new County of Cleveland following a major reorganisation of boundaries in England in 1974.

Whilst many football clubs and district leagues from Middlesbrough and other areas of Cleveland remain affiliated to the historic North Riding County FA, most pundits lump Middlesbrough FC in with Newcastle United and Sunderland as one of the North East's 'big three'. And followers of other White Rose clubs have been known to taunt 'Boro supporters with the chant: 'Yorkshire rejects'. A judgement was needed on whether or not to include Middlesbrough in the history of Yorkshire football, and if so whether to stop at 1974. Rightly or wrongly, the decision was made to exclude them from the bigger story. However, for those Middlesbrough supporters who regard themselves as dyed-in-the-wool Yorkshiremen and women, what follows is a potted history of football in their town.

Association football began in earnest in Middlesbrough in 1876 when, apocryphally over a tripe supper, members of Middlesbrough Cricket Club agreed to form their own football club as a way of keeping fit during the winter. Unsurprisingly, they called it Middlesbrough Football Club. From 1879 it shared its cricketing parent's ground on Linthorpe Road, south of the town centre. Ten years later they turned professional, an irony considering that in the same year several members broke away and formed a rival professional outfit, Ironopolis FC, over a dispute about adopting professionalism.

Ironopolis, so named in homage to the heavy industry upon which much of the town's wealth was built during Victorian times, initially gained the upper hand. In 1893 they reached the FA Cup quarter final and they won the Northern League for three consecutive seasons (1890-93), their reward for which was to be admitted into the Second Division of the Football League. But following an unsuccessful first season, and with their finances in disarray, they resigned their membership in 1894 and folded.

Big money problems had by that time forced Middlesbrough to revert to amateur status. However, subsequent success - they were Northern League champions in 1894-95-97 and FA Amateur Cup winners in 1895 and 1898 - encouraged them to give professionalism another go. Elected to the Football League in 1899, they gained promotion to the First Division three years later. In the summer of 1903 they moved to Ayresome Park, a new ground designed by Scottish architect Archibald Leitch and situated adjacent to Ironopolis's old Paradise Ground, which became their home for the next 92 years.

The club caused a sensation in February 1905 when they

paid Sunderland £1000, the first four figure transfer fee, for ex-Sheffield United inside forward Alf Common. In March 1906, they splashed out another £750 on the great Steve Bloomer from Derby County. Though outraging parts of the press, the costly signings successfully dragged 'Boro out of relegation dogfights and then helped them to reach the dizzy heights of sixth in 1908.

It was during this period that Tim 'Tiny' Williamson, a locally born goalkeeper who won seven England caps, made the first of a club record 602 appearances (1902-23). He was joined in the team by centre-forward George Elliott, the son of a naval captain, who, appropriately, skippered the team either side of the Great War. Between 1909 and 1925 he poached 213 goals in 365 games, including 31 when Middlesbrough finished third in Division One in 1913/14, the club's highest ever position. His scoring glut, though, was soon overshadowed by the phenomenal exploits of an even more potent centre forward, George Henry Camsell.

Signed for £600 from Durham City in October 1925, Camsell, an ex-miner, plundered more goals (345) than any other player in Middlesbrough's history. He top-scored in 10 consecutive seasons, hit 24 career hat-tricks and racked up 18 goals in just nine international matches for England. His *Annus Mirabilis* was 1926/27 when, at the age of 24, he took full advantage of the new attack-friendly offside law to score a record 59 goals in 37 league games. Not surprisingly, Boro stormed to the Second Division championship posting a colossal 122 goals in total. Amazingly, Camsell's scoring feat was eclipsed within the year by Everton's 'Dixie' Dean who went one goal better.

Middlesbrough fielded one of the best sides in the country in the late Thirties, one which reached the Cup quarter final in 1936 and finished in the top five of Division One in the final two campaigns before the Second World

War. The conflict interrupted the fledgling careers of a new generation of stars including; 'Gentleman' George Hardwick, a cultured left back who captained both club and country in the mid to late 40s; Micky Fenton, a short and slightly built forward whose 162 goals in 269 games puts him fifth on 'Boro's all-time goal-scoring list and Wilf Mannion, the best of the lot, considered by many critics to be the greatest player ever to wear the red and white.

Mannion was a Rolls-Royce, a golden haired inside left of style and grace whose masterful dribbling, sharp passing and stunning ball control gained him a legion of hero-worshippers at Ayresome Park. In 368 matches for 'Boro he scored 110 goals and set up countless more. A star attraction at the 1950 World Cup in Brazil, between 1946 and '51 he collected more England caps (26) than any other player in Middlesbrough's history.

Mannion entertained the crowds at a time when attendances around the country were booming to new all-time highs. At Ayresome Park they reached a peak on 27th December, 1949 when 53,596 spectators shoehorned into the old ground to watch a festive local derby with Newcastle United. The following year Jamaican-born Lloyd Delapenha, one of the first black men to make the grade in English football, was signed from League champions Portsmouth. An exciting winger/inside forward who served with the British Army during World War II, 'Lindy' captured the hearts of the Ayresome faithful and netted 93 league and cup goals in 270 matches. Alas, his eight years on Teesside coincided with a decline in fortunes for the club slipped into Division Two in 1954.

It is striking how many prolific goal-scorers have turned out for the club, from Bloomer and Elliott to Camsell and Fenton and on to Alan Peacock (141 goals, 1957-64), big John Hickton (192, 1966-78) and the selfish but brilliant Bernie

'The Wolfman' Slaven (146, 1985-93). Even amongst such illustrious company, though, one forward stands out heads and shoulders above the rest - Brian Clough.

Born and bred in Middlesbrough, Cloughie was the archetypal 'fox in the box' who utilised cunning, guile, pace and a ruthless killer instinct to dispatch his goals. Making his League debut for 'Boro in 1955, over the next six years he scored 204 goals at the breathtaking rate of virtually one every game. In the five seasons, 1956-61 he netted 40, 42, 43, 40 and 36 goals. Even so, his consistent and deadly marksmanship could not get his team promoted back to Division One. Nor could it elicit more than two full England caps, a scandalous waste of talent. In 1961 he moved to North East rivals Sunderland for £42,000. His career was wrecked, at the age of 27, by a serious knee injury sustained in a match against Bury on Boxing Day 1962. 'The finest goal-scorer in the country and one of the best the game has ever seen was no more,' Clough wrote immodestly in his autobiography.

Watched by ever shrinking crowds, Middlesbrough dropped into Division Three for the first time in their history in 1966, the same year as Ayresome Park hosted some World Cup group matches. Bouncing back at the first attempt, they then romped to the Second Division championship by 15 points in 1973/74. Managed by former Leeds United defender and World Cup winner Jack Charlton and wearing for the first time the club's now iconic red shirts with broad white band, the promotion winning team was packed with such club legends as Hickton, Jim Platt, John Craggs, skipper Stuart Boam, Willie Maddren, Graeme Souness, David Armstrong, Alan Foggon and David Mills, who briefly became Britain's most expensive player when he joined West Brom for £500,000 in January 1979. The cherry on the cake was Charlton, in his rookie season, being voted

'Manager of the Year' ahead of his old mentor Don Revie, despite the latter landing the League title with Leeds.

Brash and inspiring, Charlton guided 'Boro to within one place of qualifying for the UEFA Cup in 1975 and to the League Cup semi final in 1976, where they lost 4-1 on aggregate to Manchester City, before he quit in April 1977. Thereafter, Middlesbrough's fortunes deteriorated dreadfully. Relegated to Division Two in 1982, four years later they fell into Division Three. Attendances plummeted to below 6,000, debts mounted, taxes and players went unpaid. These were dark days. On 30th July, 1986 the Inland Revenue was granted a winding-up order by the High Court and when the iron gates at Ayresome Park were padlocked shut by the Official Receiver it seemed as if the club had taken its last breath. But at the eleventh hour it was given the kiss of life by a consortium of local big businesses, headed up by a self-made millionaire and diehard fan, Steve Gibson. Agreeing to pay outstanding debts of nearly £2 million, the takeover was completed with just 10 minutes to spare before Middlesbrough lost their 'golden share' of the Football League. And so began a remarkable renaissance.

Successive promotions shot them back to Division One, after which, for the next few years, they yo-yoed between the top two divisions. In 1990 they reached the Zenith Data Systems Cup Final, losing 1-0 to Chelsea at Wembley. Things really began to motor, though, when Gibson became the outright owner and chairman of the club in 1994. A benevolent benefactor, the former Labour town councillor possessed the vision and the financial clout to make Middlesbrough, 'synonymous with a good team rather than cooling towers and chemical plants.' He recruited Bryan Robson as manager in the belief that the ex-England captain had the necessary stature and profile to attract star players from across the globe and so it proved. In came 22-year-old

Brazilian Footballer of the Year Juninho for £4.75 million, compatriot Emerson (£4 million), Juventus star striker Fabrizio Ravanelli (£7 million) and Australia international keeper Mark Schwarzer, who for more than a decade was an utterly dependable mainstay between the sticks.

Robson lead the side back to the Premier League in his first season. That summer, Middlesbrough FC moved from their old but much loved home at Ayresome Park to the Riverside Stadium, a modern 30,000 all-seater stadium on the banks of the River Tees. Costing a relatively modest £16 million, it was the largest football stadium built in Britain for 70 years. Gates immediately rocketed to levels not seen since the halcyon days of Wilf Mannion and company in the 1940s.

In 1997 Middlesbrough came within a couple of whiskers of realising their ambitious chairman's dream. On the back of some magical midfield performances from Juninho and a bucket load of goals from Ravanelli (31 in all competitions), they reached the finals of both the FA and the Coca-Cola cups. They lost both, however, to Chelsea and Leicester City respectively. To compound matters, they were again relegated from the Premier League, a costly consequence of having three points docked mid-season for cancelling a fixture at late notice. The following year Paul Gascoigne, the most naturally gifted English player of his generation but also a fading and troubled star, joined the club from Glasgow Rangers for £3.4 million. His first match was 'Boro's second Coca-Cola Cup final in 12 months but his introduction as a second-half substitute could not prevent his new team from losing again, beaten 2-0 by their nemesis Chelsea. The bitter blow was sweetened at least by an instant return to the Premier League. As for Gazza, personal problems limited him to only a handful more appearances before being offloaded to Everton in July 2000.

Robson was given access to an open chequebook and he made some excellent buys but was not quite able to convert huge potential into tangible success. Humiliatingly, he was forced to share the managerial hot-seat with Terry Venables for much of the 2000/01 season and was shoved off it completely in June 2001. His replacement, ex-Man United assistant Steve McClaren, was a surprise choice. He spent a cool £40 million plus on new players during his five-year tenure but did little to improve the club's mediocre league form. He will, however, be remembered as the man who guided Middlesbrough to their first major piece of silverware - the League Cup in 2004 when they gloriously beat Bolton 2-1 at the Millennium Stadium, Cardiff - with a side that was indicative of the changing face of English football. The goals were scored by Job (Cameroon) and Bolo Zenden (Holland), two of 10 foreigners in a squad of 16. One of the few Englishmen on show was teenage substitute Stewart Downing, a product of the club's youth academy. An attacking left winger who delivered many a killer cross, he became a firm favourite at the Riverside. He also came very close to matching Mannion's international record, winning 23 England caps (2005-09) before a £10 million move to Aston Villa in the 2009 close season.

Hundreds of thousands of fans lined the streets to welcome home their victorious team. Gibson, a hugely popular figure among them, was awarded the freedom of the town. Reward was a place in Europe and they qualified again the following year, this time through the league, going on a magnificent run to the 2006 UEFA Cup Final. A policy of all-out attack thrillingly overturned seemingly unwinnable ties against Basle and Steaua Bucharest in the quarters and semis before becoming unstuck in the Final in Eindhoven where they were walloped 4-0 by Seville.

That summer McClaren took over as England boss in

succession to Sven-Goran Eriksson. 'Boro's cup runs, they also twice reached the FA Cup semi final during his time with the club, masked the stark fact that in the Premier League they had made no progress. Gibson had a golden opportunity to hire an experienced and proven winner as the next manager but opted for another greenhorn, promoting 35-year-old former England defender Gareth Southgate from his post as team captain.

The chairman continued to bankroll the club, pumping in another £30 million over the next three years with a club record £12.7 million being spent on Brazilian flop Afonso Alves. The heavy investment failed to pay dividends. Reaching the last eight of the FA Cup in three successive years (2007-09) in no way compensated for an abject last two-thirds of the 2008/09 season which cost 'Boro their coveted place in the Premier League and Southgate his job. It is now up to ex-Celtic manager Gordon Strachan to prove that he has what it takes for Middlesbrough to lift another major trophy and regain their place in the Premier League. It will be no easy task but so long as Steve Gibson is at the helm such dreams can come true.

Guide to black and white images

CHAPTER 1 - Sheffield FC crest - © *Sheffield FC*
CHAPTER 2 - The Youdan Cup - © *Hallam FC*
CHAPTER 3 - Charles Clegg, back row, second left, next to his brother William, playing for a Sheffield team, circa 1876 - © *Sheffield County Council*
CHAPTER 4 - Hallam FC crest - © *Hallam FC*
CHAPTER 5 - Sheffield Wednesday FC crest - © *Sheffield Wednesday*
CHAPTER 6 - Sheffield United, FA Cup winners 1901/02 - © *Sheffield United*
CHAPTER 7 - Revd Tiverton Preedy - *courtesy David Wood, Barnsley Historian*
CHAPTER 8 - Manningham FC, rugby forerunners to Bradford City AFC
CHAPTER 9 - 2nd Lieutenant Donald Bell - *courtesy The Green Howards Museum*
CHAPTER 10 - Barnsley FC crest - © *Barnsley FC*
CHAPTER 11 - Huddersfield Town in 1922 - *courtesy of Roger Pashby*
CHAPTER 12 - Sheffield United crest - © *Sheffield United*
CHAPTER 13 - Bradford-born inside-forward Len Shackleton - *source unknown*
CHAPTER 14 - Rotherham United crest - © *Rotherham United*
CHAPTER 15 - John Charles, Leeds striker, in the '50s - © *Varley Picture Agency*
CHAPTER 16 - Sheffield Wednesday's David 'Bronco' Layne - *source unknown*
CHAPTER 17 - Don Revie, Billy Bremner with FA Cup - © *Varley Picture Agency*
CHAPTER 18 - Leeds's South African Albert Johanneson - © *Varley Picture Agency*
CHAPTER 19 - Doncaster Belles, double winners 1993/94 - *courtesy Sheila Edmunds*
CHAPTER 20 - Tony Currie - © *George Herringshaw/www.sporting-heroes.net*
CHAPTER 21 - Alex Sabella - © *George Herringshaw/www.sporting-heroes.net*
CHAPTER 22 - Bradford City crest - © *Bradford City*
CHAPTER 23 - A Bovver Boy's Doc Martens
CHAPTER 24 - David Hirst - © *George Herringshaw/www.sporting-heroes.net*
CHAPTER 25 - Doncaster Rovers crest - © *Doncaster Rovers*
CHAPTER 26 - Hull City crest - © *Hull City*
CHAPTER 27 - Sheffield FC, circa 1890 - © *Sheffield FC*
EXTRA TIME - Middlesbrough Ironopolis, 1892/93 - *source unknown*

Bibliography

ADAMSON, Steve, The Official History of Scarborough FC, 1879-1998 (Yore Publications 1998)
BAGGHI, Rob, & ROGERSON, Paul, The Unforgiven: The Story of Don Revie's Leeds United (Aurum Press 2009)
BARRETT, Norman, The Daily Telegraph Football Chronicle (Colour Library Direct 1999)
BLUFF, Tony & UTTLEY, Steve, The Fall and Rise of Doncaster Rovers (Breedon Books, 2008)
BUTLER, Byron, The Official History of the FA (Queen Anne Press 1991)
BUTLER, Byron, The Football League: The Official Illustrated History (Blitz Editions 1993)
CATTON, J.A.H., Wickets and Goals (1926)
CAVENDISH, Marshall, Football Handbook: The Glory Years (Marshall Cavendish Ltd 2006)
CLOUGH, Brian, Clough: The Autobiography (Corgi Books 1994)
COLLINS, Tony, Rugby's Great Split (Frank Cass, 1998)
DAVIES, Hunter, Boots, Balls & Haircuts (Cassell Illustrated 2004)
FARNSWORTH, Keith, Sheffield Football A History, Volume 1 1857-1961 (Hallamshire Press 1995)
FARNSWORTH, Keith, Sheffield Football: A History Volume II 1961-1995 (Hallamshire Press 1995)
FIELDHOUSE, John, Hull City AFC: From Bust to Boom (Great Northern Books, 2009)
FROST, Terry, Bradford City, A Complete Record 1903-1988 (Breedon Books, 1988)
FROST, Terry, Huddersfield Town: A Complete Record 1910-1990 (Breedon Books 1990)
GALVIN, Robert & BUSHELL, Mark, Football's Greatest Heroes (Robson Books 2005)

GILLER, Norman, Football And All That: An Irreverent History (Hodder & Stoughton 2004)
GOLDBLATT, David, The Football is Round: A Global History of Football (Penguin 2007)
GREAVES, Jimmy, Football's Great Heroes and Entertainers (Hodder & Stoughton 2007)
GREAVES, Jimmy, & GILLER, Norman, Taking Sides (Sidgwick & Jackson 1984)
GREEN, Geoffrey, Soccer: The World Game (The Sportsman's Book Club 1954)
GREEN, Geoffrey, The Official History of the FA Cup (The Sportsmans Book Club 1960)
HARRIS, Bob, King John: John Charles (Headline 2004)
HART, Graham, The Guinness Football Encyclopaedia (Guinness 1991)
HART-DAVIS, Adam, What the Victorians Did for Us (Headline 2001)
HAVERS, Richard, When Football Was Football (Haynes Pub 2008)
HAY, Ian, Britain's Best Football Grounds From The Air (Myriad Books, 2008)
HEATLEY, Michael, A History of Football (Green Umbrella 2005)
HILL, Jimmy, Football Crazy! (Robson Books 1995)
HINDS, Rodney, Black Lions (Sports Books Ltd 2006)
HISTORIC NEWSPAPERS, Leeds United: A History From 1905 (Historic Newspapers 2008)
HODGSON, Derek, The Official History of Yorkshire County Cricket Club (Crowood Press 1989)
HOLT, Nick & LLOYD, Guy, Total British Football (Flame Tree Publishing 2006)
JACKSON, Paul, The Little Book Of Yorkshire (Dalesman 2007)
JARRED, Martin & MACDONALD, Malcolm, Leeds United: A Complete Record (Breedon Books1996)
KELLY, Stephen, Back Page Football (Queen Anne Press 1995)
KENYON, J.P, The Wordsworth Dictionary of British History (Market House Books 1994)
KIFT, Dagmar, The Victorian Music Hall: Culture, Class and Conflict (Cambridge University Press 1996)
LUPSON, Peter, Thank God For Football! (Azure, 2006)
MATTHEW, H.C.G, & HARRIS, Brian, Oxford Dictionary Of National Biography, Volume 45 (Oxford University Press)
MELLOR, G.J., Northern Music Hall (Hindson Reid Jordison 1970)
MURPHY, Brendan, From Sheffield With Love (SportsBooks Ltd 2007)
MYERS, Simon, Football: The Early Years (Simon Myers 2008)
NAWRAT, Chris, & HUTCHINGS, Steve, Illustrated History of Football (Reed International 1994)
PARKINSON, Michael, Sporting Profiles (Pavilion Books 1996)
PENNANT, Cass, Top Boys: True Stories of Football's Hardest Men (John Blake Publishing, 2006)

PICKERING, David, The Cassell Soccer Companion (Cassell 1994)
RIDSDALE, Peter, United We Fall (Macmillan 2007)
ROBINSON, Michael, Football League Tables 1888-2007 (Soccer Books Ltd 2007)
ROLLIN, Jack, Rothman's Book Of Football Records (Headline 1998)
ROLLIN, Jack, Soccer at War 1939-45 (Headline 2005)
SHARPE, Ivan, 40 Years in Football (The Sportsmans Book Club 1954)
SHAW, Phil, The Book of Football Quotations (Ebury Press 2003)
SOMERTON, Gerry, Now We Are United: The Official History of Rotherham United (Yore Pub 1995)
STEELE, John A, The Countrymen: The Story of Hallam FC (John Steele 1989)
TAYLOR, Matthew, The Association Game: A History of British Football (Pearson Longman 2008)
THE STAR, Legends of Rotherham United FC (At Heart Ltd 2008)
VELODY, Max, Can We Play You Every Week? (Short Books 2008)
WALVIN, James, The People's Game: The History of Football Revisited (Mainstream Publishing 1994)
WARD, Andrew, Football's Strangest Matches (Robson Books 2007)

Acknowledgements

COMPILING this book has been a mammoth task, one which could not have been undertaken without reference to some 200 books, websites and newspapers. To all those authors who I shall never know, I give my general and heartfelt gratitude.

A number of individuals have performed heroics in providing the crosses to leave me in front of goal. Firstly, a big thanks to Guy Higton, Richard Tims and Steve Hutton at Sheffield FC for providing help and photographs of Nathaniel Creswick and the 1904 FA Amateur Cup winners (as depicted on the front cover). A fascinating history of the world's oldest football club can be found at www.sheffieldfc.com.

I am also extremely grateful to Dave Atkin and Barry Crownshaw at Hallam FC for likewise supplying me with images of the club's co-founder JC Shaw and the Youdan Cup, club football's first ever knockout trophy.

For further information on Hallam, log on to www.theoldestfootballgroundintheworld.com

Thanks also to John Garrett, Operations Manager and Museum Curator at Sheffield United for his good humoured and knowledgeable assistance on the Blades' history; Dave Wood, official historian to Barnsley FC, Grenville Firth and Arthur Bower for the image of Barnsley's founding father, the Reverend Tiverton Preedy; Trevor Braithwait, Communications Manager at Sheffield Wednesday, for his checking of chapter 22; Chris Hobbs for providing useful information on Sir Charles Clegg; Mike Spick at Sheffield Local Studies Library for finding a photograph of an old Sheffield team featuring the Clegg brothers, Charles and William; Susan Langridge at the Green Howards Museum for sourcing an image of Donald Bell VC; Sheila Edmunds for her assistance and photograph of Doncaster Belles; Johnny Meynell, Halifax Town historian for the group picture of the Shaymen; Matt Carrington for the photograph of Hull City's Wembley celebrations; and Roger Pashby for the Huddersfield Town images taken from his extensive collection of cigarette cards which can be seen online at www.homepage.ntlworld.com/roger.pashby

I offer my appreciation to David Scranage (Associated Sports Photography) and Andrew Varley (Varley Picture Agency) for their professional cooperation in supplying various images. Thanks also to the following clubs for granting permission to use their club crests: Barnsley, Bradford City, Bradford PA, Doncaster Rovers, FC Halifax Town, Hallam FC, Hull City, Rotherham United, Scarborough Athletic, Sheffield FC, Sheffield United, Sheffield Wednesday and York City.

A huge thank you to everyone at Scratching Shed Publications for their efforts, in particular my editor Phil Caplan for his enthusiasm, encouragement, good humour and belief in the project, and for his excellent editing skills without which this book would be a hefty and verbose tome.

Finally, and most importantly, I thank my wife Linda for putting up with me scribbling away at my laptop night after night and for keeping my spirits up at those times of doubt which all writers experience.

Cameron Fleming,
July 2010